English Orchards

A Landscape History

Gerry Barnes and Tom Williamson

WIND*gather*
PRESS

Windgather Press is an imprint of Oxbow Books

Published in the United Kingdom in 2022 by
OXBOW BOOKS
The Old Music Hall, 106–108 Cowley Road, Oxford, OX4 1JE

and in the United States by
OXBOW BOOKS
1950 Lawrence Road, Havertown, PA 19083

Paperback Edition: ISBN 978-1-91442-719-0
Digital Edition: ISBN 978-1-91442-720-6 (epub)

A CIP record for this book is available from the British Library

Printed in the United Kingdom by CMP Digital Print Solutions

Typeset in India by Lapiz Digital Services, Chennai.

For a complete list of Windgather titles, please contact:

United Kingdom
OXBOW BOOKS
Telephone (01865) 241249
Email: oxbow@oxbowbooks.com
www.oxbowbooks.com

United States of America
OXBOW BOOKS
Telephone (610) 853-9131, Fax (610) 853-9146
Email: queries@casemateacademic.com
www.casemateacademic.com/oxbow

Oxbow Books is part of the Casemate group

Front cover: An ancient, hollowed apple tree in an old country house orchard in Norfolk (Gerry Barnes).

Contents

Acknowledgements

Many people have helped us to write this book. We would like to thank, in particular, all those involved in the Orchards East project, funded by the Heritage Fund, which first started our research into orchards, and especially Claire Adler, Gen Broad, Rowena Burgess, Sylvia Collier, Howard Jones, Andrea Lovick, Paul Read and Rachel Savage. Our gratitude also goes to Monica Askay, Martin Hicks, Peter Laws, Bob Lever and Martin Skipper, from whom we have learnt so much, and to Sabrina Barnes, Liz Bellamy, Agneta Burton, Ian Carle, Colin Carpenter, Jane Carruthers, Barry Chevallier, Stephen Coleman, Martin Collier, Louise Crawley, Joanna Crosby, Patsy Dallas, Ben Heather, Adrian Knowles, Jane Mason, Julia Masson, Sam Neal, Steve Oram, Phil Ricketts, Lorna Shaw, Jackie Ulyett, Neil Wiffen, Sally Wileman and Clara Zwetsloot for providing help and information.

Our gratitude also goes to the staff of the record offices of Bedfordshire, Cambridgeshire, Derbyshire, Devon, Essex, Hertfordshire, Huntingdonshire, Kent, Leicestershire, Norfolk, Northamptonshire, Shropshire, Suffolk, Warwickshire and Worcestershire, the Metropolitan Archives Centre, the Public Record Office at Kew, Attleborough Heritage Centre, Dacorum Heritage Centre (Berkhamsted), the Royal Horticultural Society Library and the John Innes Library (Norwich).

The photographs, maps and diagrams are by the authors, with the exception of Figures 5, Bob Lever; 13, Carol Coleman; 14, Essex Record Office; 20, Bethlem Museum of the Mind; 27 and 29, Pippa Palmar and Ivor Cooper; 28, Kevin Richardson; 33, Howard Jones; 37, Alamy Photos; 49, Paul Brock and People's Trust for Endangered Species; and 53, Judith Dainty.

Finally, we would like to thank the following for permission to reproduce images of material held in their collections: Suffolk Record Office, for Figure 8; Essex Record Office, for Figure 14; Norfolk Record Office, for Figure 15; Warwickshire Archive Centre, for Figure 17; Hertfordshire Archives and Local Studies, for Figures 31 and 42; and Tiptree Heritage Centre, for Figure 39.

Illustrations

CHAPTER I

Introducing orchards

Orchards in history

Old orchards have an irresistible appeal. The lines of trees in blossom in the spring, or laden with ripe fruit in the autumn, seem to provide a tangible and direct link with a deep rural past, with the stable, timeless world of pre-industrial England (Figure 1). Not surprisingly, over the past few decades, a significant number of books have been written about English orchards, and about the old varieties of fruit found growing within them.[1] Perhaps more importantly, ecologists have become increasingly interested in the older examples, largely, although not entirely, because of the role they play in sustaining populations of saproxylic invertebrates, that is, species that depend on decaying wood in

FIGURE I. An old, 'traditional' farmhouse orchard in Norfolk, with tall, 'veteran' fruit trees. In this case, the trees have been 'headed' at a height of a little under 2 m, creating a pollard-like appearance.

living trees. For as we shall see, fruit trees age, and 'veteranise', much more rapidly than most other species.[2] A 'wood pasture' of ancient oaks will be several centuries in the making. An orchard will provide similar environmental benefits within decades.[3]

This recent wave of interest is to be welcomed. Yet it is arguable that, to a significant extent, orchards are examined and discussed either within a kind of historical vacuum or in a fog of nostalgia. Examples planted in the 1930s or 40s are routinely described as 'traditional', while fruit varieties developed by Edwardian nursery companies are described as 'ancient'. Different kinds of orchard, planted in very different ways, for very different reasons, and at very different times, are regularly confused and conflated. The main purpose of this short book is to provide some historical precision and context to the subject, which might assist those working to conserve orchards or understand their ecology. In the chapters that follow, we outline the different kinds of orchard and explain when and why they appeared in the landscape – and when and why many have now disappeared from it.

For as we shall see, orchards are surprisingly fragile, ephemeral features, the least resilient and sustainable of habitats. They can only survive in the long or even the medium term through active human intervention. Although sometimes described as a type of 'semi-natural habitat', they are very much a part of the human world, and it is largely for this reason that the noted historical ecologist Oliver Rackham refused to deal with them, declaring in his great work, *The History of the Countryside*, that 'Orchards, garden trees and other formal plantings are outside the scope of this book', even though chapters were devoted to such topics as 'Hedges and field walls' and 'Ponds, dells and pits'.[4] The main reason why orchards are important for conservation – the fact that their constituent trees grow old very quickly – also ensures that dead trees need to be regularly replaced if the habitat is to be sustained. Moreover, active management needs to be undertaken, in the form of grazing or cutting, to prevent invasion by scrub or other tree species. A neglected orchard will soon become something else: an area of open grassland if it is regularly grazed, secondary woodland if it is not.

But more probably, an old orchard that nobody wants will simply be cleared away and its site used for something else – for housing or agriculture. Orchards have always come and gone from the landscape, and the archives are full of references, such as that to three roods of arable, 'part whereof formerly an orchard', sold at Brent Eleigh, in Suffolk, in 1725, or to the acre of land at Walsham le Willows in 1819 described as a 'meadow late converted in to an orchard'.[5] The creation, maintenance or destruction of orchards have always been the consequence of human decisions and agency and thus of broader economic and agrarian – and to an extent social and cultural – developments and influences. These, over the past six decades, have ensured the wholesale disappearance of orchards, and particularly the older examples, from the landscape, leaving little if any trace. Many, perhaps most, of those that we discuss in this book now only exist as representations on maps or as descriptions or illustrations, rather than physically, on the ground. But a significant number remain, and placing these in context – understanding their origins, character and key features – is essential for their future conservation.

Most conservationists distinguish between 'traditional' orchards, comprising tall trees growing in permanent pasture, which are of high biodiversity value, and modern commercial ones, featuring smaller trees, intensively managed and generally inimical to wildlife (Figures 2 and 3). From a historical perspective, however, the line between these two categories is very blurred. Intensive orchards, with low-growing trees, have a much longer history than is often assumed, while orchards planted in the 1970s or even 80s may, if no longer managed, have high biodiversity value. In this book we will thus be concerned with all types of orchard, the old and the not so old. For all are part of the landscape's history.

Looked at from a historical perspective, orchards can be divided and classified in a variety of ways, none entirely satisfactory. In this book we make a broad distinction, first and foremost, between 'farm orchards' and 'commercial orchards'. The former were relatively small and provided fruit – mainly apples – for domestic consumption, as well as, in most cases, a surplus for sale in local markets. These were, at least until the twentieth century, the most numerous type of orchard and could be found in almost all areas of the country. They came in a variety of sizes, but, outside of parts of western England, commonly covered between 0.5 and 1 acres (0.2–0.4 hectares), although examples covering less than 500 square metres (if arranged as a square, roughly 25 by 25 yards) are referred to in early documents, like that extending over only 15 perches (400 square metres) which was sold in Great Henny, in Suffolk, in 1669.[6] Pieces of land planted with fruit that fell below this kind of size, capable of containing perhaps a dozen trees, were usually described as 'yards' or 'gardens'.

Commercial orchards, in contrast, were those which formed the major or only source of income for their owner or tenant. They came in a much wider range of sizes than farm orchards and, by the nineteenth century, might individually extend over many hectares. Commercial orchards have existed in England since the late Middle Ages, but their number and area increased significantly in the post-medieval period, leading to the emergence, in some parts of the country, of specialised fruit-growing districts. This development was well under way by the seventeenth century, but it accelerated and intensified in the period after *c.* 1850.

This broad distinction between 'farm' and 'commercial' orchards, while useful, is not without problems. The line between the two categories is fuzzy and blurred, for a farmer might gradually expand his orchards if there was a ready market for fruit, in a local town or city, for example; the point at which he crossed the threshold to commercial production is hard to define. Particular difficulties are associated with counties like Devon, Somerset and Herefordshire, where cider was the main alcoholic beverage, produced in some quantity on

the larger farms and used to pay, in part, the wages of agricultural workers
(we refer, throughout this book, to the old county divisions of England, before
the reorganisations of the 1970s). This led to the planting of orchards more
extensive than those found on farms in eastern England, some of the fruit from
which might – from an early date – be sold to professional cider makers. These
were still, in their essential features, farm orchards, but they clearly had some
of the attributes of commercial ones. Such problems need to be remembered
in the discussions that follow.

Two other categories of orchard can usefully be identified and will be discussed in Chapter 3. One is what we might call garden orchards, attached to
stately homes, manor houses and larger middle-class residences. These share
some of the features of farm orchards but also display a number of distinctive
characteristics, most notably the fact that their location, layout and contents
were often determined by aesthetic considerations – that is, the orchard might
be used as part of an artistic landscape design. Such orchards form, in fact, an
important but largely neglected aspect of garden history. Last – far smaller in
number but again displaying a number of distinctive features – there are institutional orchards, those attached to such places as colleges, mental hospitals and
children's homes. We will accord each of these different types its own treatment
in the following chapters, while always remembering the rather arbitrary nature
of the boundaries between them.

The origins of fruit trees

Given that orchards seem such an intrinsic part of the traditional English
countryside, it is perhaps surprising that the main types of fruit grown in them
are not, in fact, indigenous to this country, although they are often related to
indigenous species. Apples, for example, first originated in central Asia. True, we
have our own indigenous apple, the crab (*Malus sylvestris*), one of many species
of the genus, which grows wild all across western Europe. But the apple of our
orchards was mainly domesticated from *Malus sieversii*, which grows wild in
Kazakhstan and surrounding countries, although other species of *Malus* have
contributed to its genetic composition.[7] The domesticated apple was probably
introduced by the Romans, although the wild crab was widely eaten in prehistoric Britain, to judge from the pips and other remains excavated from early
settlements.[8] By the end of the Middle Ages, a range of different types was
recognised. The *pearmain,* or roughly pear-shaped apple, is referred to as early
as 1204, when Robert de Evermere held the manor of Runham, in Norfolk, for,
among other annual payments, a render of '200 pearmains'.[9] The cooking apple
called the *costard* is also widely referred to in documents from the thirteenth
century, featuring (for example) in a rental payment for land near Lenham, in
Kent, in 1295.[10] *Pippin* was a term originally used for a tree grown directly from
seed, rather than one that had been grafted, but by the later Middle Ages it
was used to describe any small, crisp dessert apple. *Codlin* was used to describe

apples that cooked to a smooth mash, while *russet* was employed for apples with rough, brownish patches on their skin. As we shall see, by the time our records become abundant, in the sixteenth and seventeenth centuries, there were many varieties of these and of other broad types, and by the middle of the nineteenth century, several hundred distinct varieties were available from commercial nurseries.

Pears are slightly different. While there are many wild species and subspecies of *Pyrus*, none appear to be indigenous to Britain, and the domestic pear (*Pyrus communis*) appears to have developed from several of these, including *P. elaeagrifola*, *P. spinosa*, *P. nivalis* and *P. syriaca*. Pears were widely cultivated in the classical world, and Pliny, in his *Natural History*, distinguishes more than 30 varieties. So far as the evidence goes, they were introduced to Britain by the Romans.[11] Apples and pears were the most significant fruit grown in domestic orchards, but plums were also cultivated and were a major crop in large commercial orchards from the eighteenth century. Plums are, in fact, a very diverse group. Most domestic plums, including greengage and mirrabelle, are cultivars of the European, or domestic, plum (*Prunus domestica*), which seems to have originated in western Asia as a natural hybrid of the wild cherry plum, or myrobalan (*Prunus cerasifera*), and the sloe, or blackthorn (*Prunus spinosa*) (cherry plums have themselves been widely grown in England, although mainly as a rootstock). Damsons, in contrast, are a domesticated version of the bullace (*Prunus institia*), an indigenous species; but while this was widely eaten in prehistoric England, the true domesticated damson appears, once again, to have been introduced during the Roman period.[12]

The other main fruit cultivated in English orchards was the cherry. There are many different varieties of cherry, but all derive ultimately from just two species, the sweet cherry (*Prunus avium*), known as gean in its undomesticated state, and the morello, or sour, cherry (*Prunus cerasus*). The former is native to Britain, but the latter only to the European mainland.[13] Even *P. avium* was probably first domesticated abroad and introduced sometime in the Middle Ages, as there is no Old English word for cherry (in contrast to the other main orchard fruit). By the seventeenth century, writers were able to describe many varieties. William Ellis in 1732 listed, amongst others:

> The Kerroons, Orleans, Morella, Great-purple, Little may, Crown, Cadillac, Pomegranite, Carnation, Egriot, Merry, Cluster, Spanish, Nonesuch, Naples, Biggareaux, Kings, Prince-royal, Arch-duke, Common-duke, May-duke, Biquar, and Dwarf.[14]

He, like others, made a broad distinction between the dark or black varieties characteristic, in particular, of the Chiltern Hills in Buckinghamshire and Hertfordshire and the red or Flemish cherries, which were mainly grown in Kent.

Nuts were also grown in orchards. Cob nuts and filberts are often confused; cob nut is a domesticated form of the indigenous hazel (*Corylus avellana*), and filbert (*Corylus maxima*) is a particular species of hazel found wild in Turkey and the eastern Mediterranean. They can be distinguished, although not very easily, by their shape – cobs are roughly spherical, whereas filberts more elongated – and by other details, but have long been confused.[15] Indeed, the famous Kentish cobnuts are, in reality, a type of filbert. Other trees and shrubs, including the walnut, the medlar and the quince, were sporadically grown in orchards, together with a wide range of bush fruit, such as blackcurrants, gooseberries and the now-rare barberry (*Berberis vulgaris*). These were cultivated around the perimeter of the orchard or, in commercial examples especially, between the rows of trees.

Rootstocks and grafting

As just noted, by medieval times, apples, and other kinds of orchard fruit, already came in a range of different varieties, each exhibiting particular characteristics in terms of taste, mode of consumption, fruiting time and storage potential. And over the following centuries, new fruit varieties were developed, so that today the number of distinct types of apple alone found in English orchards exceeds a thousand. New types arose in a variety of ways. The pips produced by an individual apple tree are all genetically different – apples do not 'breed true'.[16] Most will grow into trees that produce fruit that is sour, tasteless or otherwise unappealing. But some will produce fruit that is tasty, attractive or useful. Other new types may emerge as 'sports', that is, genetic mutation on the tree itself. New varieties thus arose by chance and, in the right circumstances, might be propagated by local people or by commercial nurseries and given appropriate names. For example, the cooking apple known as Lane's Prince Albert was discovered by one Thomas Squire, a keen amateur gardener, growing in the garden of a house called The Homestead, in the Hertfordshire town of Berkhamsted. He propagated it, giving it the name Victoria and Albert, in honour of the visit of the Queen and the Prince Consort to the town in July 1841. Within a few years, it was being produced commercially by Lane's, a major nursery based in Berkhamsted, and sold all over the country.[17]

New varieties might also, however, be developed deliberately, by cross-pollinating established types in an attempt to combine the desired features of each. This was a task sometimes undertaken by the head gardeners of large estates, but more often by commercial growers – and on a larger and increasingly scientific scale in the course of the nineteenth century. Of particular note are the activities of the Laxton family of Bedford. Thomas Laxton worked as a solicitor before developing an interest in botany and plant hybridisation – he corresponded for a time with Charles Darwin – and his activities as a 'seed grower and merchant' in Bedford included the development, through cross-pollination, of new varieties of strawberry. From 1888, under his sons, Edward and William, the same technique was used to develop new kinds of orchard fruit, including as many as 22 varieties of apple, 8 of pear and 18 of plum.[18] Many are still to be found growing in orchards today all over the country, especially Laxton's Superb (1897), Fortune (1904) and Lord Lambourne (1907). All were the result of cross-pollinating established varieties. Laxton's Fortune, for example – a sweet apple with a pale yellow skin, mottled with flecks of red – was a cross between Cox's Orange Pippin and Wealthy; Lord Lambourne, a rather aromatic apple with greenish flesh and a golden skin, flushed maroon, was the result of crossing James Grieve with Worcester Pearmain.[19]

However they arose, the failure of apples to breed true ensured that such novelties could only be propagated by a process known as grafting. Small sticks, or 'scion wood', are cut from the parent tree and carefully spliced onto a dependable 'root stock', a practice carried out during the winter months. Alternatively, and more rarely, a single bud could be removed from the parent and carefully slipped beneath the bark of the rootstock; this method, more effective with apples than with other fruit, was carried out in the summer. Both approaches require training and skill. Usually, grafts are made onto very young trees, a year or less in age, but they were sometimes made into old trees, a process known as top-grafting. The rector of North Runcton, in Norfolk, recorded in his notes how one of the trees in the rectory orchard was 'a very coarse Rig setting but as the wind broke it's head in 1720 I grafted it with the best russeting'.[20] In commercial orchards, new varieties could be established wholesale in this manner. In 1948 Leslie Clarke of the National Farmer's Union, railing against the cultivation of old-established fruit varieties in a BBC radio broadcast, appealed 'to anyone who is listening and has some of these old things – put the saw through them this winter and either grub them out or top graft them to good kinds. It will pay you in the end you know'.[21]

The young rootstocks onto which grafts were, and are, made can take a range of forms. Writing about apples, early writers usually distinguished between 'crab', or 'wilding', stocks and 'paradise'. The former produced tall, vigorous, spreading and long-lasting trees, and these were the type traditionally planted in farmhouse orchards. Paradise stocks produced dwarfing or semi-dwarfing specimens and were initially a feature of gardens, rather than orchards. Commercial orchards seem to have seen a gradual replacement of vigorous rootstocks by dwarfing rootstocks, at varying rates depending on locality, through the later nineteenth and earlier twentieth centuries, a period which also witnessed the development of various intermediate rootstock types, again mainly for commercial growers, such as Doucin, Kelziners, Ided and Laune de Metz.[22] By the inter-war years, increasing concern about the vulnerability to disease of trees grown on certain rootstocks led to a programme of research by the East Malling Research Station, in Kent, which was continued into the post-war years in association with the John Innes Institute, which was at that time based at Merton, in Surrey. This led to the development of the modern range of apple rootstocks, identified by a system of letters and numbers seemingly designed to baffle those new to the subject, with 'M' standing for 'Malling' and 'MM', for 'Malling/Merton'. Among the most common now in use are MM 106, which produces semi-dwarfing trees with a fairly limited lifespan; M9 and M27, very dwarfing stocks; and M25, which produces tall, spreading trees of the kind characteristic of traditional orchards. Rootstocks, to orchard enthusiasts, are a matter of importance, with enthusiasts for 'traditional' planting regarding the use of types like MM106 with horror.

It must be emphasised, however, that the 'vigour' of an apple tree – how fast and how tall it grows – is conditioned not only by the character of the rootstock. It is also a function of the variety of the graft. Some of our best-known apple varieties, including Blenheim Orange and Bramley's Seedling, are triploids – they have three set of chromosomes rather than the usual two (diploids) – and grow with great vigour almost regardless of what they are grafted onto. Bramley's are easily recognised in an orchard, partly by virtue of their distinctive bark and partly because they always tower above their neighbours. Triploids have another characteristic, although one shared with many diploid varieties. They are not usually self-fertile and therefore require another, similar variety to pollinate them, one which comes into blossom at the same time. Indeed, even self-fertile varieties generally do better in the presence of a compatible partner which is, in the parlance of horticulturalists, in the same 'pollination group'. Many of the large commercial orchards which developed in the nineteenth and twentieth centuries contained extensive blocks of varieties unable to pollinate themselves, such as Bramley's Seedling or Cox's Orange Pippin. These were therefore interplanted with a smaller number of pollinators (often, in both cases, Worcester Pearmain).

Cherries and plums were similarly propagated by grafting, the latter, as we have noted, often onto a rootstock of myrobalan. Pears were traditionally grafted onto wild pear stock, but from at least the seventeenth century, somewhat surprisingly, onto rootstocks of quince.[23] But we should not assume that all orchard trees were produced by grafting. Greengages, for example, can be grown 'true' from seed. More importantly, in many western cider districts, apple trees were, before the later nineteenth century, routinely grown from pips. Charles Vancouver described in 1808 how nursery grounds in Devon were spread with the waste pulp from cider making and the host of plants generating from the pips gradually thinned, over a period of six years or so, to leave only those bearing fruit suitable for making cider, which were then planted out in orchards.[24] William Marshall, writing around the same time, described how a 'very large proportion' of the trees in Herefordshire cider orchards were of this type, and the practice was also common in Somerset.[25] Some nineteenth-century commercial nurseries elsewhere in England sold pips in quantity – the 1841 catalogue published by George Charlwood, a Covent Garden seedsman, offered them for 3 shillings a quart.[26] But these were probably for growing rootstocks. As we shall see, while this method of obtaining trees worked reasonably well in providing fruit for rough farmhouse cider, it would have been a highly inefficient way of obtaining dessert or culinary apples. For this, the usual practice, at least by post-medieval times, was to graft.

Sourcing fruit trees

The available evidence suggests that, before the later seventeenth century, most fruit trees were obtained as gifts of young trees, or of scion wood, from friends, relatives or neighbours and that grafting was a widely shared skill. In 1627, for example, Sir Henry Chauncy of Ardeley, in Hertfordshire, was asked whether he might provide Sir John Butler of Woodhall, near Watton-at-Stone, in the same county, with 'some younge trees, of Apples, peares and wardens', as he was 'entendinge this winter (if God permit) to plant an orchyarde'.[27] Books on fruit and orchards written before the Restoration, such as William Lawson's *A New Orchard and Garden,* of 1618; the anonymous *Countryman's Recreation,* of 1640; and *A Designe for Plentie by an Unrivalled Planting of Fruit Trees,* of 1652, seem to assume that their readers would propagate their own trees or accept grafts or young trees from people they knew.[28] Even in the more wealthy parts of the country, in the south of England and East Anglia, local exchange of plant materials and a general knowledge of grafting continued through the eighteenth century. As we shall see, this allowed the propagation of many specifically local types. But by this time, commercial nurseries were becoming widely established.

By the later seventeenth century, a number of large businesses had developed in London. Of particular note was the Brompton Park Nursery, established in 1681 by Roger Looker, Moses Cook, John Field and George London, but there were others, such as those run by John Alcocke and Leonard Gurles. These companies sold their plants, including fruit trees, to landed estates all over England.[29] They enticed customers both with new varieties developed in this country and with novelties imported from abroad, such as the 'choice pears lately obtained out of France' noted in a list of fruit trees at Wrest Park, in Bedfordshire, from 1694.[30] By this time, smaller nursery companies, catering for more local markets, were also emerging, especially in the south of England. In 1669 Joseph Blagrave described how 'very many of my Countrymen are so most abominally cheated and abused' by being sold substandard trees by 'our Nursery-men'. He evidently meant local traders, as they had premises extending over no more than 'two or three Acres of Ground'.[31] Eight years later, Henry Browne referred to the 'Gardeners and Nurserymen from all the West and South, towards *Oxford*, then towards *Cambridge*, and so all over England'.[32] By 1732 William Ellis described obtaining fruit trees from commercial nurseries in Hertfordshire, echoing Blagrave's comments about the low morals of nurserymen.[33]

In the middle and later decades of the eighteenth century, both the number and the size of provincial nursery businesses steadily increased. Thomas Rivers, for example, began his nursery at Sawbridgeworth, in Hertfordshire, in 1735, while the firm of Wood & Ingram was established in Huntingdon, in 1742. Both soon became sizeable enterprises, trading over wide areas (Figure 4).[34] The range of fruit varieties on offer also increased steadily, partly as new ones were developed, partly as types once restricted to local areas, such as the Norfolk Beefing, became available everywhere. In 1751 Thomas Coleman of Long Melford, in Suffolk, was selling 'a choice collection of fruit trees and

Figure 4. Rivers Nursery in Sawbridgeworth, Hertfordshire, established in 1735. It finally closed in 1987, but much of the area occupied by fruit trees, supplying scion wood for grafting, still remains.

best stock propergated in the best manner consisting of about an hundred of sorts of fruit'. By 1790 the Norwich firm of Mackie's, originally established as Aram's in the city in 1759, offered no fewer than 111 different kinds of apple alone.[35] Companies on this scale, active over several generations, were now appearing everywhere, not only in the south of England – Bunyards was established at Maidstone, in Kent, in 1796 – but also in the north.[36] Caldwells, of Knutsford, in Cheshire, and of Knowsley, in Lancashire, began trading in 1789, and there were numerous smaller firms, such as the nursery run by the Thompson family of Pickhill, in Yorkshire, from 1766.[37] Indeed, the earliest fully priced, printed nursery catalogues were produced by Yorkshire firms – by John and George Telford of York, in 1775, and by William and John Perfect of Pontefract, in 1777.[38]

In spite of the steady expansion of the commercial nursery industry, many people evidently continued to propagate their own fruit trees, and varieties continued to be exchanged between individuals, as scion wood or as young trees. In 1807 William Gunn of Smallburgh, in Norfolk, sent 'some beefing plants, Ribstone pippins, and another non-pareil called the Summer, with instructions for planting' to Thomas Hearn of Buckingham.[39] But this was a period in which national varieties increasingly replaced specifically local ones, for many of the grafts exchanged between friends or neighbours were themselves from trees which had been obtained from commercial firms. And as commercialisation of the plant supply proceeded apace, the advent of canals, and then of railways, allowed the larger nursery companies, such as Bunyards of Kent, to sell their fruit trees over wider and wider areas, to both private individuals and commercial growers. While the extensive commercial orchards at Bretforton, in Worcestershire, in the late nineteenth century might, on occasion, use scion wood from such sources as 'old tree in hedge by Grove's meadow gate', most of the many grafts recorded were obtained from the large Nottingham nursery of Pearsons and Co.[40] As we shall see, the large companies vied with each other to provide novel varieties. By the start of the twentieth century, both private and commercial orchards were usually planted with young trees purchased from professional nurserymen, or with trees grafted with scion wood that was directly or indirectly of commercial origin.

Pruning

With the rise of commercial nurseries, it might be possible to maintain an orchard without any knowledge of grafting, simply buying in young trees as needed. But it would still be necessary to exercise the other key orchard skill, that of pruning: the shaping and management of trees by the selective removal of twigs and branches. 'Formative pruning' mainly takes place when the tree is young, and it provides its basic shape, that is, the form of the trunk and of the permanent framework, or 'scaffolding' branches. In broad terms, the intention was to create a symmetrical, well-balanced tree, its branches not too crowded. In many contexts, there was also a desire to limit its height, although as we have seen this was also achieved by grafting on less vigorous rootstocks, and in general terms we might say that over time pruning became less important in controlling height, and rootstocks more.[41] All this being said, we note that there was much variation in pruning styles, related to such things as how the orchard was managed and what kind of fruit was being grown.

Pruning was, in general, more important in commercial than in farm orchards. Apart from the fact that the commercial grower was able and willing to invest more time on it, controlling the size and shape of the tree was more pressing where maximising the size of the crop was critical, while well-shaped and relatively low-growing trees were easier to spray with fungicides and pesticides as these came into widespread use in the second half of the nineteenth century. In farm orchards, where the land was grazed for all or part of the year and trees on vigorous rootstocks were the norm, formative pruning was often limited to the removal of the lower side branches, so that fruit and foliage were out of reach of livestock. In many old farm and cider orchards, however, the leading shoot was removed when the tree had reached a height of around 2 metres so that the scaffolding branches all rose from the same point, pollard-like. This gave the tree a neat, balanced, radial structure and ensured that most of the crop could be reached using a ladder of reasonable length (Figure 1). In commercial orchards, a more rigorous version of this form was often adopted, with trees pruned according to the 'open centre' system.

> Which involves the removal of all crossing branches and the keeping of the centres more or less free from growth. This last-mentioned type of tree has many advantages. Its airy, uncrowded condition makes for greater natural freedom from disease, and it is certainly more easily sprayed than a crowded, unpruned tree.[42]

Where orchards were not being grazed but the ground between the trees was used for growing soft fruit or vegetables or simply ploughed or mown, management and harvesting was often facilitated by creating a shorter trunk, through the removal of the central leader at an earlier stage, so that the scaffolding branches rose from a point around a metre above the ground. Again, they were carefully pruned to form an open, radial pattern. Such 'bush' trees were particularly common in the old orchards of the East Anglian Fenland, where low-growing forms were perhaps particularly favoured because of the prevalence of vigorous Bramley's Seedling trees, which, if grown as standards, might be toppled by high winds in this open landscape of damp soils (Figure 5). But they could be found in commercial orchards throughout England by the late nineteenth century, at least in those which were not grazed by livestock, and they were probably employed in some contexts from a very early date.

By the late nineteenth century, commercial orchards often featured trees whose height was even more limited, both by the use of dwarfing rootstocks

FIGURE 5. A 'bush'-
pruned, open-centred
Bramley's Seedling apple
tree in an old orchard in
the East Anglian Fens.

and by rigorous pruning, and which might be shaped not only in 'bush' form but also as 'pyramids', in which the main leader was dominant and, moving up the tree, the radiating branches decreased in size, like a narrow 'Christmas tree'. Such compact and low-growing trees were easy to harvest and spray, and various other forms developed in the middle decades of the twentieth century. These included low trees with long, horizontal branches trained in a single plane on a framework of wires; 'cordons', in which the tree is maintained as a single, low-growing trunk with very short side branches; and 'spindle' forms, similar to the first but with the leader left in place, rising above the horizontal branches and encouraging strong fruiting there, a form widely adopted in commercial orchards from the 1970s.

The rigorous pruning in commercial orchards extended, and extends, beyond the 'formative' stage. Pruning was, and is, now directed towards the maintenance of the overall 'architecture' established in the early years, by getting rid of any developing branches which threatened to disturb or distort it, as well as basal 'water shoots' and any limbs that are dead or diseased. But in addition, the size of the crop can be increased by regular removal of the smaller 'lateral' limbs, growing on the framework branches; their young replacements generally

bear more fruit.[43] The more upright laterals would also be removed (pendulous branches tend to fruit earlier), and the flat, scaly buds that develop into foliage might be trimmed away, increasing the proportion of the rounder and furry buds growing on the offshoots, or 'spurs', which will develop into fruit. In more general terms, regular thinning increases the exposure of branches to the sun, thereby encouraging blossom and thus the amount of fruit produced, helping the fruit to ripen, and increasing the circulation of air and thereby reducing the impact of certain pathogens. In the case of older trees, pruning also serves to reduce the weight of branches and the pressure on the trunk, preventing loss of limbs or even the collapse of the tree.[44] Such attention to detail might sometimes be found in old farm orchards, and especially in western cider orchards, but it was always more a feature of commercial enterprises.

So far, we have discussed pruning only in terms of practical production in farmhouse and commercial orchards. But in early gardens, as we shall see, trees on paradise stocks were often pruned in ways that were largely intended to improve their appearance. Occasionally, they might be closely cropped as topiary 'lollipops'; more usually they were trained in a single plane, against a wall or on a frame of wire. Sometimes they took the form of a fan, with branches rising and spreading from a low point, not far above the ground; sometimes they were espaliers, with a straight, vertical stem supporting a series of neatly parallel, horizontal branches (Figure 6).

FIGURE 6. An apple tree trained as an espalier in the gardens of The Vyne, Hampshire.

The geography of fruit growing

Fruit trees were not always grown in orchards. In some districts, they might be dispersed around the countryside as hedgerow trees. John Norden, writing in 1608, described this as standard practice in the west of England – in Worcestershire, Herefordshire, Shropshire, Gloucestershire, Somerset and Devon – but also in south Hertfordshire, Kent and parts of Middlesex.[45] He believed that the practice was then in decline, and it certainly does not seem to have been common in the south-east by the end of the eighteenth century. But it hung on in parts of western England into the nineteenth century, Thomas Rudge, in 1807, for example, described how 'apple and pear trees are often seen growing in the hedge-rows' in Gloucestershire, although by then it was 'not to be considered as the practice of the county, but only of a few individuals'.[46] We should also note that some kinds of fruit were seldom if ever grown in orchards. As we shall see in Chapter 3, exotic, tender fruit, such as peaches, nectarines and apricots, were a feature of gardens – and almost exclusively those of the wealthy – rather than of orchards. But most fruit was grown in orchards, the locations of which were decided by a range of factors.

Here it is important to invoke our broad distinction between farmhouse and domestic orchards, on the one hand, and commercial ones, on the other. Where orchards provided fruit for the residents of a dwelling – even if they also produced a surplus for sale – they were generally located beside it, for convenience and security and, perhaps, for aesthetic reasons. Such orchards were thus distributed with little regard for environmental conditions – their location was determined by that of the place they served. Nevertheless, circumstances of soil or climate might affect their size and number in any area, and this seems to have become increasingly true over time, as improvements in transportation made it easier to obtain fruit from somewhere else. In general, by the eighteenth century, orchards were thinner on the ground in the north of England, and especially in the north-east, than they were in the south. In 1797 John Bailey and George Culley said of the vast county of Northumberland that 'Orchards … are thinly scattered indeed. The frosty nights, the north-east winds from the German Ocean, which are so prevalent here in the spring months, are very inimical to fruit crops'. They believed that 90 per cent of the fruit consumed in the county was brought by ship from fruit-growing areas farther south.[47] Bailey, writing in 1813, thought that much the same was true of the adjacent county of Durham, while as far south as the East Riding of Yorkshire, orchards were thought to be relatively scarce at this time, although many cottage gardens contained a few fruit trees.[48] This said, we note that orchards could be found throughout the country, except on some of the bleakest uplands, and the further back in time we go, the more ubiquitous they seem to have been. Early records attest to their frequency in northern as much as in southern counties. In 1292, for example, Anne, widow of Robert de Ecclestone, was accused of having destroyed property in Eccleston, Lancashire, which included '12 orchards worth 2s'.[49] In 1628 Sir Thomas Ireland held land including '100 messuages, 50 cottages, a dovecote, a horse-mill, 100 gardens, 100 orchards…' in Pennington and Leigh in the same county.[50] Indeed, many old apple varieties – the Keswick Codlin, the Carlisle, the Ribston Pippin or the Sykehouse Russet, for example – widely planted throughout England in the course of the nineteenth and twentieth centuries were developed by northern nurserymen.

Factors of human as much as natural geography could also influence the size, and number, of farm orchards. From at least the later Middle Ages, they were, as already noted, most numerous and extensive in parts of western England, where cider rather than beer was the most important alcoholic drink. Their numbers would be limited if the land was cultivated by a few, large farms; where the landscape was farmed in a multiplicity of smaller holdings, conversely, they tended to be more numerous. How the land cultivated by each farm was disposed in the landscape was also important. Across a wide area of central England, extending diagonally from the north-east, through the Midlands, to the south coast, houses were usually tightly clustered together in nucleated villages, and most of the land comprised extensive arable 'open fields', in which the holdings of the various farmers lay intermingled, in unhedged strips. These were cultivated according to strict communal rules and regulations and were subject to communal grazing after the harvest and during the fallow year.[51] In such 'champion' districts, orchards could only be established on the enclosed 'tofts', each covering a few acres of ground, located beside the farmhouses, but these also had to cater for a range of other uses – including grazing and the cultivation of vegetables. This was rather different from the situation in the so-called 'woodland' areas found to either side of the champion belt, in the south-east and the west of England, where farms were more widely scattered across the landscape and usually surrounded by continuous blocks of private property, making the creation of an orchard straightforward. Bedfordshire was a 'champion' county, and at the start of the nineteenth century it was said that:

> The orchards are in general very small…. There are a few that may contain a 100 fruit trees of various kinds, and new ones of an acre or two may be occasionally met with, planted sometimes in squares of about seven yards [*c.* 6.5 metres] between each tree, but there are frequently no other orchards than what are included in the gardens, consisting of four or five trees.[52]

In neighbouring Northamptonshire in the same period, it was thought that 'Respecting orchards, the county is not wholly without them, although not famous for them', while in Huntingdonshire, they were said to be 'generally very small'.[53] This argument should not be taken too far, however. Surveys and maps show that orchards were by no means uncommon in most 'champion' districts, at least in the period before the eighteenth century. A detailed survey of the manor of Milcombe, in Oxfordshire, made in 1656, included a list of 'what wood and timber is growing on the premises' of the tenants, and as well as listing the ash, elm and other trees densely crammed into the toft hedges, the surveyors noted that 'there be very pretty orchards to all these farmes Except Robert Credwells'.[54] As we shall see, in some 'champion' villages, where the soils were particularly well suited to the cultivation of fruit, as in south Cambridgeshire, orchards were already thick on the ground, and a degree of specialised production for the market was established, before the majority of their associated open fields were enclosed. But for the most part, in a broad band of countryside extending across the centre of England from north-east to south, farm orchards tended, before the later eighteenth century, to be fewer and smaller than in the 'woodland' regions lying to either side, where, in the words of one sixteenth-century writer, each man lived 'in the midst of his own occupieng'.[55] To some extent this remained true even in the early twentieth century, long after enclosure of the open fields had been completed.

Some aspects of the distribution of farm orchards are clearly a consequence of the complex interplay of a range of factors, and further research is required to ascertain the relative importance of each. In particular, orchards were often thin on the ground, by the nineteenth century at least, in areas of very light and porous soils, formed in chalk or sand, such as the Wiltshire chalklands, west Norfolk or the wolds of Yorkshire and Lincolnshire. In part this reflects the fact that fruit trees generally do poorly in such conditions, suffering from drought and attacks of chlorosis, which could seriously reduce yields.[56] But it was also a consequence of social and economic geography. Many areas of light land were 'champion' countryside, and many, in the course of the post-medieval period, fell into the hands of large, landed estates and were leased out as extensive arable farms. Gentleman farmers running what were, in effect, industrial grain factories extending over 500 acres (*c.* 200 hectares) or more had little interest in the money to be made from a small surplus of fruit. Orchards were, on the whole, a more important part of small farm businesses than of large ones.

Fruit trees will tolerate a wide range of environmental conditions, as the near ubiquity of farm orchards attests. But those wishing to make a living from fruit growing needed to be more careful in choosing where to plant. In eastern districts, in particular, late frosts posed a serious threat, destroying blossom and reducing yields, sometimes to nothing. Every effort was therefore made to avoid 'frost pockets', such as those which might develop in deep and narrow valleys: 'Let the fruit planter look first for open country, as valleys are a snare for the unwary'.[57] Equally important were considerations of soil quality. In 1754 William Ellis suggested that, with the right care and attention, fruit trees would tolerate soil derived from 'a stiff cold Clay, or binding Gravel, or a light, sandy or hollow Earth … if it run not into the Extremes of any of these'.[58] But commercial growers required the optimum soil conditions. Fruit trees do not thrive and crop well when subject to either winter waterlogging or summer drought. Loamy and silty soils, rather than those formed in heavy clays, chalk, sand or gravel, were thus considered the best for commercial production, especially where they overlay some freely draining substrate, such as chalk or sandstone, at no great depth. Hoare in the 1920s thus recommended sites 'in the neighbourhood of chalk', although not actually on it.[59] He described, in particular, the orchard districts of the Chiltern Hills, where sandy clays and loams overlay chalk, as ideal for fruit growing. The trees could be assured sufficient water for summer growth, but the porous nature of the underlying geology guarded against waterlogging. The cherry in particular did best in such locations because it is 'a surface rooting tree', prone to suffer from both excess water and 'from a too-rapid drying out of soil moisture'.[60] Plums, in contrast, flourished when planted on rather heavier soils, 'fairly heavy calcareous loams', although again where these overlay a porous substrate.

All this said, commercial orchards could be established on most soils. Heavy clays could be planted, especially if steps were taken to improve their drainage, using pipe drains, for example. So, too, could freely draining chalky and sandy soils, although always with the dangers of summer drought and rapid leaching of nutrients, leading to attacks of chlorosis. By the twentieth century, soil treatments, including the application of potash to remedy potassium deficiency on sandy soils, widened the range of potential planting sites.[61] But only within limits. The key fruit-growing areas which emerged in the course of the post-medieval period were almost all to be found where soil conditions were particularly favourable, although as we shall see, other factors, most notably relating to markets and transport systems, were also critical in structuring their development and distribution.

Conclusion

In the course of this book, we will explore in more detail the character and development of the main orchard types defined earlier, before going on to outline the contrasting histories of orchards in the three key fruit-growing regions of England: the western cider counties, Kent and the south-east, and East Anglia. Subsequent chapters explore the decline of orchards in England since the middle decades of the twentieth century and the significance of orchards for sustaining wildlife and in cultural terms. For as we have already intimated with reference to garden orchards, we must be careful not to concentrate solely on the economic, practical aspects of this important subject. Orchards had, and have, other significances, both aesthetic and symbolic. To the early modern mind, an orchard was laden with religious meanings, and when in 1653 Ralph Austen published, along with his *Treatise on Fruit-trees,* a long pamphlet on the *Spiritual Use of an Orchard,* he was treading familiar ground. From the nineteenth century, in such things as the paintings of Helen Allingham, orchards became one of the symbols of unspoilt, picturesque rural England, a role they have continued to fulfil to this day. The orchard as imagined, the orchard of the mind, is as important as the orchard as a place of practical horticultural production; the image has always helped to shape the reality to some extent, although now, perhaps, more than ever.

Notes

1   See, for example, B. Short, P. May, G. Vine and A-M. Bur, *Apples and Orchards in Sussex* (Lewes, 2012); M. Gee, *The Devon Orchards Book* (Wellington, 2018); C. Masset, *Orchards* (Princes Risborough, 2012); L. Copas, *A Somerset Pomona: the Cider Apples of Somerset* (Wimbourne, 2001); P. Brown, *The Apple Orchard: the Story of Our Most English Fruit* (London, 2016); R. Blanc, *The Lost Orchard: A French Chef Rediscovers a Great British Food Heritage* (London, 2020); M. Quinion, *Cider Making* (Princes Risborough, 2008); I.D. Rotherham (ed.), *Orchards and Groves: Their History, Ecology, Culture and Archaeology* (Sheffield, 2008); W. Muggleton, *The Apples and Orchards of Worcestershire* (Malvern, 2017); J. Morgan and A. Richards, *The New Book of Apples,* revised edn (London, 2002); P. Blackburne-Maze, *The Apple Book* (London, 1986); M. Clarke, *Apples: a Field Guide,* revised edn (Tewin, 2015); R. Sanders, *The Apple Book* (London, 2010); Common Ground, *Orchards: a Guide to Local Conservation* (London, 1989).

2   A 'veteran' tree is one that is old for its species, rich in cavities and dead wood. K.N.A. Alexander, The Special Importance of Traditional Orchards for Invertebrate Conservation, with a Case Study of the BAP Priority Species the Noble Chafer *Gnorimus nobilis.* In Rotherham (ed.), *Orchards and Groves,* 12–18.

3   A wood pasture is an area of woodland that is grazed by livestock, with an understorey of grass and other herbage, rather than coppiced underwood.

4   O. Rackham, *The History of the Countryside* (London, 1986), 65.

5   Suffolk Record Office, Bury St Edmunds branch, TEM.173/261/6 (b) and 754/1/177.

6   Suffolk Record Office, Bury St Edmunds branch, 613/411.

7   J.E. Jackson, *Biology of Apples and Pears* (Cambridge, 2003), 21–23; Morgan and Richards, *New Book of Apples,* 9; A. Cornille, T. Giraud, M.J.M. Smulders, I. Roldán-Ruiz and P. Gladieux, The Domestication and Evolutionary Ecology of Apples, *Trends in Genetics* 30, 2 (2014), 57–65.

8   Historic England, *Environmental Archaeology: a Guide to the Theory and Practice of Methods, from Sampling and Recovery to Post-excavation* (2011), 29, https://historicengland.org.uk/images-books/publications/environmental-archaeology-2nd/environmental_archaeology/.

9   F. Blomefield, *An Essay towards a Topographical History of the County of Norfolk,* second edn, Volume 11 (London, 1810), 241.

10 The National Archives, Kew, E40/4939.

11 G.J. Silva, T.M. Souza, R.L. Barbieri and A.C. de Oliveira, Origin, Domestication, and Dispersing of Pear (*Pyrus* spp.), *Advances in Agriculture* 20 (2014), 1–8.

12 J. Janick, The Origins of Fruits, Fruit Growing and Fruit Breeding, *Plant Breeding Review* 25 (2005), 255–320, at 282.

13 Janick, Origins of Fruit, 281.

14 W. Ellis, *Chiltern and Vale Farming Explained, According to the Latest Improvements* (London, 1733), 145.

15 Suffolk Traditional Orchards Group, Cobnuts in Suffolk: https://issuu.com/suffolkbis/docs/stogan__6_cobnuts_in_suffolk_v3_aug?ff=TRUE&e=25146667/41601866, accessed 12 April 2021.

16 Morgan and Richards, *New Book of Apples,* 11, 18 and 296–98.

17 FruitID, https://www.fruitid.com/#view/670, accessed 3 May 2021.

18   B. Ricketts, The Laxtons in Bedford (1879–1957), *Bedford Architectural Archaeological & Local History Society, Newsletter* 82 (October 2008), 14–28; , http://virtual-library. culturalservices.net/webingres/bedfordshire/vlib/0.digitised_resources/high_street_ history_laxton.htm, accessed 14 June 2020.

19   Morgan and Richards, *New Book of Apples*, 214 and 237.

20   Norfolk Record Office, PD 332/20.

21   Essex Record Office, D/F 152/7/1.

22   Blackburne-Maze, *The Apple Book*, 45–49.

23   Pears grafted on quince rootstocks are recorded in the grounds of Wrest Park, in Bedfordshire, in 1693: Bedfordshire Record Office, L 31/295.

24   C. Vancouver, *General View of the Agriculture of the County of Devon* (London, 1808), 236.

25   W. Marshall, *The Rural Economy of Gloucestershire, Including Its Dairy; Together with the Dairy Management of North Wiltshire; and the Management of Orchards and Fruit Liquor in Herefordshire*, Volume 2 (London, 1796), 217.

26   Catalogue of Tree, Shrub and Herbaceous Shrub Seeds, George Charlwood, Covent Garden, 1841. Private collection.

27   W.B. Gerish, *Sir Henry Chauncy, Kt; Serjeant-at-Law and Recorder of Hertford* (London, 1907), 28–29.

28   Anon., *A Designe for Plentie by an Unrivalled Planting of Fruit Trees* (London, 1652), 17–20; Anon., *The Country-Man's Recreation, or the Art of Planting, Grafting, Gardening* (London, 1640), 19–32; W. Lawson, *A New Orchard or Garden* (London, 1618), 25–30.

29   J.H. Harvey, The Stocks Held by Early Nurseries, *Agricultural History Review* 22 (1974), 18–35.

30   Bedfordshire Record Office, L 31/301, L BRO 31/303.

31   J. Blagrave, *The Epitome of the Whole Art of Husbandry* (London, 1669), 299.

32   H. Browne, *Nurseries, Orchards, Profitable Gardens and Vineyards Encouraged* (London, 1677), 14.

33   W. Ellis, *The Timber-Tree Improved* (London, 1738), 151–52.

34   L.J. Drake, *Wood & Ingram: A Huntingdon Nursery: 1742–1950* (Cambridge, 2008); E. Waugh, *Rivers Nursery of Sawbridgeworth: the Art of Pomology* (Ware, 2009), 25; E. Waugh, Planting the Garden: the Nursery Trade in Hertfordshire. In D. Spring (ed.), *Hertfordshire Garden History Volume 2: Gardens Pleasant, Groves Delicious* (Hatfield, 2012), 177–201, especially 191–95.

35   John Mackie and Sons catalogue, 1790: https://archive.org/details/JohnMackieSons NorwichACatalogueOfForestTreesFruitTreesEvergreenAndFloweringShrubs1790/ page/n85, accessed 1 June 2021.

36   E. Wilson, *The Downright Epicure: Essays on Edward Bunyard 1878–1939* (London, 2007).

37   Cauldwell Archives, the Caldwell Nurseries Project, https://www.caldwellarchives. org.uk/places/nursery-sites.html, accessed 1 March 2021; J. Harvey, *Early Gardening Catalogues* (Chichester, 1972), 33, 51 and 43.

38   Harvey, *Early Gardening Catalogues*, 36.

39   Norfolk Record Office, WGN 5/3/10.

40   Worcestershire Record Office, 705/273/7775/27ii.

41 J. Wright, *Profitable Fruit Growing* (London, 1891), 79–82; R. Bush, *Tree Fruit Growing*, Volume 1 (London, 1951), 101–20; A.H. Hoare, *The English Grass Orchard and the Principles of Fruit Growing* (London, 1928).

42 Hoare, *Grass Orchard*, 120.

43 Wright, *Profitable Fruit Growing*, 82–84.

44 Hoare, *Grass Orchard*; Morgan and Richards, *New Book of Apples*, 293–98.

45 J. Norden, *The Surveyor's Dialogue* (London, 1608), 209.

46 T. Rudge, *General View of the Agriculture of the County of Gloucester* (London, 1807), 212–13.

47 J. Bailey and G. Culley, *General View of the Agriculture of the County of Northumberland* (London, 1797), 123.

48 J. Bailey, *General View of the Agriculture of the County of Durham* (London, 1813), 184; H.E. Strickland, *General View of the Agriculture of the East Riding of Yorkshire* (London, 1812), 174.

49 W. Farrer and J. Brownbill (eds), *The Victoria History of the County of Lancaster*, Volume 3 (London, 1907), 363.

50 Farrer and Brownbill, *Victoria History of Lancaster*, Volume 3, 429.

51 D. Hall, *Medieval Fields* (Princes Risborough, 1982); T. Williamson, *Shaping Medieval Landscapes: Settlement, Society, Environment* (Macclesfield, 2003), 1–12.

52 T. Batchellor, *General View of the Agriculture of the County of Bedford* (London, 1813), 438.

53 W. Pitt, *General View of the Agriculture of the County of Northampton* (London, 1809), 140; R. Parkinson, *General View of the Agriculture of the County of Huntingdon* (London, 1811), 164.

54 Northamptonshire Record Office, C(A) Box104 4 1656.

55 G. Edelen (ed.), *William Harrison's Description of England* (Ithaca, NY, 1968), 217.

56 Chlorosis is the yellowing of leaves resulting from a lack of chlorophyll.

57 Hoare, *Grass Orchard*, 28.

58 W. Ellis, *The Compleat Cyderman: or, the Present Practice of Raising Plantations of the Best Cyder Apple and Perry Pear-Trees* (London, 1754), 14.

59 *Grass Orchard*, 37.

60 *Grass Orchard*, 41.

61 N.B Bagenal (ed.), *Fruit Growing* (London, 1939), 27–31.

CHAPTER 2

Types of orchard: farmhouse and commercial

....

Farm orchards: numbers and economics

For most of history, the overwhelming majority of orchards were attached to farmhouses, and as late as 1948, L. Dudley Stamp was able to describe how farm holdings in England 'usually' included a small orchard.[1] But it is generally difficult, before the nineteenth century, to estimate with any degree of accuracy the area covered by orchards in any district, or the proportion of farms that possessed one. A survey of the Manor of Wilburton, in Cambridgeshire, drawn up in 1636, thus records 'the dwelling houses, orchards, gardens or yards in the Town with the number of acres, roods and perches that each of them contain'.[2] Of the village farms, in addition to the manor house and parsonage, 18 had an orchard, several of them more than one, but 19 were described as having a 'yard' or 'homestead' only. It is unclear whether this means that they lacked any fruit trees or whether they had small numbers in their 'yards' and 'homesteads' and, if so, how many fruit trees needed to be present before the surveyor recognised these areas as an 'orchard'. In surveys, and to an extent on early maps, what constituted an orchard was very much in the eye of the beholder.

Allowing for such uncertainties, our sources suggest that while in medieval times all farms of any size probably possessed their own orchard, by the eighteenth century some farmers kept only a few fruit trees, if any, for their own use, and made no attempt to produce a surplus for sale. These tended to be the larger farmers, and especially large grain producers. Orchards were generally more important on smaller farms, whether tenanted or owner occupied, where the sale of surplus fruit provided an additional income stream, if only a small one, in what was often a portfolio of enterprises. As John Sinclair put it in 1818, orchards were beneficial:

> To a small farmer, who attends personally to the whole business, and whose wife and children are his assistants. In various cases also, the produce of an orchard, in favourable seasons, will pay the rent of an industrious cottager. But whether it is the profitable appendage of a large farm, and advantageous on an average of years, either to the landlord or the tenant, is a different question.[3]

There was also, as already intimated, significant geographical differences in the size, and economic importance, of farm orchards. In particular, in many western districts, a major aim was the provision of apples and pears for making the cider and perry (a similar beverage but made from pears) which, as well as being

FIGURE 7. A 'tall-tree', 'traditional' cider orchard at Whimple, Devon.

consumed domestically, might be used to pay casual workers and day-labourers, especially at harvest time. A surplus of apples might be sold to a local cider-maker or, by the late nineteenth century, to one of the big industrial producers, such as Bulmers. West Country orchards therefore tended to occupy a rather greater proportion of the farm acreage than elsewhere in the country, where beer was the most widely consumed alcoholic beverage (Figure 7). In many parts of Devon, Somerset, Herefordshire and the adjacent counties, orchards might, by the seventeenth or eighteenth centuries, account for as much as 3, 4 or 5 per cent of the total farm acreage, and occasionally even more. In parts of south-east England, close to London, farm orchards might be similarly extensive. But in most parts of the country, they usually made up only 1 acre or so of a 100-acre farm, and proportionately less of a smaller one.

While such an area would have produced, in most years, more than could be consumed by even the largest farming household, the sums received from selling the surplus, either locally or in a nearby market town, should not be exaggerated. In December 1798 Randall Burroughes, a farmer at Wymondham, in Norfolk, recorded how he retained 15 sacks of apples harvested from the farm orchards for his own use but sent 28 sacks to be sold at Norwich market for 6 shillings a sack.[4] The sum received, £8 2 shillings, was about the same as the net profit he gained for each of the bullocks which he bought and fattened for a year. Burroughes was a fairly substantial farmer, with orchards covering nearly 2 acres (0.8 hectares), and profits like this probably represent the upper range of what might be received. Fruit from farm orchards was subject to tithe payments, made to the rector or vicar (or other tithe owner), and they were usually part of the 'small' tithes, along with livestock, eggs and hay. By the seventeenth and eighteenth centuries, payments in kind had often been commuted, on an ad hoc, local basis, to cash equivalents, and the various values attached to different produce seem to suggest that in most districts farm orchards were not a major source of profit. At Boxworth, in Cambridgeshire, in 1632, the tithes from orchards were compounded at 1 shilling, 2 shillings or 4 shillings, depending on their size; but 6 shillings was paid for each cow, 5 shillings 6d for each lamb, and 6 shillings for each sow.[5] At Diss, in south Norfolk, in the early eighteenth century, the rector received 1 penny per annum 'for every orchard and garden plot', the same as was due 'for every hive of bees ... except it be the first year they swarm, and then nothing'.[6] At Barley, in Hertfordshire, in 1773, the total value of the tithes received was £250 5 shillings 1¼d, but of this, orchards contributed only 10 shillings, that is, less than 0.2 per cent.[7] Orchards in most areas provided a useful additional income stream but were not a major source of profit. Only in western cider areas, in parts of the south-east, and in a few other places close to large population centres were they becoming, by the later seventeenth century, a major element in the economies of many farms. But as they did so, the fuzzy line between 'farm' and 'commercial' orchards was, as we emphasised earlier, beginning to be crossed.

Orchards nevertheless had an importance in the lives of early farming communities which it is hard to appreciate today. Fruit was of critical importance in a world in which other forms of sweet-tasting food were expensive or unavailable. Its value is clear from the way that yeomen, when drawing up their wills, made provision for their widows which frequently included a proportion of the produce of their orchard. In 1597 John Battell of Eastwood, in Essex, for example, left to his wife 'during her widowhood, yearly out of my orchard six bushels of the best apples, if they be growing there', while the will drawn up in the following year by William Baker of Great Chishall, in the far north of the same county (and now in Cambridgeshire), left to Alice, his widow, 'the use of my twist [intertwined] walnut tree in my garden' and allowed her to take nuts from the orchard and to 'choose 2 of the apple trees in my orchard and gather the apples'.[8] As late as 1817 the will of Joseph Reed of Tregathenau, Sithney, in Cornwall, stipulated that his sons were to regularly provide his widow Anne with 'coal, a pint of milk and apples from the little orchard...'.[9] Orchard fruit featured frequently as an element in rents and similar payments, not only in the Middle Ages, as at Wood Norton, in Norfolk, in 1290, or at Lacock and Natton, in Wiltshire, in 1304, but also, on occasions, into the eighteenth century.[10] In 1701 part of the payment for a piece of land in Downham Market, in Norfolk, comprised '3 lbs. potatoes and the fruit of three fruit-trees each year', to be made to Thomas Buckingham and his wife for the duration of their lives.[11] When the vicarage house at Lillington, in Warwickshire, was leased in 1714, the tenant agreed to present to the vicar, as part of the rent, 'an equal share of apples and pears that shall grow upon the Golden-Runnet & Warden Pear Trees'.[12]

Where farms were owned by their occupier, the orchard would have been planted and managed according to the needs and wishes of the farmer or, perhaps more usually, his wife. Most evidently would have agreed with the advice offered by Thomas Tusser in his *Five Hundred Points of Good Husbandrie* in 1573:

> Good fruit and good plenty doth well in the loft,
> Then make thee an orchard and cherish it oft.[13]

But farms were often owned by someone else, and increasingly, in the course of the post-medieval centuries, they were owned by a large landed estate. The lease agreement which was drawn up at the start of the tenancy often included stipulations about how the orchard attached to the farm should be managed – what stock might be grazed there, for example, or how the trees should be looked after. When in 1584 Richard Swanne leased a property in Tanworth, Warwickshire, with an attached orchard, the agreement bound him 'not to crop or lopp any fruit trees growing on the said land but to nourish and increase the same by proyning, muckeing, earthing and Dressinge the said trees and by setting of stokes and graffyng'.[14] Some estates went further, actively encouraging the planting of orchards by providing fruit trees for their tenants. In 1844, for example, a member of the Howell family, of Ethy, in Cornwall, described how they were busy establishing 'a nursery for apple trees' for the estate farms.[15] Estate administrators sometimes tried to limit their employer's more philanthropic tendencies in this respect. In 1682 Lord Hatton of Kirby, in Northamptonshire, received a letter from his steward, John Simpson, describing:

> 2 or 3 of your Honours tenants that would have some young apple trees to set in your Lordships grounds. If your Honour pleases to give them. Kat: Wade saith your Honour Promised him some. Mr Jeffreys sent his shepherd one John Sotchill your Honours tenant, to have som to plant a little orchard if they are to be spared and Mathew Brathit of Groaton if your Honour pleases to bestowe som on him. I fear all your Lordships tenants will look for the same if they may have them for nothing but I shall give them none till your Honour pleases to order me.[16]

Farm orchards: location and management

We know a reasonable amount about the location, character and management of farm orchards, at least in the post-medieval period. First, it is clear that almost all were placed in close proximity to the farmhouse. There were a number of reasons for this. It facilitated day-to-day management – the removal of windfalls before they were damaged by birds, for example – as well as the movement of harvested fruit to the kitchen or storage place. Almost certainly, it also reflects the aesthetic value placed on orchards in the past – the displays of blossom, the beauty of trees heavily laden with fruit, the birdsong. Early writers waxed lyrical on such subjects, and for many, the intended audience was the prosperous yeoman as much as the wealthy landowner. In William Lawson's words, 'whereas every other pleasure commonly fills some one of our senses, with delight; this makes all our senses swim in pleasure, and that with infinite variety, joined with no less commodity'.[17] But above all, proximity to the house afforded some protection against predators, animal or human. Amongst the former we might note not only the fieldfares which feasted on windfalls, but also the bullfinch (*Pyrrhula pyrrhula*), which attacked the buds of fruit trees in spring, seriously reducing the scale of the autumn harvest. This is why birds of this species were, along with crows, rooks, jackdaws, ravens, magpies, jays, red kites and unspecified 'hawks', among the vermin listed in the 1566 Acte for the Preservation of Grayne, for which bounties were to be paid by churchwardens in order to protect crops or livestock.[18] The bullfinch was viciously targeted: 6,600 were killed over a period of 36 years in just one Cheshire parish – 452 in 1676 alone. As late as 1955, following meetings between the Ministry of Agriculture Food and Fisheries and the Fruit Committee of the National Farmer's Union, the Wild Birds (Bullfinches) Order was issued, adding bullfinch to the list of wild birds which owners or occupiers of land in the main orchard counties were allowed to kill because they were a threat to crops.[19] But human intruders posed, in many ways, a more serious threat to the orchard crop.

Sometimes this was a simple case of children 'scrumping' – in 1840 Mary Edwards, of Cuddra, in Cornwall, wrote to her neighbour Mrs Carlyon, asking for steps to be taken to prevent boys stealing apples: 'they have stolen nearly all the quarantines[20] and broken the tree...'.[21] But sometimes theft was the work of impoverished adults, and as such could be severely punished, as in 1812, when Richard Chipmas, of Sithne, in the same county, was sent to Bodmin jail for a week for stealing 12 apples from the orchard of James Bullier.[22] In many cases, intruders appear to have been bent on vandalism more than theft, as when in 1734 Elias Snelling, of Ashburton, in Devon, was convicted of 'breaking and entering a close of land of John Eales, commonly called the orchard. For breaking down the gates and hedges, tearing and spoiling the apple trees there'.[23] Such behaviour might have been due to drunkenness or a desire to settle a personal score, or it might be a manifestation of the same kind of class antagonism that encouraged the sporadic maiming of livestock, and which also affected other forms of planting, such as young plantations.[24] Often, perhaps, it was a combination of all these things. Court cases sometimes hint at complex stories. In 1636 a Worcestershire farmer described in court how Robert Darwin, of Tenbury, was 'a man who doth lead low and disorderly courses and one that doth continually wander by night when all else are in bed. Item he doth threaten to cut down all the fruit trees in my orchard and I go daily in fear of him. Item he hath beaten my wife and taken my fruit from her...'.[25] These kinds of attacks continued well into the nineteenth century. In 1863, for example, Thomas Snowball, of Crayke, in north Yorkshire, a tailor, was convicted for rooting up fruit trees in the grounds of John Haxby, a gentleman of Easingwold.[26] Whatever the particular reasons, orchards seem to have been a frequent target for thieves and vandals and were thus best planted where the owner could keep a good eye on them, although this might mean they were not best placed for the production of fruit. Worgan, writing about Cornwall in 1805, described the problems which arose 'from a partiality in the inhabitants to plant orchards close adjoining to their houses (to prevent plunder), however much these houses are exposed to the sea winds, which not only hinder the trees from bearing fruit, but in a few years destroy them'.[27]

After proximity to the residence, the second notable feature of farmhouse orchards was the character of their planting. Most contained tall, spreading trees planted on vigorous rootstocks, although with some local exceptions: in parts of Devon and Cornwall, for example, the trees in farm orchards were often pruned low, at a height of 4 or 5 feet (*c.* 1.2 or 1.5 metres), in part because of the damaging effects of winds and gales.[28] The trees, moreover, were usually planted on a rough grid – Gervase Markham in 1613 thought they should stand in 'such arteficiall rowes that which way soever a man shall cast his eyes yet hee shall see the trees every way stand in rows making squares, alleyes and divisions according to a man's imagination'.[29] And they were usually quite widely spaced. True, Markham advocated very dense planting, with trees only 12 feet (*c.* 3.6 metres) apart, but most writers suggested leaving much more open ground between them. William Lawson, in his *New Orchard and Garden,* of 1618, advised that 'trees should be well spaced', at a distance of 20 yards (*c.* 6 metres). The orchard planted by Mary Birkhead at Thwaite, in Norfolk, in 1734 had ' trees planted in rows look which way you please', which were spaced at '36 foot one way and 26 the other' (11 metres and 8 metres).[30] An orchard at Hasketon in Suffolk, planted in 1814, contained seven rows of nine trees, mainly apples, with the trees spaced at 14 yards (13 metres) along the rows and the rows spaced 7 yards (6.5 metres) apart (Figure 8).[31] In most surviving farm orchards, trees are spaced at intervals of between 6 and 10 metres, although both wider and narrower intervals are known.

Most farm orchards appear to have been dominated, often overwhelmingly, by apples, their numbers in some cases rivalled by pears, but with fewer plums and cherries. This, for obvious reasons, was especially true in cider areas, but was generally the case everywhere. In the orchard at North Runcton rectory, in Norfolk, in 1719, for example, there were 14 apples but only 2 pears listed; the orchard at West End Farm in Wormley, Hertfordshire, in 1784 contained 18 apple but only 2 other trees, both walnuts, while all the trees in the orchard at Ayott St Lawrence parsonage, in Hertfordshire, in 1806 were apples.[32] There were sound practical reasons for this emphasis. Plum trees only cropped for three months in the summer, cherries only in June and July, and neither fruit could be kept more than a few days unless processed or preserved in some way. In contrast, by planting a good range of varieties, apples could be cropped from late July until November, while particular varieties, such as the Norfolk Beefing, could be stored successfully well into the following year. Pears had a shorter cropping season, but the large 'warden' varieties, in particular, could keep for many months.[33] The desire for a long cropping season, but also the need for

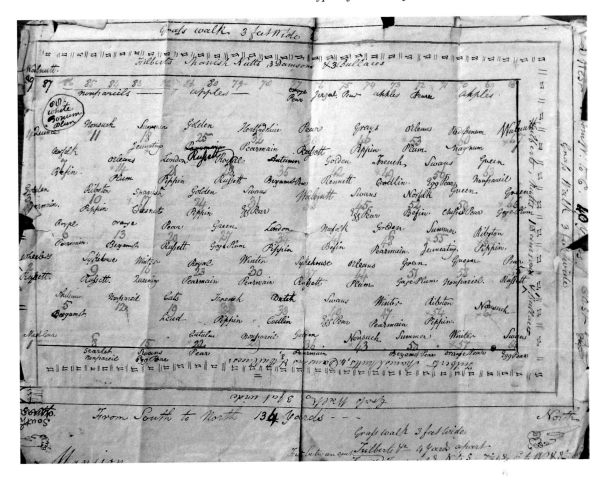

FIGURE 8. Plan of an orchard at Hasketon, Suffolk, drawn up in 1814. Mainly planted with apples, but with some pears, plums and other fruit, it was surrounded by rows of 'filberts, Spanish nuts, damsons and bullaces'. Suffolk Record Office, V5/11/4.2.

fruit that could be used in a variety of ways, ensured that the yeoman farmer's orchard often boasted a large number of different varieties. That at Thwaite, in Norfolk, just described, included no fewer than 21 different types of apple and 6 of pear.[34]

Other factors may have played a part in the dominance of apples. In particular, cherry trees tended to grow taller and faster than other types of fruit and, if liberally intermixed with apples in an orchard, might overshadow them and supress their growth. At large country houses, as we shall see, they were often grown in a separate 'cherry ground', and, while this was not usually an option at less socially elevated residences, cherry trees might be relegated to the gardens or yards away from the orchard. So, too, could other fruit. All the 15 trees growing in the orchard at the rectory at Carleton Rode, in Norfolk, in 1758 were apples, but there were plums, pears and cherries in the garden, as well as two almonds and a mulberry (although even here nearly half the trees were apples).[35] Where significant numbers of fruit other than apples and pears were planted in an orchard, one common arrangement was to place them as a border or hedge around the margins. Birkhead's orchard at Thwaite was surrounded

FIGURE 9. Veteran
cobnut stools, planted
around the margins of
the orchard at Parkgate
Farm, Saxmundham,
Suffolk.

by a perimeter fence against which were planted several sorts of plum, quinces, barberries and unspecified 'nuts', and on one side a single row of six walnut trees.[36] A number of early writers suggested that orchards should have a perimeter planting of plums, in part to act as shelter for the slower-growing apples in the main body of the orchard. The orchard planted at Hasketon, in Suffolk, in 1814 mainly comprised apples, but with some pears and plums, two walnuts, a quince, a sweet chestnut and a medlar. But it was surrounded on all sides by rows of 'filberts, Spanish nuts [sweet chestnuts], damsons and bullaces', beyond which was a grass walk (Figure 8).[37] Where cobnut or filbert stools survive in an old orchard, they are usually found towards the edges, although whether they were originally accompanied by less long-lived plums is usually unclear (Figure 9). In reality, there was much variety in the character of the fruit trees planted in farm orchards, over both time and space.

Soft fruit, such as blackcurrants and gooseberries, might also be planted around the margins of the orchard. So, too – as in Birkhead's orchard at Thwaite – might barberry, widely cultivated as a culinary and medicinal plant before the late nineteenth century (according to Worlidge in 1675, 'The barberry is a common plant in orchards, and bears a fruit very useful in housewifery').[38] William Lawson, in his *New Orchard and Garden,* of 1618, described how an orchard should have 'borders on every side hanging and droopy with Feberries [gooseberries], Rasberries, Barberries, Currans'.[39] Occasionally, soft fruit or even vegetables might be grown in lines between the trees, but in farm orchards (as opposed to many commercial enterprises) this was usually a temporary

FIGURE 10. Sheep grazing in an orchard. It was more usual to graze sheep in orchards than larger livestock, such as cattle, as sheep did less damage to trees and fruit. But even they would harm young trees if these were not carefully protected.

arrangement made when the orchard was first planted: as the trees matured, this kind of underplanting came to an end.

Indeed, the evidence leaves no doubt that – outside parts of western England – most farm orchards were 'grass' orchards, with a continuous covering of turf between the trees. This might be mown for hay, although some early writers, such as Arthur Young, thought that this could damage the trees by depleting the soil of nutrients.[40] References to orchard hay often appear in tithe accounts, and payments to mowers are sometimes noted in farming journals and similar sources: in 1708 the rector of Fowlmere, in Cambridgeshire, paid 'Old William Thrift' for a day spent mowing the orchard and carrying out the grass, 'though he could not be a day about it'.[41] The will of Margaret Haward, of Writtle, in Essex, drawn up in 1729, refers to apples, walnuts and plums in the orchard, and to 'one hay cock' standing there.[42] But orchards were also grazed, for all or part of the year, and this was their principal secondary use.

In general, small stock, such as sheep, were more easily kept in orchards than horses, cows or bullocks, as they were less able to reach the fruit and leaves and less likely to damage trees by rubbing against them (Figure 10). Lease agreements sometimes included terms which prohibited the pasturing of cattle and horses. One for a farm in Rushden, in Hertfordshire, dating to 1687 ordered the lessor to keep cows out of the orchard.[43] Another, for the vicarage house at Lillington, in Warwickshire, from 1714 ordered the tenant 'not to put or suffer to be put any cattle (except sheep) into the orchard'.[44] Nevertheless, cows could be kept in orchards if appropriate measures were taken to protect the trees. These could take elaborate forms. Arthur Young described how, in the orchards on the Dengie peninsula in Essex at the start of the nineteenth century, 'they buckle a circingle round the body across the chine, and to this attach a sort of halter on the head, which passes between the legs, to keep them from raising the head high enough to browse the trees'.[45] Alternatively, as in some West Country orchards, the trees had long boles, so that all the fruit was out of reach of even the most determined animal. Poultry were also often kept in orchards – especially geese, which could graze the grass – and pigs were a regular feature. In 1612 a property in Diss, in Norfolk, was conveyed 'with part of an orchard or hogs' yard'.[46] The pigs were presumably ringed to reduce damage to roots and trees or were only kept there for relatively short periods, probably in the autumn, to browse on windfalls.

It was mainly because farm orchards were mown for hay and grazed that they were planted with tall, 'standard' trees on vigorous rootstocks. Low-growing trees on dwarf stocks would have cast more shade, reducing the grass growth, and would, more importantly, have been vulnerable to grazing, even by sheep or geese. It is true that some early nineteenth-century writers bemoaned 'the too common, but destructive practice, of turning all sorts of cattle into orchards, pigs being the only animal that should not always be excluded'.[47] But most farm orchards were grazed, if only after a hay crop was taken, and this also limited the extent to which low-growing soft fruit – or indeed anything else – could be cultivated within them.

Orchards had a number of other uses. One was bee keeping, as Ralph Austen emphasised in 1653:

> Now beside all the profit, and pleasure that may be made of an Orchard in an ordinary way, by *Cider, Perry, sale of the fruits, and use of them all the yeare in the house*: there may be another profit made of them, by the labour of the industrious *Bees*, which will gather *store of Honey* all the *blossoming time* from the *fruit-trees*, and the more, and the sooner because they (in such a place) neede not labour far for *Honey*, as having it neere hand...[48]

The presence of a large bee population would increase pollination rates and thus the size of the fruit crop. Bee keeping is not frequently referred to in documents, but there are sporadic examples. When William Baker, of Great Chishall, in Essex, died in 1598, for instance, he left his widow Alice '1 hive of bees standing in my orchard...'.[49] In addition, early writers emphasised the contribution that orchards might make to the nation's fuel needs, a matter of regular concern before improvements in transport systems – the advent of canals and, in particular, railways – ensured that coal was available even in the most remote rural areas. Ralph Austen listed the importance of the wood from orchard trees above that of the cider and perry that could be made from their fruit:

> It is well known how usefull, and profitable they are, from yeare to yeare, not only in respect of the *Fruits*, all the yeare long, but likewise for *Fuell*, by the *prunings of the Trees*, and *old dead Trees*.[50]

The lopping of fruit trees, or felling of old trees, to provide fuel was a private matter if the orchard was the property of its occupier and only appears in the documentary record when others were paid to carry out the task – a seventeenth-century list in the Cornwall Record Office gives the locally agreed rates of pay for 'cutting the orchards and cutting and making a hundred faggots, faggots from apple trees, furze faggots'.[51] But where farms were tenanted, lease agreements sometimes include references to such practices. One for a farm in Northamptonshire drawn up in 1824, for example, instructed the tenant to:

> Keep the gardens, orchard and close in neat and good order and well and sufficiently manured and stocked with fruit trees; not to cut or lop, carry away etc the timber or fruit trees nor make faggots from the same without the consent of the lessor in writing (except such as shall be decayed and fruitless in order to replant and except for pruning).[52]

Orchards, in short, were – like the olive groves of Spain, so ably studied by Juan Amante Infante – multi-use environments.[53] While their primary purpose was the production of fruit, they were also valued for the grazing they provided, as well as for the fodder, fuel, honey and, on occasions, soft fruit which they produced. Indeed, such was their importance that leases and other legal agreements often divided their use and produce between two or more parties. One farm at Kirkandrews, Orton, in Cumbria, was leased in 1763 with 'one third of the fruit trees in the orchard excluding the grass or hay in the orchard'.[54]

Yet it is important to emphasise, once again, that orchards were also valued for reasons less practical and less easy to quantify. Not only did past generations delight in their appearance, especially in spring and autumn, but the lives of individual family members were inextricably linked to those of their fruit trees, the two growing old together. When, in 1582, William Gough, of Marlborough, in Wiltshire, leased his farm to William Harrys and his sons, a clause was added to the agreement that Alice Coles, 'kinsman of William Gough, might take yearly for her life, half the apples growing on a little apple tree on the premises, which tree she had to be planted.'[55] When Mary Birkhead, of Thwaite, in Norfolk, reflected in 1734 on the many years of hard work she had invested in the orchard, now in the hands of her daughter, she concluded: 'But this year I had the pleasure of seeing my two Grand Children run a striving [in competition] which should get most Filberts and such fruit as pleased them, a full recompense for all my past care'.[56]

Commercial orchards

As we have already emphasised, it is not easy to draw a neat or firm line between what we have defined above as farm orchards and as commercial ones, given that the former usually produced a surplus for local sale. By 'commercial', we essentially mean orchards which formed the main, if not the only, business of the owner or tenant, but in many cases, as we shall see, farmers gradually expanded the scale of fruit growing, adding to their existing orchards, so the precise threshold was blurred.

For an individual owner or tenant to move decisively into fruit growing, as a main or only enterprise, required a degree of investment and confidence. As one witness before the 1839 Parliamentary Select Committee on Fruit put it:

> In my humble opinion there is not a single article of consumption, either in agriculture or horticulture, that requires so much outlay of capital, time, and trouble, as apples, pears, and cherries, to bring to perfection. The farmer gets an annual return for his capital, outlay, and skill; and when his crops are housed he has nothing to fear from the effects of frost, and is protected by a duty. The hop-planter can raise a plantation in two years comparatively at a trifling expense, after which – he gets his annual return; and when his crop is bagged, he may sell the whole of his year's produce in one day, and is protected by a duty. The horticulturist, planting an orchard, is obliged to purchase his trees at a very considerable expense, which are liable to numerous casualties; and after paying the greatest attention to them, at an expense of at least 50 *L* per acre, he cannot get them into profitable bearing in less than from 14 to 20 years, and a very large portion of his produce he is obliged to put into storehouses to supply the market during the winter and spring months...[57]

For an entire district to move into specialised fruit production, conditions had to be particularly favourable. Three things, in particular, were necessary. First, environmental conditions needed to be suitable in terms of both soils and climate. While orchards which mainly served the domestic needs of the farmer and produced only a small surplus for sale could be, and were, established everywhere, the investment in land and labour required for commercial production would only make sense if the fruit crop was large and relatively dependable. Second, there needed to be a good market in the immediate vicinity or else transport systems which allowed a more distant one to be reached. There was no point in growing large volumes of fruit if there was nobody in the locality to purchase it or if it rotted before it reached some more distant destination. And, third, fruit growing needed to be a more profitable use of the land than any alternative: it made no sense to devote a piece of ground to fruit growing if more money could be made by doing something else with it, especially growing arable crops. Fruit production therefore tended to expand during periods of agricultural depression, when the prices for grain in particular were low.

To these three pre-conditions we might add a fourth. Although some owners or occupiers of extensive acreages have always tried their hand at fruit production, it was only really from the late nineteenth century, and especially in the middle decades of the twentieth century, with the rise of extensive commercial 'fruit farms', that large commercial growers became common. In most contexts, fruit growing was a small farmer's game – especially in times of depression, when it was hard to compete against neighbours farming larger acreages, who were able to benefit from economies of scale – and specialised fruit growing therefore tended to emerge in districts characterised by small farms. The interaction of these various factors explains much about the geography and chronology of the rise of the main 'orchard countries' in England, which we will explore in some detail in Chapters 4, 5 and 6. But the development of specialised fruit growing in such regions, or indeed more generally, did not simply involve the gradual expansion of orchards on small and medium-sized farms. 'Small farms' shade imperceptibly (again, problems of definition!) into smallholdings – tiny enterprises, sometimes operated as a part-time business, which produced vegetables, poultry, eggs and fruit. Smallholdings, as we shall see, have always played a prominent role in commercial fruit production.

Such small producers had existed, albeit in limited numbers, for centuries, especially in the vicinity of the larger towns and cities. Typical was 'William Burridge, gardener', who in 1781 took a lease for seven years of a property on Maldon Lane, in Colchester, Essex, comprising a small parcel of land with a cottage and 89 fruit trees.[58] The trees in these small commercial orchards appear to have been more frequently interplanted with soft fruit, such as gooseberries or blackcurrants, or with vegetables than those found on farms. A lease for land in Heigham, in Norwich, from 1684 described it as being 'in form of a triangle planted with 60 fruit trees and 200 gooseberry and currant bushes'.[59] An inventory of the trees and bushes growing in a garden in Lower Olland Street, in Bungay, in Suffolk, in 1831, occupied by a Mrs Whiskin, lists a total of 678 plum, peach, apricot, nectarine, cherry, apple, pear and bullace trees; 37 nut bushes; and 2,040 'currant and gooseberry bushes'.[60]

The inhabitants of the larger towns and cities and of emerging industrial areas in early modern England were supplied with fruit by a plethora of such places, as much as from the orchards of the farms in their hinterlands. By far the biggest urban centre was London, which by 1700 had a population of well over half a million. Not surprisingly, by the middle of the seventeenth century, extensive acreages of orchards had developed in its hinterland, particularly in Kent, Middlesex and Hertfordshire. Similar, if less dramatic, stimulus was provided by the growth of other major cities in the early modern period, such as Norwich and Bristol. But the development of commercial orchards only really gathered pace from the later eighteenth century, ushering in the hundred years of expansion from the 1850s until the 1950s – a period which we term the 'orchard century'.

This great period of growth was fuelled by a rapidly rising population; by urban expansion, in particular the emergence of large industrial conurbations in the Midlands and the north, which provided huge markets for fruit growers; and by the development, from the 1830s, of a national railway network, which allowed fruit of all kinds to be transported long distances with considerable speed. The second half of the nineteenth century accordingly saw both the expansion of production in existing fruit-growing districts, such as the East Anglian Fens and the Vale of Pershore, in Worcestershire, and the emergence of entirely new orchard areas, such as the 'Aylesbury Prune' district, in Buckinghamshire and Bedfordshire. Growth continued through the late nineteenth and the first half of the twentieth century, now also stimulated by changes in the wider agricultural economy. From the late 1870s, English farming entered a period of depression, largely caused by imports of grain and meat from the Americas and elsewhere, which continued with only limited interruptions up until the outbreak of the Second World War.[61] Where soils and climate were suitable – and in some places where they were not – farmers diversified production, making up for declining markets in cereals and livestock by growing fruit. Moreover, the number of smallholdings expanded significantly, in part encouraged by large estates, but largely as a consequence of government initiatives. A series of parliamentary acts – in 1882, 1887, 1892 and 1907 – gradually empowered local authorities to acquire land to create smallholdings for local people, through compulsory purchase if necessary. Between 1908 and 1914, a total of 205,103 acres (83,000 hectares) were duly acquired in England and no fewer than 14,045 smallholders settled on the land, some buying their properties by hire purchase but most holding it as council tenants.[62] There was more rapid expansion at the end of the First World War, when the 1919 Land Settlement (Facilities) Act provided a fund of £20 million to buy and equip smallholdings for ex-servicemen.[63] Many of these diminutive farms included orchards, some of which survive – like that at Dunsley, on the outskirts of Tring, in Hertfordshire, accompanied by its original timber-framed bungalow and combined cartshed/piggery, which was built for its first tenant, Mr Jaycock, in 1920. But we should not exaggerate the importance of smallholders in the expansion of commercial production. From the late nineteenth century, larger farmers, members of the local gentry, and even major landowners were increasingly involved, because of the poor prices received for more conventional agricultural produce and the low levels of rental income resulting from this.

Another important factor in the great expansion of the 'orchard century' was the development, from the late nineteenth century, of various kinds of fruit processing industry. The steady decline, from the 1850s, in the price of sugar – particularly after the removal of the duty on sugar in 1874 – made the large-scale production and sale of jams and preserves economically viable for the first time. Improvements in food hygiene, which reduced anxiety about processed foods, were a further encouragement.[64] Large industrial jam manufacturers emerged, increasing in particular the demand for plums, although apple growers also benefitted, as apples were often used to bulk out jam ostensibly made from other fruit. In the last decades of the nineteenth century, moreover, cider making became an industrial process, not only in western England, but also, to a surprising extent, in East Anglia.

The expansion of commercial orchards from the mid-nineteenth century radically changed the geography of fruit production. In 1850, at the start of the 'orchard century', the main concentrations of orchards were in the west of England – in Devon, Herefordshire, Gloucestershire and Somerset – were farmers planted large orchards of apples, and to an extent of pears, for making their own cider or, increasingly, for sale to professional producers. In the east, only Kent could boast a similar county density. But the expanding urban and industrial markets required, not more cider apples, but more dessert or culinary varieties, together with plums and cherries, all of which grew as well or better in eastern and south-eastern England, where low summer rainfall and long periods of sunshine provided ideal ripening conditions. As a result, the gap between east and west narrowed significantly, and by 1950, the density of orchards in

Cambridgeshire or Essex was similar, averaged across county area, to that in Gloucestershire or Somerset, and greater than that in Devon (Figure 11).

This is not to suggest that the 'orchard century' saw no changes in the west. As we shall see, there was a significant expansion of commercial orchards in Worcestershire and Gloucestershire. But these mainly grew plums or other fruit for eating, and while there was some planting of new cider-apple orchards, mainly in Herefordshire, to provide fruit for industrial manufacturers like Bulmers, for the most part the industry continued to be supplied by long-established small farm orchards. In 1948 one National Union of Farmers official contrasted orchards in the west of the country, which tended to be small and scattered and often contained a wide range of apple varieties, to those in the east of the country, where 'we tend to plant big blocks of trees of one variety so that we can cultivate and spray with modern machinery'.[65]

The phenomenal expansion in orchard acreage between the mid-nineteenth and the mid-twentieth century was, indeed, associated with the adoption of increasingly intensive forms of cultivation. As Hoare explained in 1928:

> The control of pests and diseases involves, in a good many cases, the work of spraying the trees with insecticidal, ovicidal and fungicidal washes. Furthermore, the trees are often sprayed with cleansing and "cover" washes, such as caustic-soda preparations, hot lime or lime and salt.[66]

All this, he believed, was an 'essential feature of modern fruit-growing'. Plums and cherries were usually sprayed twice a year, but apples, between four and six times.[67] Contemporary photographs often show orchard workers spraying the trees, wearing minimal protective clothing, if any at all (Figure 12). The widespread use of sprays was one of the main reasons why, from the end of the nineteenth century, commercial orchards were increasingly characterised by low-growing trees – half-standards, pyramids or dwarf bush trees – although these offered other advantages, in terms of facilitating picking. In Worcestershire, one observer, writing in 1906, described how 'The old pear orchards that were allowed to grow up as they pleased ... are dying out'.[68] Height could be controlled by pruning but also by the use of dwarfing rootstocks, which were already widely employed in many areas by the early twentieth century. Nevertheless, many commercial apple orchards even in the 1940s were planted with half-standard or standard trees, and cherries in particular were often grafted on rigorous rootstocks and pollarded at a height of around 2 metres.

To begin with, commercial orchards, like farm orchards, were 'multi-use environments'. Well into the inter-war period, many were underplanted with soft fruit, flowers, vegetables or even arable crops. Some observers believed that this served to improve yields, of apples at least, by evening out yearly fluctuations in the harvest.[69] Sheep continued to be grazed in many examples, and those run by smallholders often doubled as poultry farms. In 1937 an orchard in Willingham, Cambridgeshire, was said to contain '4 boarded and corrugated iron poultry houses', while sales particulars from 1949 for a property in Haynes, Bedfordshire, describe one of the parcels as an 'Accredited poultry farm' with

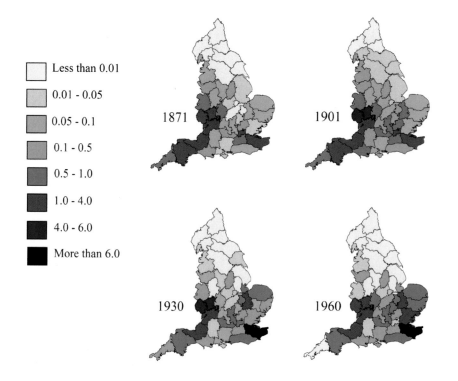

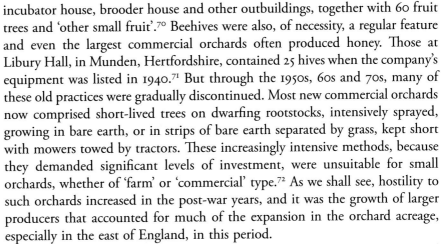

incubator house, brooder house and other outbuildings, together with 60 fruit trees and 'other small fruit'.[70] Beehives were also, of necessity, a regular feature and even the largest commercial orchards often produced honey. Those at Libury Hall, in Munden, Hertfordshire, contained 25 hives when the company's equipment was listed in 1940.[71] But through the 1950s, 60s and 70s, many of these old practices were gradually discontinued. Most new commercial orchards now comprised short-lived trees on dwarfing rootstocks, intensively sprayed, growing in bare earth, or in strips of bare earth separated by grass, kept short with mowers towed by tractors. These increasingly intensive methods, because they demanded significant levels of investment, were unsuitable for small orchards, whether of 'farm' or 'commercial' type.[72] As we shall see, hostility to such orchards increased in the post-war years, and it was the growth of larger producers that accounted for much of the expansion in the orchard acreage, especially in the east of England, in this period.

There is a tendency amongst orchard enthusiasts to regard commercial orchards, and especially those dating from the middle and later decades of the

twentieth century, as inherently uninteresting, compared with those of 'traditional' farmhouse type. But in many districts, in eastern and south-eastern England especially, commercial orchards account for the majority of surviving examples. Those no longer intensively managed, moreover, can have considerable importance in sustaining biodiversity (Figure 13). In Chapters 4, 5 and 6, where we chart the contrasting histories of the key orchard districts of England, much of our attention will be focused on the early development of fruit growing. But we will not entirely neglect the later, less picturesque phases of orchard history.

Notes

1   L. Dudley Stamp, *The Land of Britain: Its Use and Misuse* (London, 1948), 108.
2   Cambridgeshire Record Office, R/106/091.
3   J. Sinclair, *The Code of Agriculture* (London, 1818), 308–9.
4   S. Wade Martins and T. Williamson (eds), *The Farming Journal of Randall Burroughes of Wymondham, 1794–99* (Norwich, 1995), 113.
5   Cambridgeshire Record Office, P15/28/1.
6   F. Blomefield, *An Essay Towards a Topographical History of the County of Norfolk*, Volume 1 (London, 1805), 20.
7   J.C. Wilkerson (ed.), *John Norden's Survey of Barley, Hertfordshire: 1593–1603* (Cambridge, 1974), 13.
8   F.G. Emmison, *Elizabethan Life: Home Work and Land: From Essex Wills and Sessions and Manorial Records* (Chelmsford, 1976), 31 and 194.
9   Cambridgeshire Record Office, X413/6. 1817.

10   Norfolk Record Office, DCN 44/128/3; The National Archives, Kew, WARD 2/27/94B/68.

11   Norfolk Record Office, SF 431/19, 308X5.

12   Warwickshire Record Office, DR0426/21/1–2.

13   T. Tusser, *A Hundreth Good Pointes of Husbandry* (London, 1570), Fol. 12.

14   Shakespeare Birthplace Trust, Stratford on Avon, DR37/1/1462.

15   Cornwall Record Office, HL/2/518/1–3.

16   Northamptonshire Record Office, FH/D/B/A/2442.

17   W. Lawson, *A New Orchard or Garden* (London, 1618), 56.

18   A.H. Cocks, Vermin Paid For by Churchwardens in a Buckinghamshire Parish, *Zoologist* Series 3, 16 (1892), 61–64. C. Oldham, Payments for Vermin by Some Hertfordshire Churchwardens, *Transactions of the Hertfordshire Natural History Society* 18 (1929), 79-112. R. Lovegrove, *Silent Fields: the long decline of a nation's wildlife* (Oxford, 2002).

19   The National Archives, Kew, MAF 131/78.

20   The Devonshire Quarrendon, an old West Country variety – a temptingly good eating apple.

21   Cornwall Record Office 1171.

22   Cornwall Record Office, QS/1/8/71–83.

23   Devon Record Office, QS/4/1734/Easter/PR/33.

24   C.J. Griffin, 'Some Inhuman Wretch': Animal Maiming and the Ambivalent Relationship between Rural Workers and Animals, *Rural History* 25, 2 (2014), 133–60; C.J. Griffin, 'Cut Down by Some Cowardly Miscreants': Plant Maiming, or the Malicious Cutting of Flora, as an Act of Protest in Eighteenth- and Nineteenth-Century Rural England, *Rural History*, 19, 2 (2008), 29–54.

25   Worcestershire Record Office, 1/1/62/18.

26   North Yorkshire County Record Office, QSB 1864 4/10/3/8.

27   G.B. Worgan, *General View of the Agriculture of the County of Cornwall* (London, 1815), 95.

28   W. Marshall, *The Rural Economy of the West of England,* Volume 1 (London, 1805), 13.

29   G. Markham, *The English Husbandman* (London, 1613), 36–37.

30   Norfolk Record Office, BRA 926 122.

31   Suffolk Record Office, Ipswich branch, V5/11/4.2.

32   Norfolk Record Office, PD 332/20; HALS DE/Bb/E27; HALS D/P10 1/3.

33   For Warden pears, see M. Roberts, *The Original Warden Pear,* revised edn (Bedford, 2018).

34   Norfolk Record Office, BRA 926 122.

35   Norfolk Record Office, PD 254/60.

36   Norfolk Record Office, BRA 926 122.

37   Suffolk Record Office, Ipswich branch, V5/11/4.2.

38   J. Worlidge, *Systema Agriculturae; The Mystery of Husbandry Discovered* (London, 1675), 103.

39   W. Lawson, *A New Orchard and Garden* (London, 1618), 71.

40   A. Young, *General View of the Agriculture of the County of Hertfordshire* (London, 1804), 143.

41   P. Brassley, A. Lambert and P. Saunders (eds), *Accounts of the Reverend John Crakanthorp of Fowlmere 1682–1710* (Cambridge, 1988), 112.

42 Emmison, *Elizabethan Life*, 265.

43 Hertfordshire Archives and Local Studies, 74499.

44 Warwickshire Record Office, DR0426/21/1–2.

45 A. Young, *General View of the Agriculture of the County of Essex*, Volume 2 (London, 1807), 132.

46 Norfolk Record Office, MC 257/55, 684X3.

47 Worgan, *General View of the Agriculture of the County of Cornwall* (London, 1815).

48 R. Austen, *A Treatise on Fruit Trees* (London, 1653), 119.

49 Emmison, *Elizabethan Life*, 194.

50 Austen, *Treatise on Fruit Trees*, unpaginated introduction.

51 Cornwall Record Office, RP/1/67.

52 Northamptonshire Record Office, ZB0584/10.

53 J. Infante-Amate, The Ecology and History of the Mediterranean Olive Grove: The Spanish Great Expansion, 1750–2000, *Rural History* 23, 1 (2012), 161–84.

54 Cumbria Archives Centre, Carlisle, DYB/1/102.

55 Wiltshire Record Office, 9/6/272. 1582.

56 Norfolk Record Office, BRA 926 122.

57 House of Commons, *Reports from Committees*, Volume 3 (London, 1839), 104.

58 Suffolk Record Office, Bury St Edmunds branch, HA 519/949.

59 Norfolk Record Office, COL 1/39.

60 Suffolk Record Office, Lowestoft branch, 880/D1/96/13.

61 P.J. Perry, *British Farming in the Great Depression: an Historical Geography* (Newton Abbot, 1974); R. Perren, *Agriculture in Depression 1870–1940* (Cambridge, 1995).

62 Q. Bone, Legislation to Revive Small Farming in England 1887–1914, *Agricultural History* 49 (1975), 653–61.

63 S. Wade Martins and T. Williamson, *The Countryside of East Anglia: Changing Landscapes, 1870–1950* (Woodbridge, 2008), 55–60.

64 P. Atkins, Vinegar and Sugar: The Early History of Factory-made Jams, Sauces and Pickles in Britain. In D.J. Oddy and A. Drouard (eds), *The Food Industries of Europe in the Nineteenth and Twentieth Centuries* (London, 2016), 41–54; D. Harvey, Fruit Growing in Kent in the Nineteenth Century, *Archaeologia Cantiana* 79 (1964), 94–108, especially 96–97.

65 Stamp, *Land of Britain: Its Use and Misuse*, 122; Essex Record Office, D/F 152/7/1.

66 Hoare, *English Grass Orchard*, 161.

67 Stamp, *Land of Britain: Its Use and Misuse*, 111–13.

68 H.A. Doubleday, J.W.W. Bund and W. Page (eds), *Victoria History of the County of Worcestershire*, Volume 1 (London, 1901), 313.

69 Stamp, *Land of Britain: Its Use and Misuse*, 110.

70 Suffolk Record Office, Bury St Edmunds branch, 1432/.170; Cambridgeshire Record Office, K515/L/2069; Bedfordshire Record Office, PK1/4/181.

71 Bedfordshire Record Office, BML 10/44/153.

72 Stamp, *Land of Britain: Its Use and Misuse*, 108.

CHAPTER 3

Types of orchard: gardens and institutions

Country house gardens before *c.* 1760

So far, we have discussed orchards largely in economic and practical terms. But, as we have noted, they were also valued in the past for their appearance – for their blossom in season – and for birdsong, and they were thus a prominent feature of gardens and designed landscapes during the Middle Ages and into the sixteenth and seventeenth centuries. Gardens were places for gentle recreation, and orchards associated with great houses made agreeable places in which to take the air. They were thus regularly provided with sanded or gravelled paths, as at Stiffkey Hall, in Norfolk, in the 1590s.[1] William Lawson in 1618 recommended a square shape for an orchard in part because this made it easier to lay out paths, and 'one principall end of orchards is recreation by walks'.[2] But there were particular stylistic reasons why orchards were prominent features of early designed landscapes. Before the middle decades of the eighteenth century, gardens were usually enclosed by walls or hedges and were geometric in layout and highly artificial in appearance, their design dominated by formal planting – knots, parterres and topiary. Orchards, with their evenly spaced rows of well-pruned trees, fitted in well with this aesthetic. In addition, the immediate setting of even the greatest houses also included functional areas, such as farmyards, and features which had both a productive *and* an aesthetic role. The ornamental garden ponds called 'canals' doubled as 'stews', in which fish were kept prior to consumption; dovecotes were elaborately constructed and proudly displayed within the garden area.[3] Here, too, orchards, with their combination of beauty and productivity, had an obvious appeal. Like many other features in the grounds of elite residences, they constituted eloquent statements of abundance in a world dogged by dearth.

There was a further layer of complexity. Orchards in the early modern period were imbued with complex layers of biblical and classical meanings, making them appropriate places for thoughtful meditation in a religious age – a subject recently explored by Liz Bellamy. Not only was the 'forbidden fruit' in Genesis commonly, if erroneously, described as an apple, Eden itself was sometimes depicted or described as an orchard and, according to one seventeenth-century account, contained 'every tree that is pleasant to the sight, and good for food'.[4] Orchards also featured prominently in the various Greek or Latin texts which, from the sixteenth century, were widely read in original or in translation. Here, too, they were associated with golden age myths, lands of lost plenty and abundance. Homer's description of the grounds of King Alcinous was thus rendered, in George Chapman's translation of 1616, as 'a pretty orchard-ground … of near ten acres'.[5] Religious symbolism may explain, for example, why an orchard was such a prominent feature of the gardens created by the recusant Catholic Sir Thomas Tresham around his extravagant, unfinished summer house, the New Bield, at Aldwinkle, in Northamptonshire.

It is thus not surprising that orchards featured prominently in the designed landscapes associated with grand residences in the sixteenth and seventeenth centuries. Some great houses had more than one. Radwell Hall, in Hertfordshire, had both 'an orchard beneath the house and another above the house, both well planted with fruit' when it was surveyed in 1650.[6] In some cases, as on the farms of yeomen, one may have been intended as a replacement for an old orchard, perhaps suffering from honey fungus (*Armillaria mellea*) or some other pathogen, which would be grubbed out when the new one had matured. At Chatsworth, in Derbyshire, in the late sixteenth century, there was both a 'New Orchard' and an 'Old Orchard', the latter being shown as devoid of trees on a map of 1617.[7] In other cases, one may have been planted with cherries, the tall, vigorous growth of which, as we have seen, tended to supress that of other kinds of fruit tree. A map of Hethel Hall, in Norfolk, from 1756 shows the 'Cherry Ground' lying within a courtyard adjacent to the hall. But elsewhere, as at Somerleyton, in Suffolk, in 1659, one orchard seems to have fulfilled a more aesthetic role, the other a more utilitarian one.[8]

In the sixteenth and early seventeenth centuries, orchards were often planted very close to the house. At Redgrave Hall, in Suffolk, the great mansion of the Bacon family, the new garden laid out in 1540 was divided into two sections, the half nearest the house comprising an orchard dissected by walks, or *allées*.[9] A map of New Peverels Hall, in West Hanningfield, in Essex, drawn up in 1601, shows the orchard, as was typical, adjacent to the mansion, crossed by paths, and clearly considered an aesthetic as much as a practical feature (Figure 14). In these cases, proximity was clearly intentional, but in others it was enforced by the fact that house, gardens and orchard were all clustered together on an artificial island surrounded by a water-filled moat. Moats were mainly a fashion of the twelfth, thirteenth and fourteenth centuries, but their construction continued, albeit on a declining scale, into the seventeenth century; only in the eighteenth century did they really go out of fashion (along with damp, low-lying sites for great houses more generally). They were then routinely filled in, or the mansion was rebuilt on some higher, drier site. Maps from the period before the mid-seventeenth century are often rather schematic, but they suggest the while in some cases the orchard accounted for a relatively small part of the central 'island', elsewhere it was more extensive. A map of 1633 thus suggests that fruit trees covered well over half of the 2 acres (0.8 hectares) enclosed by the moat of Mole Hall, Iden, in Sussex, where in the 1470s Sir William Scott spent over 6 shillings on planting an orchard.[10] In some places there were two connected or conjoined moats, one occupied by the house and gardens but the other by an orchard, as at Channonz Hall, at Tibenham in Norfolk, in 1640, or

FIGURE 14. New Peverels Hall, West Hanningfield, Essex, as shown on a map of 1601. The orchard clearly formed an aesthetic as much as a practical feature in the grounds of this small manor house. Essex Record Office, D/DZt 5.

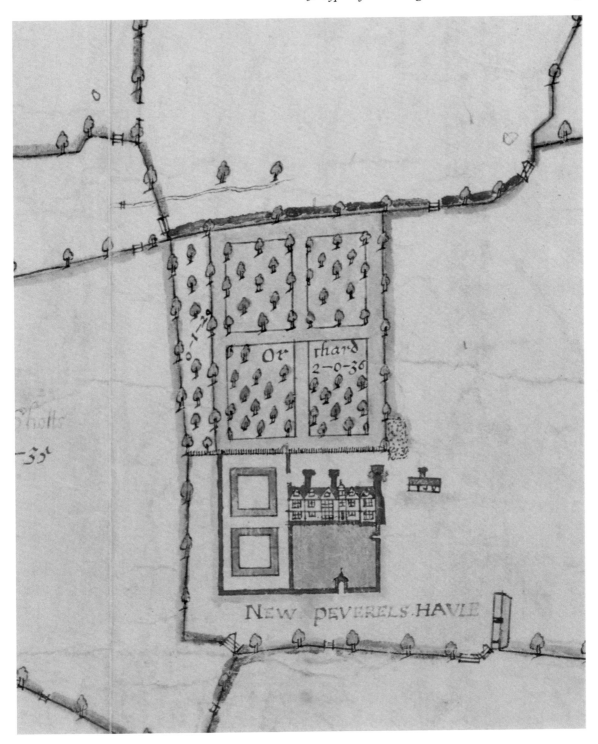

Or   rhard
2-0-36

NEW·PEVERELS·HAVLE

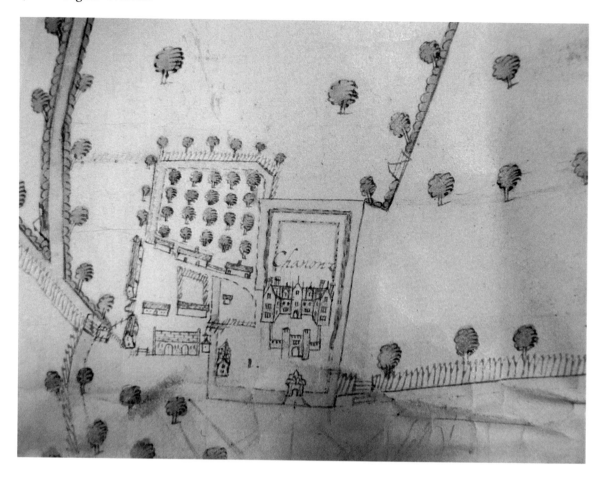

at Guilden Morden in Cambridgeshire, as late as 1797 (Figure 15).[11] At Little Linton, in the same county, in 1600 the second moat also contained a network of rectangular ponds, presumably fishponds: a document of 1771–72 described the area as 'summer house, boathouse, land, orchard and fishpond'.[12] Moats had an enduring aesthetic appeal, were important status symbols, and also had practical functions in terms of drainage and security. Lawson and others recommended that orchards should be moated, regardless of whether the house itself was so enclosed, on the grounds that it would 'afford you fish, fence and moisture to your trees; and pleasure also'.[13] Indeed, even when moats went out of fashion as the setting for the house, the moat around an adjacent orchard might be retained, as at Childerley, in Cambridgeshire.[14]

Orchards continued to be a feature of great gardens right through the seventeenth century, but over time they tended to be located farther from the house. At Somerleyton, in Suffolk, a map of 1652 shows the extensive 'North Orchard' lying immediately beyond the 'Great Garden', overlooked by a transverse terrace and ranged either side of the axial walk.[15] A similar arrangement is described at Moor Park, in Hertfordshire, by William Temple, in his *Upon the Gardens*

FIGURE 15. Channons Hall, Tibbenham, Norfolk, as shown on a map of 1640. The hall stands on a moated site, its orchard within a separate but connected moat enclosing nearly 2.5 acres (*c.* 1 hectare). Norfolk Record Office, MC 1777/1.

of Epicurus, written in 1685 but looking back into the 1650s: terraced gardens were arranged down a slope below the house, the lowest of which was 'all fruit trees ranged about the several quarters of a wilderness which is very shady'.[16] 'Wildernesses', areas of formal planting in spite of their name, became increasingly prominent in gardens from the late seventeenth century onward, and by the 1720s often accounted for the majority of their area.[17] They comprised networks of hedged paths running through blocks of ornamental woodland and shrubbery, and, as Temple implies, the line between 'wilderness' and 'orchard' might be very blurred. At Stow Bardolph, in Norfolk, in 1712, the wilderness 'quarters' were planted with '14 pears, 14 apples, 14 plums, 7 cherries all for standard trees'; Celia Fiennes described in 1685 an 'orchard or wilderness' at Budsworth Hall, in Staffordshire, 'which Lookes very nobly'.[18]

A lease for Harrold Hall, in Bedfordshire, drawn up in 1653, bound the tenant 'From tyme to tyme [to] preserve and keepe the Orchyards, gardens, Cort yards and the Mounts and Walkes therein with prunninge, weedinge, new gravellinge and rollinge in such sort as the beauty thereof may be preserved and maynteined'.[19] The attached schedule described how the grounds included a garden containing '30 trees of wall fruit'; how there were 28 fruit trees 'in quarters'; and how there were '4 grass quarters encompassed with an apple hedge before the door opening out of the chief house eastward'. The term 'wall fruit' is an important one, referring to the trees trained against garden walls, as fans or espaliers. These were not restricted to particular parts of the garden but were a prominent feature of even the most ornamental areas. Jan Woudstra has described how at Hampton Court Palace in the seventeenth century, 'fruit was present in varying forms in virtually every part of the garden', and even a cursory glance at contemporary paintings or engravings of country houses shows that this was invariably the case.[20] The presence of fruit trees in ornamental areas, and their prominence more generally, were typical of that intermixture of beauty and productivity which was the hallmark of great gardens before the middle decades of the eighteenth century.

Peaches, apricots and nectarines were the most important wall fruit. These were all high-status fruit, rarely grown in the gardens of mere farmers because they required walls for shelter and warmth, together with a considerable amount of management to ensure high yields.[21] In 1682 John Simpson informed Lord Hatton that he had finished planting the consignment of new trees which had been ordered for Kirby Hall, in Northamptonshire: 'I have taken care of the names of them a Peach and Apricot and a Pare, and soe mixed them all a longe a wall. I had left 2 Apricots and one Elroage Nectarine and them I have planted under the old brick wall.'[22] Plans and descriptions from places as diverse as Wormley Bury, in Hertfordshire (1741); Sharnbrook and Hinwick, in Bedfordshire (1740); and Honing, in Norfolk (1758), suggest that peaches were generally more numerous than nectarines and apricots, which were themselves present in roughly equal number.[23] But there was much variation. Cherries and plums were also often grown against garden walls, together with pears, but this was much less true of apples. Some might be found as standards, in the more productive areas of the garden, and occasionally these took the form of free-standing specimens, clipped in ornamental fashion, in the more decorative parts. But most were to be found in separate orchards (Figure 16). Fruit trees in walled gardens were usually grafted on dwarfing, or paradise, rootstocks; those in wildernesses and orchards were more likely to be tall 'standards', grafted on crab, or wilding, rootstocks.

The numbers of fruit trees present in the grounds of quite minor country houses could be considerable. So, too, could the range of varieties represented. At East Turnbull Hall, in Berkshire, in 1696, the new orchard and garden contained no fewer than 450 fruit trees comprising 90 different varieties of apple, pear, peach, nectarine and apricot.[24] Such diversity was partly, as in the orchards of farmers, intended to provide an extended fruiting season, and fruit with a range of tastes, storage potential and uses. But it was also an assertion of social status, for the more unusual varieties of pear, apple and plum, as well as exotic fruit, such as peaches, nectarines and apricots, were often difficult to source and had to be obtained from a distance. Local nurseries proliferated in the second half of the seventeenth century, as we have seen, and were relatively

FIGURE 16. Dwarf apple trees, trimmed in an ornamental fashion, in the gardens of Hanbury Hall, a National Trust property in Worcestershire.

common in most districts by the eighteenth, but large landowners usually sourced much of their fruit from the big London firms. The Brompton Park Nursery supplied fruit trees to country houses all over the country in the late seventeenth and early eighteenth centuries, not only to ones within easy reach of London, such as Wrest Park, in Bedfordshire, or nearby Ampthill, where the Dowager Countess of Ailesbury built a new house in the 1680s, but as far afield as Chatsworth, in Derbyshire, in 1690.[25] Fruit trees from Brompton Park were sometimes supplied as part of larger landscaping schemes, as at Chatsworth, because George London and Henry Wise were the leading garden designers of the late seventeenth and early eighteenth centuries and laid out parterres and other features at most of the greatest gardens in the land. But other London nurserymen also traded widely to great landowners, including Leonard Gurle of Whitechapel[26]; and the wealthiest landowners, even those living in the more distant parts of the country, routinely visited the capital for political or business reasons or to enjoy the social 'season', and many owned a 'town house' there. They were thus able to visit the city nurseries, be tempted by the displays, and place their orders accordingly. London was where the latest varieties could be obtained, developed by the great nurseries or newly imported from distant places. Sometimes, however, new and exotic varieties were imported directly from abroad, and occasionally these were given new names by wealthy landowners. The horticulturalist Peter Collinson recorded how, in the 1720s, Sir William Gage, of Hengrave Hall, near Bury St Edmunds, in Suffolk, received a shipment of fruit trees from France which included the plum called Reine-Claude, which either he or his gardener renamed Green Gage, after the family name.[27]

Country house landscapes: the late eighteenth and nineteenth centuries

Gradually, through the first half of the eighteenth century, the gardens of the wealthy became less rigidly geometric and more 'naturalistic' in appearance, and at the highest social levels it became fashionable to remove walled enclosures and all useful and productive clutter from around the mansion. This trend culminated in the 1760s and 70s, when Lancelot 'Capability' Brown and his contemporaries banished avenues and all geometric plantings, so that large country houses came to stand in simple landscapes of sweeping pastures, casually scattered with individual trees and clumps. These 'landscape parks' were surrounded in whole or part by perimeter belts of woodland and ornamented (if the owner was rich enough and the terrain amenable) with a serpentine lake. Ornamental gardens did not entirely disappear, but they now took the form of informal 'pleasure grounds', featuring serpentine paths, mown grass, specimen trees and flowering shrubs, which were mainly located to one side of the main facades of the house and separated from the surrounding parkland by a sunken fence, or 'ha ha'.[28] The only walled garden was now the kitchen garden, primarily used for growing food for the household. With fashion now demanding that the mansion stood free of all walled enclosures, this was sometimes located at a distance, occasionally as much as a kilometre or even more away. More usually, however, it was discretely tucked away behind a screen of trees and shrubs a few hundred metres from the house, close to the stables (the main source of manure).

In the latter circumstances, the kitchen garden could usually be accessed directly from the ornamental gardens, and this signals the fact that, to some extent, it occupied an ambivalent position in the landscape of gentility. For as well as vegetables, the cut flowers used to decorate the rooms of the house were usually grown there, while the sheltering walls made for a warm place in which to take an early spring walk.[29] The kitchen garden was thus a place to be visited and enjoyed, even if it could not be a part of the main views away from, or towards, the house. Not surprisingly, some of the aesthetic of the old formal gardens lived on within it. In particular, fruit trees were still trained as espaliers or fans against the walls, clearly for ornamental as much as for practical reasons. These were still, moreover, dominated by exotics, such as peaches and nectarines, accompanied by smaller numbers of plums, cherries and pears. The new kitchen garden at North Elmham Hall, in Norfolk, in 1765, for example, contained 6 different varieties of nectarine, 12 of peach, 19 of pear, 14 of plum, 13 of cherry, and a medlar, but only 2 varieties of apple.[30] Apples, usually accompanied by some pears, were mainly grown in a neighbouring orchard, although this was not an invariable rule, and towards the end of the century they might occasionally be planted in substantial quantities in the larger kitchen gardens. The 80 dwarf apple trees and 80 dwarf pear trees purchased by the Duke of Bedford in 1791 from Samuel Swinton's nursery in Sloane Street, London, were specifically destined for his new kitchen garden at Woburn Abbey.[31] The continuing importance of fruit trees in kitchen gardens encouraged attempts to increase the length of south-facing walls by, for example, providing a curved north wall, as at Blenheim and at Greys Court, in Oxfordshire, or at West Acre, in Norfolk; by laying them out on a polygonal plan, as at Raynham, in Norfolk; or by adding internal walls. Blossom could be protected from frost by constructing walls heated by internal flues, an expensive but increasingly popular device from the middle decades of the eighteenth century.

On smaller properties, those of the minor gentry or the upper middle class, there was less space available to ensure the spatial segregation of the completely aesthetic and the largely productive, and there are signs that the old habit of planting fruit trees within the more overtly ornamental areas of the grounds often continued through the late eighteenth and into the early nineteenth century. One interesting example is shown on a plan from the 1850s of an unlocated house and its grounds, probably owned by the Newdegate family of Warwickshire but evidently not their residence at Arbury Hall, for it is a small 'villa', a residence of some affluence but without a landscape park. A kitchen garden is shown in close proximity immediately to the north of the house, while to the west of this is a pleasure ground, ornamented with shrubs and roses, laid out around a diminutive lake.[32] What is striking is that the serpentine path winding through this area is flanked for its entire length by fruit trees (Figure 17). On smaller properties, such as that owned

FIGURE 17. A plan of the grounds of an unlocated house in Warwickshire, *c.* 1850. The serpentine path winding through the pleasure grounds and around the diminutive 'lake' is flanked for its entire length by fruit trees, the varieties of which are individually listed in the margin. Warwickshire Record Office, CR1199/35.

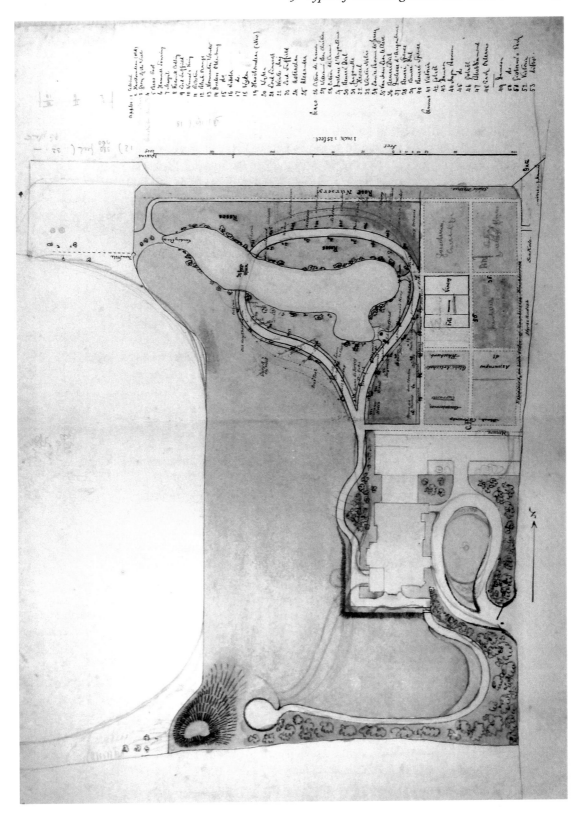

by 'Dr Bloxham' of Rugby, in the same county, mapped in 1818, gardens often remained more geometric in character, and certainly more functional. Fruit trees were here liberally scattered throughout the grounds, but the main feature of the property was an extensive orchard.[33]

In the first half of the nineteenth century, the pendulum of style began to swing back in favour of structure and formality, and by the 1860s, many country houses stood within complex geometric gardens featuring terraces and even parterres. But there was no return to prominence of useful and productive features. Orchards and kitchen gardens remained at a respectful distance, although they were now, perhaps, of even greater interest to their owners. Some of the wealthiest estates boasted 'conservative walls' for the cultivation of exotic fruit. These were a kind of narrow glasshouse attached to the south-facing walls of kitchen gardens, a novelty first developed by Joseph Paxton at Chatsworth House, in Derbyshire, in the 1840s.[34] By the end of the century, simpler and cheaper versions – 'Peach Cases for Garden Walls' – were being widely marketed by companies like Messengers of Loughborough, alongside other forms of protection, including glass coping which could be fixed to the top of garden walls to help protect trees from frost. Companies like Messengers, or Boulton and Paul of Norwich, now supplied wire frame systems for training fruit trees against walls: 'By this method, nails and shreds are entirely dispensed with, the walls are not injured, and no harbour is afforded to insects'.[35] Fruit trees were also now often trained on free-standing frames of wrought iron and wire or on open ironwork tunnels ('continuous covered-way espaliers') erected beside or across the kitchen garden paths, all indicative of higher densities of fruit trees within their walls (Figure 18).

There are clear signs that, in the course of the nineteenth century, apple trees became a more prominent feature of kitchen gardens. In 1834 the fruit in the walled garden at Ensdon House, near Shrewsbury, in Shropshire, for example, comprised 13 peaches, 12 nectarines, 4 apricots, 4 plums, 4 pears and 4 cherries, as well as figs and a vine, but there were no apples. These were all grown in the neighbouring orchard, where 170 apple trees are recorded, comprising 39 different varieties (there was also a separate pear orchard, with more than 180 trees).[36] The fruit trees growing in the kitchen garden, and against the 'New Walls', at Linton Park, in Kent, in 1840 similarly included 16 peaches, 10 nectarines, 11 cherries and 4 apricots, along with 24 pears and 12 plums. Again no apples are listed, and these were presumably grown in the orchard which, the near-contemporary tithe map shows, lay a little to the north.[37] In contrast, lists and plans from the second half of the century often suggest significant numbers of apple trees within the walls. A plan of the kitchen garden at Brereton, in Worcestershire, for example, drawn up in 1875, shows numerous apple trees – varieties like Blenheim Orange, New Hawthornden, Wyken Pippin and Baddow Pippin – in the interior of the garden, lining the grid of paths, accompanied by pears and plums.[38] Most were free standing, but some appear to have been trained on iron frames. None were planted against the walls, which were instead filled with peaches, nectarines, apricots and plums, and this appears to have been typical. In 1848 Jane Loudon described how:

> The principal fruits grown against a wall in England are those containing stones; and of all these the most valuable are the peach, the nectarine, and the apricot. The plum and the cherry are also frequently grown against a wall, but they are most common as standards. The kernel fruits, such as the apple and pear, are generally standards; the apple being very rarely trained against a wall in England…[39]

The Victorian period was the great age of country house horticulture, and the achievements of famous head gardeners, such as Joseph Paxton, were widely celebrated in publications like the *Gardener's Chronicle*, including their involvement in the discovery and propagation of new fruit varieties. The late-season dessert apple called the Duke of Devonshire was raised in the Chatsworth gardens by Paxton's predecessor, Mr Wilson, in 1835; 'Lady Henniker' (an excellent dual-purpose apple) was discovered in 1873 by Mr Perkins, the head gardener at Thornham Hall, in Suffolk, as a seedling growing in the discarded

FIGURE 18. Apple trees, trained on iron frames, lining the paths in the kitchen garden of a country house in Suffolk.

waste from cider making.[40] There are many other examples. Head gardeners sometimes penned books on fruit cultivation, such as John Taylor Fisher, who worked in the gardens of Scone, in Scotland, and later at Hardwick Hall, in Suffolk, and who in 1879 published *The Peach and Nectarine: Their History, Varieties and Cultivation*.[41]

To an even greater extent than before, landowners in the nineteenth century eagerly sought out interesting or unusual varieties of fruit tree for their gardens. While they often acquired many of their trees from local nurseries, they still sourced rarities from London firms or from large companies elsewhere in the country. They sometimes looked farther afield. Lord Bristol, of Ickworth Hall, in Suffolk, corresponded regularly with the noted horticulturalist and botanist Thomas Knight, who in 1824 supplied him with Italian varieties of apple and Belgian varieties of pears, 'which the public nurseries do not afford, or at least from which there is much uncertainty of obtaining them'.[42] Even on relatively small estates, a phenomenal range of fruit might be grown. A small country house called The Pines, in Mettingham, Suffolk, placed on the market in 1896, had an orchard containing 200 trees, including 55 different varieties of apple alone, and more fruit was grown in the kitchen garden.[43]

The location of orchards in the country house landscape is of some interest, and can be studied with some ease using the late-nineteenth-century Ordnance Survey 6-inch and 25-inch maps. Most of these orchards seem to have been placed beside the kitchen garden, under the watchful eye of the head gardener. There was no preferred relative location – orchards can be found to the north, south-east or west – but in a number of places there are indications that they were positioned so that they could be directly accessed from walks leading from the house, through the pleasure grounds, to the kitchen garden (Figure 19).

In the last decades of the nineteenth century, the economic health of large landowners was challenged by a raft of factors, including agricultural depression and death duties, while social and political changes gradually rendered a large country house an expensive encumbrance, rather than a necessary expression of status and precondition of political success. These pressures culminated in the first half of the twentieth century, when many landed estates were broken up and numerous country houses were demolished or given new uses – as schools or hotels or, after subdivision, as flats.[44] The collections of fruit trees and orchards that we can still sometimes find at country houses today generally date from this phase of relative decline, rather than from earlier periods. They are often in a decayed and fragmentary condition. Even where country houses survived as private residences, fruit trees and orchards were often neglected by owners, along with kitchen gardens and other food-producing facilities, due to high labour costs and the existence of other sources of good-quality food. This said, many owners have, over the past few decades, replanted their orchards and, occasionally, replenished their wall fruit. More importantly, many kitchen gardens – even when converted to some new use, as sheltered enclosures for swimming pools or as pheasant release pens – still have some fruit trees trained, as fans or espaliers, against the walls or on frames beside the paths. The walls are

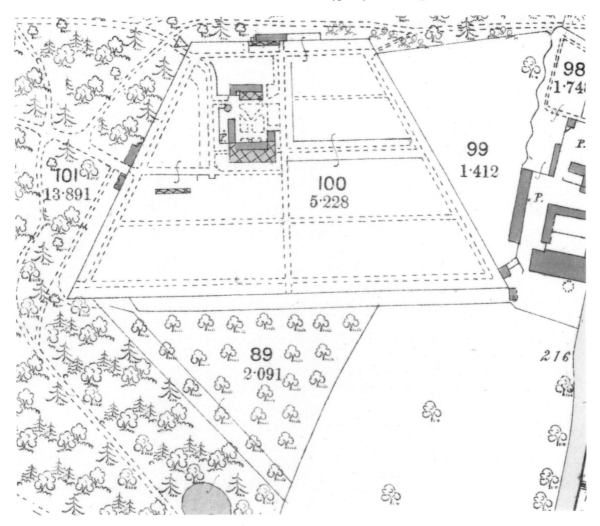

FIGURE 19. The walled kitchen garden at Raynham Hall, Norfolk, constructed in the 1780s, as shown on the Ordnance Survey 25-inch map of 1885. The unusual, trapezoid shape, designed by John Haverfield, was intended to increase the length of south-facing walls; the triangular area to the south is an orchard. Note the paths threading through the woodland screen to the west, which connect the kitchen garden to the pleasure grounds beside the hall.

usually pock-marked with small holes, left by the nails against which the trees were tied, and sometimes the metal plaques giving the variety of some lost tree can be found, fixed to the wall or lying at its base. Country house orchards, where they survive, are broadly similar to those associated with farmhouses and tend to be dominated by apples, of varieties popular in the late nineteenth or early twentieth century – Ribston Pippin, Blenheim Orange, Dumelow's Seedling and, in particular, Bramley's Seedling. But they often include a scattering of rarer types or ones unusual for the locality. An apple like Calville Rouge d'Hiver, for example, is more likely to turn up there than in a farmhouse or commercial orchard.

Arts and Crafts, and suburbs

Perhaps surprisingly, the challenged financial circumstances of the traditional landed estates from the late nineteenth century gave orchards and fruit trees a new lease of life as elements in designed aesthetic landscapes. From the 1870s, leading architects increasingly turned their attention to the erection of new houses, usually on new sites, for successful businessmen or professionals rather than established landowners. These were houses in the country, rather than country houses on the old model, lacking extensive parklands or an attached estate, although large enough residences compared with most readers' homes. Architects like Phillip Webb or Charles Voysey were inspired by vernacular farmhouse architecture, especially that of the Cotswolds and the Home Counties.[45] Those who designed gardens in a broadly Arts and Crafts style, providing the grounds in which such houses were set, drew on similar romanticised models – referencing the gardens of old manor houses – and created designs which combined strongly architectural features with irregular planting, and which were often divided into a series of separate compartments, of which one was often an orchard. In 1899 Gertrude Jekyll, one of the most influential of these designers, provided advice on the creation of 'orchard gardens' containing scattered fruit trees and grass, mown once or twice a year for hay.[46] In 1919 she provided more details:

> For what is more lovely than the bloom of orchard trees in April and May, with the grass below in its strong, young growth; in itself a garden of Cowslips and Daffodils. In an old orchard how pictorial are the lines of the low-leaning Apple-trunks and the swing and poise of their upper branches... But the younger orchard has its beauty too, of fresh, young life and wealth of bloom and bounteous bearing.[47]

William Robinson devoted an entire chapter of his book *The English Flower Garden*, of 1913, to 'The Orchard Beautiful', filled with fruit trees but also underplanted with 'Daffodils, Snowflakes, Snowdrops, wild Tulips'.[48] He, like other writers, advocated the use of tall trees on vigorous rootstocks, like those found in traditional farmhouse orchards:

> When we plant for beauty we must have the natural form of the tree. Owing to the use of dwarfing stocks, fruit gardens and orchards are now beginning to show shapes of trees that are poor compared with the tall orchard tree. However much these dwarf and pinched shapes may appeal to the gardener in his own domain, in the orchard beautiful they have no place.[49]

A number of such orchards, associated with houses and gardens designed in the Arts and Crafts style, can still be seen, such as that in the grounds of the house called Rodmarton, in Gloucestershire, built in 1909 to designs by the architect Ernest Barnsley. The spirit of the times also encouraged the newly wealthy to buy, and renovate, relatively small and neglected medieval or Elizabethan manor houses and provide them with fashionable gardens, and these, too, might feature an orchard, as at the Manor House, Upton Gray, in Hampshire, where the grounds were designed by Jekyll herself. Indeed, it is striking that a number of famous Arts and Crafts houses have names which reference orchards – Voysey's Orchard House, Chorleywood, Hertfordshire, and Lutyens' The Orchards, at Bramley, in Surrey.

In the late nineteenth and early twentieth century, such enthusiasms were widely shared, and many large houses built for affluent businessmen in suburban or rural locations were provided with an orchard or with collections of fruit trees more widely scattered. Typical was a house at Ampthill, in Bedfordshire, advertised for sale in 1910, which included 'ornamental pleasure and kitchen gardens which are most productive and contain upwards of 40 varieties of apple, pear, plum and other fruit trees...'.[50] A surprising number of old orchards which survive in the landscape are attached to such properties, and their trees – usually half-standards, in spite of Robinson's advice – have now attained 'veteran' status. There are traps here for the orchard historian. A collection of old fruit trees beside a farmhouse may not be quite the 'traditional farmhouse orchard' that it seems. Already by the late nineteenth century, wealthy businessmen and professionals – especially in the hinterland of London – were acquiring old farmhouses and modernising them, planting new orchards or adding extensively to existing ones.

The thousands of smaller suburban villas, terraced houses and 'semis' erected in the first half of the twentieth century were accompanied by gardens which normally contained fruit trees, although hardly in numbers sufficient to merit the term 'orchard'. Indeed, space usually precluded the planting of more than a handful of trees. In 1911 F.H. Harding, in his book *Saturday in My Garden*, bemoaned the fact that it was rare to see 'in the ordinary suburban back garden any real attempt to cultivate hardy fruit trees!' due in large measure to the fact that 'sixty feet by eighteen feet ... is the customary space allotted by the builders of suburban middle-class homes' (18.3 by 5.5 metres).[51] Nevertheless, both he and other writers of gardening books aimed at the occupiers of such residences, such as H.E. Helier and M. James, provided advice on the cultivation of apples, pears, plums and cherries on dwarfing or semi-dwarfing rootstocks, as cordons or half-standards.[52] But interesting as such plantings might be in terms of social history, they take us away from the true orchards that are our principal concern.

Institutional orchards

There is one other kind of orchard which we need to briefly discuss, not least because it accounts for a number of important surviving examples: those attached to residential institutions. From an early date, almshouses and other charitable establishments might be provided with an orchard to supply fruit for the residents and sometimes for others in need. At Braughing, in Hertfordshire, in 1579, for example, Thomas Jenyns left in his will 'a Cottage with an Orchard, containing an Acre of Ground, for an ancient Couple to dwell in without payment of any Rent, on Condition to take Care of the Trees and Fruit, which the Minister and Church-wardens shall yearly distribute among the Poor of the Parish; and upon the Vacancy of the House, they shall put in others.'[53] Some early boarding schools were provided with orchards. In 1827 90 apples and pears were planted in a new orchard at the Friends (Quakers) boarding school at Brookfield, Wigton, in Cumbria, a year after it had opened.[54] Early workhouses were also sometimes equipped with quite extensive food-producing facilities, which might include orchards as well as gardens. At Wickhambrook, in Suffolk, in 1822, an agreement was made for cutting a ditch across the orchard of the workhouse.[55] Orchards do not seem to have been a feature of many workhouses built under the terms of the 1834 New Poor Law, although fruit trees were often a feature of their kitchen gardens; where orchards did exist, they were often small. It is possible that overseers did not think that dependent paupers should be provided with anything as appealing as ripe fruit. As the nineteenth century progressed, moreover, orchards were less frequently maintained at elite residential institutions, such as boarding schools. Most large surviving institutional orchards are instead associated with a new range of institution which emerged in the second half of the nineteenth century.

Mental hospitals, which began to be erected on a large scale following the passing of the 1845 Lunatics Act, which made it a duty for counties and boroughs to provide asylums for their 'pauper lunatics', were regularly provided with a range of food-production facilities which included not only kitchen gardens and orchards, but also, in many cases, farms. To some extent, the practice reflected the influence of the Frenchman Phillipe Pinel, whose *Traité Medico-Philosophique sur l'Alienation Mentale*, of 1801, was translated into English as *A Treatise on Lunacy*, in 1806. This emphasised the therapeutic value of 'interesting and laborious employment' and suggested that asylums should be provided with 'a sort of farm' to this end.[56] But growing food on site also made economic sense. In Sarah Rutherford's words, 'The asylum estate was essentially a closed market with a potentially large source of "free" labour which would otherwise be absorbing revenue rather than offsetting it'.[57] Maps suggest that orchards and farms were initially located some distance from the main wards, but it is noteworthy that in suburban locations, where the hospital farm was absent or located at a distance — as with the two mental hospitals in Nottingham — the orchard was in close proximity and that in the course of the twentieth century additional orchards were often established closer to the wards, as at Leavesden or at Napsbury, both in south Hertfordshire. When Bethlem Hospital in London was relocated to its new site in Beckenham, on the outskirts of the capital, in 1930, the area immediately to the west of the main wards was laid out as a football pitch, but in the 1940s it was planted up as an orchard (it still survives, in beautiful condition, and is open to the public) (Figure 20). Orchards were thus also regarded as bringing more direct benefits to residents, as calming places to sit and walk. As early as 1891 Sir Henry Burdett, in his *Hospitals and Asylums of the World*, recommended that the courts between hospital wards 'should be laid out as gardens, and orchards, and lawns'.[58] But in most cases, orchards only seem to have been planted close to wards at English hospitals in the 1940s or 50s.

FIGURE 20. The orchard
at Bethlem Hospital,
Beckenham, south
London, planted in the
1940s. As is typical in
institutional orchards, the
trees are predominantly
cooking apples – mainly
Bramley's Seedling – with
a smaller number of
dessert varieties.

Many other kinds of residential institution were provided with orchards, but usually only where inmates were expected or encouraged to work. Children's homes had them, public schools did not; psychiatric hospitals were given them, but general medical hospitals only seldom. It is striking that, at least by the twentieth century, the only Cambridge colleges with orchards – Girton and Homerton – were both attended exclusively by women; orchards may have been thought appropriately 'domestic' in such a context. Most surviving examples of institutional orchards are dominated, as we might expect, by culinary or dual-purpose apples, such as Bramley's Seedling, Lane's Prince Albert or Dumelow's Seedling, and contained rather smaller numbers of common dessert varieties. Unlike the orchards associated with country houses, they seldom feature rare or archaic types, although that at Girton, planted around three decades after the date the college was founded in 1869, is something of an exception. Here the original trees include the old East Anglian apples Dr Harvey and Norfolk Beefing, probably a self-conscious attempt to evoke tradition and antiquity in an orchard planted beside a new building designed in medieval gothic style.

There is a particular concentration of former 'institutional' orchards in the Home Counties, reflecting the high concentration of psychiatric hospitals, children's homes and the like surrounding London. Even when, in the post-war years, their associated institutions were closed down, they sometimes found new roles, as 'community' orchards, for example. In Hertfordshire alone they include the orchard formerly associated with Shenley Psychiatric Hospital, now run by a community group, and that at The Oval in Harpenden, a former children's home, as well as the wonderful example attached to the St Elizabeth Centre in Much Hadham, a place which still fulfils its original function as an institution for the care of people living with epilepsy.

Conclusion

It is easy to concentrate on the practical and commercial roles of orchards and fruit, and to forget their ornamental and recreational significance. Even farmhouse orchards, as we have noted, were probably appreciated for their beauty in the past, but it is at the residences of the wealthy that this aspect appears most prominent. Even in the later eighteenth and nineteenth centuries, when kitchen gardens and other food-producing facilities were separated from the more ornamental areas in the grounds of great houses, orchards and fruit trees were still visited, enjoyed and celebrated. The calming pleasures of the orchard may in part explain their prominence at certain kinds of residential institution, for the infirm or the destitute, but here, as we have seen, economic factors were probably, in most contexts, more important. Either way, although always less numerous than those attached to farmhouses or run as commercial enterprises, the types of orchard briefly discussed in this chapter have their own characters, and histories, and in some parts of England now account for many of the most interesting surviving examples.

Notes

1   A. Taigel and T. Williamson, Some Early Geometric Gardens in Norfolk, *Journal of Garden History* 11, 1 and 2 (1991), 5–111, 97.

2   W. Lawson, *A New Orchard or Garden* (London), 11.

3   C. Currie, Fish Ponds as Garden Features, *Garden History* 18 (1990), 22–33; T. Williamson, *Polite Landscapes: Gardens and Society in Eighteenth-Century England* (Stroud, 1995), 31–35.

4   L. Bellamy, *The Language of Fruit: Literature and Horticulture in the Long Eighteenth Century* (Philadelphia, 2019), 16.

5   G. Chapman, *Chapman's Homer: the Iliad and the Odyssey*, ed. Jan Parker (Ware, 2002), Book 7, line 155.

6   Hertfordshire Archives and Local Studies, DE/X450/E1.

7   Chatsworth House archives, bound collection of estate surveys by William Senior.

8   Suffolk Record Office, Lowestoft branch, 295 and 942.64 Som.

9   A. Hassell Smith, The Gardens of Sir Nicholas and Francis Bacon: an Enigma Resolved and a Mind Explored. In P. Roberts (ed.), *Religion, Culture and Society in Early Modern England* (Cambridge, 1994), 125–60; discussed on 144.

10 B. Short, P. May, G. Vines and A.-M. Bur, *Apples and Orchards in Sussex* (Lewes, 2012), 56.

11 Norfolk Record Office, MC 1777/1; T. Mowl and L. Mayer, *The Historic Gardens of England: Cambridgeshire and the Isle of Ely* (Bristol, 2013), 40–41.

12 Mowl and Mayer, *Cambridgeshire*, 42–43.

13 Lawson, *New Orchard or Garden*, 14.

14 Mowl and Mayer, *Cambridgeshire*, 55.

15 Suffolk Record Office, Lowestoft, 295 and 942.64 Som.

16 W. Temple, *Miscellanea: the Second Part* (London, 1690), 129.

17 J. Bartos, Wilderness and Grove: Gardening with Trees in England 1688–1750. Unpublished PhD thesis, University of Bristol, 2013; J. Woudstra, The History and Development of Groves in English Formal Gardens, 1600–1760. In J. Woudstra and C. Roth (eds), *A History of Groves* (London, 2017), 67–85.

18 Norfolk Record Office, HARE 5531 223 X 55; E.W. Griffiths (ed.), *Through England on a Side Saddle in the Time of William and Mary: the Diary of Celia Fiennes* (London, 1888), 285.

19 Bedfordshire Record Office, TW685.

20 J. Woudstra, Fruit Cultivation in the Royal Gardens of Hampton Court Palace 1630–1842, *Garden History* 44, 2 (2016), 255–71.

21 Bellamy, *Language of Fruit*, 46–54.

22 Northamptonshire Record Office, FH/D/B/A/2442.

23 Royal Institute of British Architects Library, London, Mylne Drawing Collection SC 122/21; Bedfordshire Record Office, 2331/11 and X800/32; private collection; Norfolk Record Office, PD 254/60.

24 Berkshire Record Office, D/Ed F14.

25 Wiltshire Record Office, 1300/669/29; Bedfordshire Record Office L 31/297; Chatsworth House archives, First Series, 70.1.

26 As at Ryston, in Norfolk, in the 1670s: Norfolk Record Office, MF/RO 219/1.

27 L.W. Dilwyn, *Hortus Collinsonianus: an Account of the Plants Cultivated by the Late Peter Collinson* (Swansea, 1843), 60.

28 D. Brown and T. Williamson, *Lancelot Brown and the Capability Men: Landscape Revolution in Eighteenth-Century England* (London, 2016); J. Phibbs, *Place Making: the Art of Capability Brown* (London, 2016).

29 Brown and Williamson, *Lancelot Brown*, 126–29.

30 W. Roberts, Richard Milles' New Kitchen Garden, *Norfolk Archaeology* 62 (1937), 501–7.

31 Bedfordshire Record Office, R3/2114/534.

32 Warwickshire Record Office, CR1199/35.

33 Warwickshire Record Office, CR 1861/1.

34 *Magazine of Botany* 12 (1843), 62–63, 180–84.

35 Boulton and Paul *Catalogue*, 1888, 56.

36 Shropshire Record Office, 552/11/888 and 552/11/112.

37 Kent Archives, U24/F25.

38 Worcestershire Record Office, 705/273/7775/27ii.

39 J. Loudon, *Gardening for Ladies* (London, 1848), 219.

40 J. Morgan and A. Richards, *The New Book of Apples* (London, 2002), 208 and 233.

41 J.T. Fisher, *The Peach and Nectarine: Their History, Varieties and Cultivation* (London, 1879).

42 Suffolk Record Office, Bury St Edmunds branch, 941/56/25.

43 Suffolk Record Office, Lowestoft branch, 1117/285/29.

44 J.M. Robinson, *Felling the Ancient Oaks* (London, 2012); G. Worsley, *England's Lost Houses: from the Archives of Country Life* (London, 2002).

45 P. Davey, *Arts and Crafts Architecture* (London, 1995); W. Hitchmough, *CFA Voysey* (London, 1997); S. Kirk, *Philip Webb: Pioneer of the Arts and Crafts Movement* (London, 2005).

46 G. Jekyll, *Wood and Garden* (London, 1899), 181–83.

47 G. Jekyll, *Colour Schemes for the Flower Garden* (London, 1919), 140.

48 W. Robinson, *The English Flower Garden* (London, 1890), 382.

49 Robinson, *English Flower Garden*, 376.

50 Bedfordshire Record Office, HN7/1/AMP3.

51 F.H. Farthing, *Saturday in My Garden* (London, 1911), 317.

52 H.E. Hellier, *Practical Gardening for Amateurs* (London, 1935); M. James, *Complete Guide to Home Gardening* (London, 1932).

53 H. Chauncy, *The Historical Antiquities of Hertfordshire*, Volume 1, second edn (London, 1826), 449.

54 Cumbria Archives Centre, Carlisle, D FCF 7/1.

55 Suffolk Record Office, Bury St Edmunds branch, FL 652/8/1.

56 P. Pinel, *Traité Medico-Philosophique sur l'Alienation Mentale* (Paris, 1801), translated into English as *A Treatise on Lunacy* (London, 1806).

57 S. Rutherford, Landscapes of Lunatic Asylums. Unpublished PhD thesis, de Montfort University, Leicester (2003), 226.

58 H. C. Burdett, *Hospitals and Asylums of the World: Asylum Construction* (London, 1891), 13.

CHAPTER 4

The orchard countries: western England

Orchards could, and can, be found throughout England, and even in the far north of the country some areas of specialised fruit production existed from an early date. In Cumbria, for example, the Lythe valley to the west of Kendal was famous for its damson orchards, and in north Yorkshire, the village of Nunnington, in Ryedale, had numerous orchards in the early nineteenth century which supplied the markets of Leeds and other cities.[1] But orchards are a particularly important aspect of the landscape history of three regions: the West Country, the Home Counties and East Anglia. It is the first of these which people perhaps associate most readily with orchards, mainly intended to provide the raw ingredients for cider and, to a lesser extent, perry. And indeed, when the first detailed government surveys of agriculture were undertaken in the 1870s, the prominence of the west of England in this respect was very clear (Figure 11, above). In some western districts, orchards, including those of 'traditional' type, remain a prominent feature of the landscape (Figure 21).

Devon, Somerset and Herefordshire were the prime cider counties, but the drink was also produced and consumed on some scale, and extensive cider-apple orchards were accordingly planted, in Cornwall, Dorset, Shropshire, Worcestershire and Gloucestershire. They were also a prominent feature of the old county of Monmouthshire, variously considered part of Wales and part of England (especially on the lower, drier ground around Raglan, where, in 1803, Barber described 'teeming orchards sweeping over hills').[2] Yet fruit other than apples and pears was also grown on a substantial scale in many parts of western England from an early date, and orchards attached to farms did not only produce cider apples. A tithe agreement drawn up in 1630 in Feock, Cornwall refers to the payments made for the 'apples, pears, plums and cherries' grown in the village.[3] Nevertheless, it was the production of cider which, for centuries, principally shaped the character of western orchards and determined their extent.

Cider orchards before 1850

It is unclear when cider became the alcoholic drink of choice in the west of England, but by the later Middle Ages there are frequent references to its production, not least in the form of the obligation of manorial tenants to use the

FIGURE 21. A typical 'tall-tree' cider-apple orchard at Whimple, east Devon. The parish has a long tradition of cider making, with more than 7 per cent of its area occupied by orchards when the tithes were commuted in 1842. Whiteways cider factory was established here in 1897, beside the railway line. It was provided with its own sidings.

lord's cider press. The Abbot of Tavistock, for example, received a significant income from the exercise of this right on his Devon manors between 1392 and 1489.[4] Manorial demesnes also produced cider, for both consumption and sale, as in the Devon parishes of Exminster in the 1280s, Tynhyd in 1297 and Bishops Clyst in 1372.[5] In 1461 7 shillings and 5d was paid to 'diverse men and women for gathering apples' on the manor of Collington, and 2 shillings and 6d to 'to one man for watching the press and pressers at the time of making the said Lady's cider'.[6] There are many other references; the manorial accounts of the Devon manor of Lanchernes thus record in 1383 payments for 'collecting apples in the garden, carrying them to the presser, hiring 1 presser to make 2 casks of cider, milling the apples, carrying home 2 casks of cider, purchase of 1 empty cask.'[7] Similar evidence could be quoted from the other western counties.

But we should not, perhaps, exaggerate the importance of cider in this period, or the extent of the orchards used to provide the apples required for its production. A survey made of the Devon lands of Cicily, Marchioness of Dorset, in 1525 shows that most orchards on her properties were small and that many farms lacked them.[8] The evidence, so far as it goes, suggests that the scale of cider production expanded steadily through the sixteenth and early seventeenth centuries, and in the 1590s, John Vowell, writing about the people of Devon, could describe how 'They have of late years much enlarged the orchards, and are very curious in planting and grafting all kinds of fruits, for all seasons, of which they make good use and profit … but most especially for making of cider'.[9] Herefordshire saw particularly rapid growth, and in 1657 John Beale could characterise the county as 'The Orchard of England', where 'From the greatest persons to the poorest cottager, all habitations are encompassed with Orchards and Gardens', which were used, in particular, to provide fruit for the production of perry and cider.[10] In terms of its fruit cultivation, he argued, the county was 'a Pattern for all England'. The growing importance of orchards by the second half of the seventeenth century is reflected in the clauses in the many West Country leases which refer to their establishment or maintenance as a condition of a tenancy. Examples from Dorset include stipulations that the tenant was to 'plant an orchard with 100 fruit trees…' (1648, Monkton);[11] 'replenish and plant with fruit trees 1 acre of ground adjoining the house and to fence and maintain it as an orchard' (Tatworth, 1655);[12] 'replenish the orchard with good fruit trees when necessary' (Shute, 1672).[13]

An even greater expansion came in the second half of the seventeenth century and the first half of the eighteenth. In Devon and Somerset, the orchard acreage grew 'sometimes slowly and sometimes briskly throughout the period 1640–1750', while in south Worcestershire, the cultivation of cider apples 'developed a reliable and sustained market' and references to gathered fruit, cider mills and cider itself began to feature prominently in probate inventories and other documents.[14] By the mid-eighteenth century, while in absolute terms the area covered by orchards in the western counties was still small, compared with other regions it was remarkable. In 1757 Dean Jeremiah Milles conducted a survey of agriculture in the parishes of the Exeter Diocese by sending a questionnaire to incumbents, 263 of whom replied. One parish, Paignton, reputedly had as much as 300 acres

(121 hectares) of orchard, amounting to around 6.8 per cent of its total area. A further 14 parishes had between 150 and 300 acres (*c.* 60 and 120 hectares) under fruit trees, which in most cases was between 3 and 5 per cent of the parish area.[15] In most, orchards accounted for only around 2 per cent of the land area, but even this was roughly twice the usual figure in other parts of England. As an indication of the scale of production, moreover, the extent of orchards is misleading because, as noted earlier, large quantities of fruit came from trees planted, not in conventional orchards, but in the wider countryside.

While John Beale, as we have seen, praised the number of orchards in Herefordshire, he also noted that 'in most places our hedges are inriched with rowes of fruit-trees, pears, or apples, Gennet-moyles, or crab trees'.[16] Fifty years earlier, John Norden had commented on the abundance of fruit trees in the hedges of Devon, Gloucestershire, Shropshire, Somerset and Worcestershire.[17] Edward Leigh, writing in 1657, similarly commented on their ubiquity in Herefordshire, while Timothy Nourse, writing in 1700, described how fruit trees were widely planted in hedges in 'Herefordshire, Worcestershire, some parts of Gloucestershire'.[18] Apple trees, free-standing in the hedgerows, are often mentioned in documents describing farms in the western counties. Deeds relating to Bye Farm, Old Cleeve, in Somerset, from 1577, for example, refer to 'all apples and pears in hedgerows'; 72 'crab apple, apple trees and beech' were recorded in a survey of a holding at Roughton, near Bridgenorth, in Shropshire, in 1720.[19] Leases sometimes include clauses intended to increase their number. One for land at Whitton and Ludford, in Shropshire, drawn up in 1653, instructed the tenant to plant 'ten oaks, ten ashes and ten apple trees' on the farm each year.[20] Similar clauses appear in other Shropshire leases: from Whitton in 1660, Woodbatch in 1661 and 1724, Bishop's Castle in 1732, and elsewhere.[21] Other leases include clauses intended to protect fruit trees already present. At Bishop's Castle, in 1654, for example, the tenants could take wood for *hedgebote* and *firbote* – for their fences and their fires – 'crab trees excepted'.[22] In some western districts fruit trees were still being maintained in hedges into the nineteenth century. In 1807, for example, Rudge criticised those in Gloucestershire as a 'temptation to theft and plunder'.[23] But the impression conveyed by such sources is that by this stage, fruit production was becoming concentrated more and more in orchards.

How far the gradual decline of hedgerow planting led to a further increase in the area of orchards is unclear, but the tithe maps from *c.* 1840 show that they were thick on the ground in most, although by no means all, parts of the West Country. In the majority of Somerset parishes, they occupied between 2 and 5 per cent of the land area, although towards the south-east the figure was sometimes higher, reaching more than 8 per cent in parishes like North Barrow.[24] In Devon, similarly, parishes in which orchards accounted for between 2 and 5 per cent of the land area were the norm, but here there was more variation. A significant number of places on the lower, drier ground in the east of the county, on loamy soils formed in Devonian, Permian or Triassic sandstone, had between 5 and 10 per cent of their land under orchards. Such parishes were noticeably clustered in the vicinity of the largest towns, especially Exeter and Newton Abbot, where places such as Broadclyst (7.6 per cent), Clyst St George (7.5 per cent), and Whimple (7.2 per cent) were clearly producing a significant surplus of cider to supply urban markets, or of cider apples to supply commercial manufacturers (Figure 22). Conversely, there were a significant number of parishes in the county, well over a quarter, in which orchards accounted for less than 2 per cent of the land area, and around one sixth in which the figure was less than 1 per cent. These were mainly on the higher ground and in the wetter west of the county, towards Cornwall. In the latter county, with its high rainfall and acidic soils, orchards were similarly sparse, accounting for less than 2 per cent of the area of most parishes. The only significant densities were to be found in places like Landulph (7.2 per cent) and Calstock (6.8 per cent), which occupied sheltered ground in the Tamar valley and formed an extension of a small cluster on the Devonshire side of the river, perhaps supplying a surplus to the port of Plymouth, a few miles to the south.

By *c.* 1840 the greatest densities of orchards, by far, were to be found in Herefordshire. Here most parishes had more than 5 per cent of their land area under fruit, although again there was much variation. Mirroring the situation elsewhere, orchards tended to be fewer and smaller in the higher, wetter north-west of the county than in the lower, drier south-east (Figure 22). In the

FIGURE 22. A map showing the percentage of land area occupied by orchards, by parish, in two western counties, *c.* 1840, based on tithe apportionments. Left, Devon (100 per cent sample); right, Herefordshire (50 per cent sample). The highest densities are in parishes located on lower ground and on loamy soils overlying sandstone.

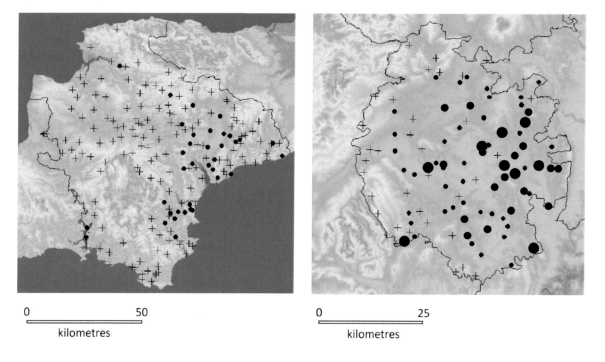

```
0              50
===============
   kilometres
```

```
0              25
===============
   kilometres
```

+ Less than 5 per cent   ● 10 - 14.9 per cent

• 5 - 9.9 per cent   ⬤ 15 per cent or more

latter area, and in the adjacent parts of Gloucestershire, a significant number of places had 10 per cent, 15 per cent, or even more of their land planted as orchards; in some, including Aston Ingham and Bromyard, over a quarter of the land area was so occupied. Most of these places were located on loamy soils formed in the Devonian Old Red Sandstone. Most were also within 10 miles (*c.* 16 kilometres) of Hereford but also within reasonable distance of industrial areas in the west Midlands – Stourport-on-Severn and the Wyre Forest coalfield, for example, lay only 15 miles (*c.* 24 kilometres) as the crow flies from Bromyard.

Why cider?

By the eighteenth century, cider orchards appear to have been ubiquitous in the western counties and cider making a regular domestic activity. Even as late as this, leases sometimes insisted that cider apples grown on a farm had to be milled or even pressed using the landowner's equipment: a lease drawn up for one Dorset farm in 1760, for example, stipulated that 'apples grown on the premises to be crushed at the manor apple ground...'.[25] But the larger farms now usually had their own mills and presses and the buildings to house them, to judge from references in deeds and leases, such as the 'Cider House with Orchard' on a farm at Colbourne, in Dorset, in 1803;[26] the 'Messuage with cider house and small orchard...' at Keate, in the same county, in 1810;[27] or the 'House, cider house, small orchard' at Castleton, in 1815 (Figure 23).[28] Small farmers used the equipment of neighbours or hired one of the mobile presses, their design based on equipment used in Cuban sugar plantations. Cider was deeply embedded in rural life and in social and economic relations – until the passing of the second Truck Amendment Act, in 1887, it was routinely used to pay part of the wages of agricultural workers. The very high densities of orchards in some districts, however, also reflects the market for cider presented by urban populations, in market towns and in cities like Exeter, Hereford and Bristol and the existence, from an early date, of professional cider makers.

Eighteenth- and nineteenth-century commentators marvelled at the amounts of cider both produced and consumed. In Monmouthshire it was said in 1800 that 'Cider is a common beverage in every house'.[29] Yet the reasons why cider became the alcoholic drink of choice across much of western England, but not to any significant extent elsewhere, have received little attention from modern historians, or indeed from early writers, although the latter often drew attention to the marked concentration of production here,

FIGURE 23. A stone cider mill for crushing apples prior to pressing, in the fourteenth-century Leigh Court Barn, in Worcestershire. The great stone, or 'runner', would be moved through the trough by a horse. Worcestershire was, with Gloucestershire, the most easterly of the cider counties.

and its equally striking absence from districts only a little farther to the east. As William Marshall put it in 1796:

> The cultivation of fruit trees, for the sole purpose of liquor, is peculiar to the western provinces. The southern counties, when the London markets are over-stocked with fruit, make a sort of liquor from the surplus: but the eastern, the northern, and the Midland counties, may be said to be as unacquainted with the business of a liquor-orchard, as they are with that of a vineyard.[30]

It is certainly clear that the bounds of the cider-drinking region were, at least by the eighteenth century, fairly sharp. Somerset was famous for its cider, but in the next county to the east, Wiltshire, it was said in 1811 that 'orchards are little known' and cider making was restricted to a small number of villages close to the main towns.[31] Shropshire, albeit to a lesser extent than Herefordshire, was essentially a cider-producing county, but in 1796 Pitt thought that in Staffordshire, which lies immediately to the east, 'the orchards … are inconsiderable, little or no cyder or perry is made'.[32] Marshall likewise described how the same county, although 'divided from the cyder country by a narrow ridge of hills only, has not, generally speaking, a barrel of cyder made within it'.

In all probability, the popularity of cider had little to do with the particular suitability of the west for the cultivation of apples and pears, or even for growing the kinds of varieties best suited to the production of cider or perry. Instead, it arose from wider aspects of agriculture and the environment which militated against the successful production of beer, the drink of choice elsewhere in England amongst the working population. Beer was made from malted barley, and it was the quantity and quality of the barley crop that was critical in shaping regional preferences in alcoholic drinks. Barley was cultivated throughout England, for it was the main cereal crop grown in rotation with wheat, especially on lighter land. Little of it appears to have been consumed directly, at least by the sixteenth century – as barley bread, for example. Most, if not converted to malt, was used as animal feed. Before the modern period, grain crops were to some extent cultivated in all parts of England, because limitations on transport ensured a greater degree of local agricultural self-sufficiency than exists today. But the higher rainfall and, in many cases, more elevated terrain found in the west ensured that the arable acreage was always more restricted than in the east. Moreover, from the sixteenth century, the area under cultivation, especially in Devon and Somerset, contracted further, as a more integrated national economy emerged, and as many western areas began to concentrate on stock rearing and dairying. In Harrison's words, 'The increasing importance of pasture farming represented a positive shift towards specialisation in that branch of agriculture to which the south-west was best suited, and which the dawning of a national economy increasingly allowed it to pursue'.[33] Although barley was widely cultivated in western England, in many districts it was on a comparatively small and declining scale, and not in sufficient abundance to sustain a significant local malting industry.

This said, there were some parts of western England with large areas under arable cultivation, especially in Herefordshire. Perhaps of more importance was the fact that much of the barley grown in western districts was not very suitable for malting. Good malting barley needs to contain a high proportion of starch but only a small proportion of protein, because it is the starch that is converted by the malting process to maltose, which is combined with yeast to produce the fermented liquid.[34] Such barley requires a relatively dry climate and light, well-drained soils, preferably ones which are calcareous in nature. Not surprisingly, the chalklands of eastern and southern England were, as a national economy emerged in the course of the post-medieval period, the main areas of production, although good-quality malting grain also came from areas of limestone soils, such as eastern Northamptonshire. Reasonable malting barley could be made in areas of neutral soils, but only if the rainfall levels were modest. In areas with a damp climate, and especially those in which the soils were generally acidic, it could not be produced. Most of the soils in the principal 'cider counties' have a natural pH above 6, and although the seventeenth and eighteenth centuries saw increasing applications of lime to farmland, this could never improve the soil enough for the successful cultivation of malting-quality barley. It is striking, in this context, that early writers sometimes observed how, near the eastern boundary of the cider country, in areas where good barley land lay close to areas rich in orchards, cider and beer were effectively in competition, their relative fortunes determined by the availability of their raw materials. Pitt thus reported that Staffordshire farmers kept a careful eye on the apple crop in the adjacent county of Worcestershire, 'conceiving a large production of cyder and perry would affect the price of their great favourite, barley'.[35] A shortage of good-quality malting barley thus seems to have encouraged the development of alternative forms of intoxication, in the form of cider and perry, in the west of England. To some extent, of course, similar conditions obtained in the northern counties, where beer *was* the preferred drink. Rainfall levels were high, and the area under pasture, as in the western counties, likewise increased steadily throughout the post-medieval centuries. But the extent of lime-rich soils, developed in limestone, was here greater. More importantly, in cooler conditions, the apple harvest itself was smaller and less dependable.

This essentially environmental, agrarian argument should not be taken too far. Malt was produced on some scale in many western districts, especially on the fertile Herefordshire plane, where the area under arable cultivation always remained extensive: in 1830 there were 20 maltsters in Hereford alone, 13 in Leominster, and others elsewhere.[36] Beer certainly was available, and widely consumed, in the west of England, although in Devon and Cornwall especially much was made from oats and was widely criticised by outsiders. By the nineteenth century, a number of industrial beer producers had emerged, in Herefordshire especially, such as the Imperial Brewery and the Hereford and Tredegar Brewery. A shortage of malting barley may have been an important reason for the dominance of cider in the western counties, but other factors were probably also at work.

In particular, cider production may have been encouraged by the fact that much of the west was enclosed at an early date, in small fields, providing ample opportunities for planting apple trees in hedges, in the manner just described. Early writers usually associated the apples from hedgerow trees specifically with cider production, rather than with dessert or culinary use. John Norden suggested that, even allowing for losses through theft, to which they were prone:

> The fruite thus dispersedly planted, hath made in some little Farmes … a tunne, two, three, foure, of *Syder*, and *Perry*, which kinde of drinke resembling white wine, hath without any further supply of ale, or beere, sufficed a good householder and his family, the whole yeare following, and sometimes hath made of the overplus twenty nobles, or ten poundes, more or lesse.[37]

Many areas on the eastern side of England were similarly enclosed in small fields by the sixteenth century, but their hedges were filled with ash, oak and elm trees, the vast majority of which were pollarded on a regular basis in order to provide a source of firewood. In East Anglia, and in most parts of south-east England, other forms of fuel were often in short supply before improvements in transport in the eighteenth and nineteenth centuries made coal more widely available. In the western cider counties, the situation was generally different. Already by the end of the seventeenth century the Shropshire coalfields were producing over 230,000 tons of coal a year.[38] Some of this went to the adjacent county of Herefordshire, which was also served by the mines in the Forest of Dean. As early as the fifteenth century, the mines in north Somerset not only supplied the county itself, but also provided fuel – via ships sailing down the Bristol Channel – for Devon, which also received coal from the mines of south Wales. True, coal was not available to everyone. As late as 1805, it was said of Herefordshire that 'Coal is in general use as fuel as by as many of the inhabitants as can afford the purchase of it'; while in Devon in 1792 it was the primary fuel in the 'Houses of Creditable People, but the poor burn no Coals, and very little Wood, on Account of the Expense… most of their Fuel is Turf or Peat'.[39] But as this last comment attests, extensive moorlands in Devon, Somerset and Shropshire, as well as wetlands, provided an ample store of peat, while commons supplied gorse and heather in abundance. Many hedgerow trees were, especially in parts of Shropshire and Herefordshire, routinely cropped for fuel or grown for timber.[40] But in most western districts, blessed with a relative abundance of combustible materials, it was possible to find space for fruit trees, and this may have been another factor which encouraged the early preference for cider.

We might also note again the greater emphasis on pastoral agriculture in the western counties. This tended to spread the demand for labour fairly evenly across the farming year, whereas in arable areas, autumn ploughing, harrowing, and sowing generally coincided with the apple harvest, perhaps discouraging too great an emphasis on orchards and cider. In addition, the strong sea-faring tradition of the west of England may have played a part: one early writer described how 'The merchants who make great voyages to sea, find it a very useful drink in their ships and so buy up a great store of it, for one ton of cider will go as far as three of beer and is found more wholesome in hot climates'.[41] A number of factors, in other words, probably encouraged the dominance of cider in western England. But the most important were probably the relatively small (and steadily contracting) arable acreage and the unsuitability of much local barley for malting. Whatever the precise balance of influences, this preference, once established, became a regional taste, deeply sown into the fabric of local culture.

The character of western cider orchards

It is sometime suggested that West Country orchards were invariably 'grass' orchards, mown for hay or grazed by livestock and dominated by tall, spreading trees. Surviving examples of old orchards in the western counties are certainly like this. But the situation was more complex in the past, and eighteenth-century commentators made a distinction between 'grass orchards', 'arable orchards' and what some described as 'close orchards'. Arable orchards were, according to William Marshall in 1796, a particular feature of Herefordshire and Gloucestershire, although they could certainly be found, scattered more thinly, elsewhere in the west. In such orchards, the trees were widely spaced – at intervals of 18, 20 or even 25 yards (*c.* 16.5 to 23 metres) – and the ground between them was planted, not merely with vegetables, but with arable crops, such as wheat, barley and turnips.[42] Of necessity, tall trees, with clear stems 2 metres or more in height, were favoured, as 'a tall-stemmed tree … is much less injurious to whatever grows under it, than a low-headed tree'.[43] The tithe apportionments for Herefordshire make it clear that this form of management was widely practised in the county in the middle of the nineteenth century, although it may by then have already been in decline. They do not always consistently distinguish between different kinds of orchard in each parish, but where they do, they suggest that a little over one half were of 'arable' type; most of the rest were described as 'pasture orchards', with a small minority (around 5 per cent) described as 'meadow orchards', although again not all apportionments make this distinction. Perhaps unsurprisingly, parishes in which more than 75 per cent of the orchards were 'arable', such as Aston Ingham (85 per cent) or Yarkhill (92 per cent), were mostly located in the drier, lower south and east of the county, where arable land was itself generally more extensive. The small size of some of the 'arable orchards' suggests that they were cultivated as market gardens, for vegetable crops, but many were extensive, covering 5, 10 or more acres (2, 4 or more hectares). With their widely spaced trees, they might appear more as farmland scattered with fruit trees than as 'orchards' as usually conceived. Indeed, in his *General View of the Agriculture of Herefordshire,* of 1798, Clarke referred to debates in the county over the relative advantages of planting apple trees in orchards or 'in the arable fields'.[44]

Marshall, among other writers, believed that ploughing around the trees was beneficial to them, especially in their early stages of growth, but he was less enthusiastic about the effects that the trees would have on the crops growing beneath them, in terms of shade and dripping water.[45] It was probably for this reason that arable use was sometimes, although by no means usually, only one phase of an orchard's life: that is, cultivation continued while the trees were young, but the orchard was grassed down as the trees matured.[46] Arable orchards had largely disappeared from Herefordshire and Gloucestershire by the end of the nineteenth century. Inter-planting and replanting of such orchards after they had been laid to grass has generally ensured that the trees, while still quite widely spaced, are more closely planted than was originally the case – often at around 8–10 metres, rather than the 15, 20 or more described by early writers (Figure 24).

The high proportion of arable orchards was not the only feature that distinguished Herefordshire from other parts of western England. In Devon, Somerset and other western counties, most orchards were located close to farmhouses, as was usually the case elsewhere. But while this was true of many Herefordshire examples, others were 'scattered abroad, in every part of the township; perhaps half a mile from any habitation'.[47] The difference was one of degree, not absolute: scattered orchards could be found, to some extent, in most western counties, but eighteenth-century writers certainly associated them closely with Herefordshire and to an extent with Gloucestershire. The result was a landscape, not simply full of orchards, but strewn with fruit trees – planted in hedges and across both arable and pasture fields. In 1793 John Eyre, travelling from Ross-on-Wye, in Herefordshire, to Gloucester, described at one point how 'the road winds thro' short abrupt vallies, their green sides hung with coppice wood or Orchards, for all their pastures, meadows, & corn fields are stuck with apple trees, which in themselves are ugly, but as the source of commerce to these parts of the Kingdom we respect them, & when thrown together in a map under the eye enrich the view'.[48]

Herefordshire was the only cider county in which the tithe apportionments show that the extent of arable land exceeded that of pasture, mainly a consequence of the relatively low levels of rainfall which characterised areas lying in the lee of the Brecon Beacons and the Black Mountains. If large areas of land were to be devoted to orchards, then in an economy largely geared towards the production of crops, their area, too, needed to be ploughed and cultivated: the land use in extensive orchards, of necessity, reflected that which predominated in the wider landscape.

In other parts of the west, where climatic conditions encouraged a specialisation in livestock farming, orchards were more likely to be laid to grass, serving as a useful place to keep young or sick animals or in which to carry out calving or even milking. In Devon, in particular, 'Orchards often doubled as 'mowbartons' or rickyards – the trees providing shelter for the ricks'. Younger trees would be protected from livestock with posts and rails or, in many cases, with bundles of thorns staked around their base. But cattle farming was the main agricultural pursuit in many of these cider-producing areas. Orchards were sometimes used for calving and certainly as a place in which to keep young calves, rather than

FIGURE 24. An old cider-apple orchard at Mansell Lacey, Herefordshire. Now under pasture, this was an arable orchard when the tithe map was surveyed in 1842.

FIGURE 25. Cattle grazing in an orchard in Whimple, east Devon. Cattle were grazed in West Country orchards, especially in Devon, more often than in orchards in eastern England. The trees, in consequence, were often 'headed' rather higher above the ground, at a height of 2.5 or even 3 m.

just sheep.[49] Even grown cattle might be grazed in them on occasions. Like the arable orchards, western grass orchards therefore sometimes contained particularly tall trees, with clear stems more than 2 metres long, so that the branches and fruit were out of reach of the cows and their offspring. In many districts, including Herefordshire, they were often pruned pollard-fashion, sometimes as high as 3 metres above the ground (Figure 25). Tall trees – surviving veterans are often very tall indeed – could be tolerated because the cider apples were

usually shaken from the tree, rather than picked and the hard varieties used for cider making were less easily damaged than most culinary or dessert types

Early writers, as noted earlier, distinguished a third and rather different kind of West Country orchard, sometimes described as 'Close Orchards'. These could, once again, be found throughout the west but were evidently a particular feature of Devon, and especially of the west of that county and the adjacent parts of Cornwall. In many ways they resembled modern commercial orchards. They were composed of trees kept very low by rigorous pruning – with stems no more than 4 or 5 feet (*c.* 1.5 metres) high – and which were very densely planted, at intervals of 4 or 5 yards (*c.* 3.5–5.5 metres).[50] This was in part to prevent wind damage, a particular concern in coastal areas and districts of elevated terrain, but also because such an arrangement made it easier to pick the fruit and provided higher yields per acre than orchards of more conventional, 'grass' or 'arable', type. Where trees were so densely packed together it was impossible to grow arable crops between them and difficult, although not impossible, to cultivate vegetables or soft fruit. Such orchards were thus grass orchards, but the low growth of the trees limited the extent to which they could be grazed by livestock. As Sinclair put it in 1832, in such circumstances 'the use of the land is in a great measure lost. Horses are sometimes allowed to run through them; and calves in early spring; but grown cattle and sheep are at all times prohibited; likewise swine, when the fruit is on the trees'.[51] The close spacing of the trees also made a hay crop problematic. Indeed, instead of being mown for hay, the grass was often simply cut and laid around the base of the trees, as a mulch against weeds.[52]

Other western orchards: Gloucestershire and Worcestershire

As early agricultural writers often pointed out, not every orchard in western England was dedicated to the cultivation of apples for the production of cider or of pears for the production of perry. Other kinds of fruit were also grown, both for domestic use and for local sale. Even in Devon 'mazzard' cherries were widely cultivated in the north of the county, while in Monmouthshire eating as well as cider apples were grown in the orchards, in part to supply 'the iron works on the hills where the climate will not allow of their being produced from the soil'. [53] But the most diversified fruit-growing industries developed in the counties of Worcestershire and Gloucestershire. Both were 'cider counties', and both continued to be major producers of cider apples well into the nineteenth century. But both, by this time, were more famous for other kinds of fruit, and especially for their plums.

Pitt described in his *General View,* of 1808, how orchards had 'been long and successfully cultivated' in Worcestershire, particularly in 'the middle, south and western parts' of the county.[54] But Pomeroy, who contributed to Pitt's volume, drew a distinction between 'old' orchards and 'new' ones. The former were small, farm orchards, which were mainly stocked with apples and pears for domestic consumption and in particular for cider making. The 'new' orchards were more carefully sited with respect to soils and more carefully managed and, by implication, more commercial in character.[55] Pitt himself discussed how they produced cherries, plums and walnuts, as well as apples and pears. The cherries in particular were taken to Birmingham and Wolverhampton, and sometimes as far away as Lancashire or Yorkshire. This was possible because of the existence of the new canal network: 'I have been very creditably informed, that in some such year, £2000 has been paid for tonnage of fruit upon the Trent and Severn Canal, passing to the north'. He calculated that this was equivalent to nearly 7,000 tons of fruit.[56] Pitt and Pomeroy together thus imply that orchards mainly geared to growing cider apples were a long-established feature of Worcestershire, as they were of the counties to the west, but that industrialisation and urban growth in the west Midlands had encouraged both an expansion and a diversification of production in the second half of the eighteenth century, with the development of the canal network in the 1780s and 90s providing access to more distant markets, and a further stimulus.

The situation in Gloucestershire appears to have been broadly similar, except that in some parts of the county – especially in areas of amenable soils lying close to the navigable River Severn – specialisation and diversification began at an earlier date than in Worcestershire, in part because of the market provided by the great city of Bristol, the third largest centre of population in England in the early modern period. As early as 1600, a legal case was fought concerning the tolls paid at the Port of Bristol on apples and pears brought by boat along the Severn from Gloucester, Newnham, Tewkesbury and Barkley.[57] The tithe maps suggest that this north-western part of the county, around the Severn and bordering on Herefordshire and Worcestershire, was already characterised by a high density of orchards. Nevertheless, in both counties, large-scale commercial production only really took off in the second half of the nineteenth century.

This development was, as we have seen, shared by many other areas in England, being the consequence of rising demand as the country industrialised and urbanised; of improvements in transport, with the development of a national rail network; and, from the 1870s, of the onset of agricultural depression. Worcestershire and Gloucestershire were less badly affected by the latter than the more intensively arable districts of eastern England, but many farmers were, nevertheless, obliged to diversify into the production of new commodities. The rise of food processing, and in particular industrial jam making, was also a factor. Initially based in major cities, at the end of the century the industry tended to migrate out from urban areas, into the districts where the fruit was actually produced, leading to the establishment of new factories in villages or hamlets, usually close to rail lines. One example was at Toddington, in Gloucestershire, where from the 1880s, Lord Sudeley planted 500 acres (*c.* 200 hectares) of fruit trees on his estate and converted one of the estate farms and its outbuildings into a jam factory, which was leased to T.W. Beach, a Middlesex manufacturer.[58] The orchards were provided with their own tramway system for moving the fruit. In 1907 the factory was taken over by Deakin's of Wigan, and Beach's company shifted its attention to a new factory established by Sudeley's neighbour, the Earl of Coventry, at Pershore, to process fruit from his tenant's orchards. Deakin's now built a fruit canning plant at Toddington, taking full advantage of the possibilities presented by the construction of the Great Western branch line to Cheltenham and Gloucester, opened in 1906, which ran through the estate, now owned by the industrialist Hugh Andrews.[59] The orchards continued to increase in area, covering around 1,000 (c. 400 hectares) acres by 1914.

By 1873 there were 11,620 acres (4,808 hectares) of orchard in Gloucestershire, and this figure had risen to over 20,000 by 1905. In Worcestershire the figures were 12,707 and 22,636, with a peak of over 24,000 acres (c. 9,700 hectares) around the start of the First World War. While some this expansion reflected a growth in demand for cider apples, most of the new orchards produced dessert or culinary fruit, or plums for processing into jam. There was some decline in the overall orchard area during the inter-war years, but this was largely a consequence of the grubbing out of old cider-apple orchards.[60] By the start of the Second World War, both counties, but Worcestershire in particular, contained some of the most important fruit-growing districts in England.

Different areas in the two counties came to specialise in the cultivation of different kinds of fruit. In Gloucestershire, cider apples continued to be a major item of production in the orchards in the Forest of Dean and the Vale of Severn, while in Worcestershire their cultivation was concentrated in the west of the county, and in particular in the far north-west (in the Upper Teme valley, around Tenbury and in the area between Stourport-on-Severn and the Shropshire border, near Ludlow), and in the far south-west, to the south of Malvern. Cherry orchards were also clustered in the north-west of Worcestershire, especially in the parishes of Leigh, Suckley and Alfrick. But plums were most numerous in the south-east of the county, in the Vale of Evesham, where the towns of Evesham and Pershore gave their names to the Evesham Wonder, Pershore Yellow Egg and Purple Pershore varieties.[61] The calcareous clay soils of the area, derived from the Lower Lias, were ideal for growing plum trees (Figure 26). All this said, many districts grew a range of fruit, especially those lying close to large towns, such as Cheltenham and Gloucester, or – in the far south of Gloucestershire – within easy reach of the Bristol markets. Even in the Vale of Evesham, apples, pears and cherries were widely grown, alongside the famous plums. In the orchards on the Bretforton Manor estate, for example, 5 miles (3 kilometres) east of Evesham, the Blenheim orchard was planted in 1862 with both apples and Pershore plums; the Bakehouse Close orchard in 1862 with cherries; the Upper Close in 1867 with apples and pears of mixed varieties; and Fulland Bank in 1870 with 'Cherries, plums, damsons and prune damsons'.[62] Such diversity continued into the late nineteenth century (orchards in the neighbouring village of Badsey were producing large numbers of apples and pears, as well as plums, in the 1890s) and into the inter-war years.[63] Stamp was able to describe in 1941 how dessert apples were increasing in significance in the locality, especially on the higher ground, and

FIGURE 26. The phenomenal density of orchards around Pershore, Worcestershire, in 1884, as shown on the First Edition Ordnance Survey 6-inch map. Note how the boundaries of the individual plots have 'fossilised' the boundaries of the strips and furlongs in the former open fields, enclosed piecemeal over the previous centuries.

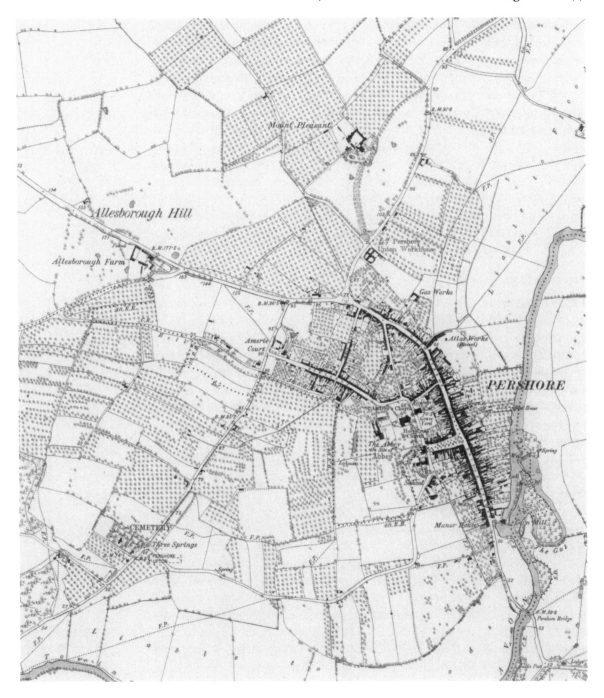

were an even more important item farther west, around Pershore. Nevertheless, he described the Evesham and Pershore district as 'the leading centre for plum orchards in the whole of England'.[64]

At the start of the nineteenth century, Worcestershire orchards were sometimes under grass and sometimes ploughed and, as elsewhere in the west, they sometimes began life as arable orchards but were grassed down as the trees matured and their canopies closed. In Gloucestershire, there was also a mixture of orchard types, with arable orchards common in the north-west, towards the Herefordshire border, but with most of the county dominated by grass orchards, mown for hay and grazed by stock, including cattle. As elsewhere, in both circumstances the trees needed to be tall, and grafted on vigorous rootstocks. The proportion of grass orchards in the two counties increased steadily through the second half of the nineteenth century, but this should not conjure up idyllic images of romantic, effortless production, leading to environments rich in wildlife. These orchards were, by the second half of the nineteenth century, rigorously managed and often intensively sprayed with pesticides, as well as being heavily manured. An orchard in Bretforton, planted in 1863, had its turf rolled back in 1870 to allow heavy applications of dung, bones and guano.[65]

The later history of cider orchards

In the middle years of the nineteenth century, cider orchards were extensive in many western counties and already served more than domestic needs. Cider and perry were supplied to the region's numerous ports, and to major towns and cities, such as Exeter, Hereford, Gloucester and Bristol; some went farther afield, to London. But the later decades of the century saw further growth. Government figures show that between 1873 and 1905 the area of cider orchards rose in Devon from 24,448 acres to 27,472 (9,894 to 11,118 hectares), in Somerset from 18,192 to 25,405 (7,362 to 10,281 hectares), and in Herefordshire from 21,373 to 27,081 (8,650 to 10,960 hectares) – increases of 12.4 per cent, 39.6 per cent and 26.7 per cent, respectively.[66] One important factor in this expansion was the rise of industrial cider production. Between 1870 and 1900, no fewer than 12 cider factories opened around Hereford, including Godwins of Holmer (1898); Westons of Much Marcle (1880); Ridlers of Clehonger (1870); Symonds of Stock Lacey; and, above all, Bulmers of Hereford, established in 1887 and still in business today. And others could be found in Devon, Somerset and Gloucestershire, including S.W. Arnold of Taunton (1876) and Whiteways of Whimple (1897).[67] Much of the cider produced by these firms was sold locally– domestic production was replaced by factory production – but the railways allowed a wider, urban market to be reached, especially in the Midlands and the north. It is true that beer remained, by a long way, the preferred beverage in these areas; it is also true that the West Country factories faced stiff competition in the eastern parts of the country from Gaymers in Norfolk, a company that, somewhat surprisingly, was established before many of these West Country firms. But this was, nevertheless, a period of significant growth in cider production in the west of England.

Initially, the apples used by the cider factories continued to be sourced from existing farm orchards. So far as the evidence goes, most of these were now grass orchards with standard trees – there are fewer references to the intensive, 'close' orchards characteristic of Devon, and by 1900 most of the arable orchards of Herefordshire seem to have been laid to grass, in part perhaps as a consequence of the agricultural depression.[68] But in the early years of the twentieth century, problems with the poor quality of fruit, together with the logistical problems associated with gathering fruit from numerous small, scattered orchards, led to the planting of some new, more modern examples, especially in Herefordshire. This was part of a wider process of modernisation. In 1903 the National Fruit and Cider Institute (later the Long Ashton Research Station) was established at Long Ashton, near Bristol, by C.W. Radcliffe-Cooke, with the support of the Board of Agriculture; the Bath and West Society; and the county councils of Devon, Gloucestershire, Somerset, Worcestershire and Herefordshire.[69] This worked to develop new varieties of cider apple and to encourage better forms of pest control and pruning, as well as improved manufacturing processes. Practical demonstrations and technical instruction were provided.

Replanting intensified in the inter-war years. In the area lying to the north-east of Hereford especially, the 'old neglected orchards of cider-apples and perry pears' were, by the 1930s, being replaced by 'modern orchards well laid out and managed'.[70] As Stamp explained in 1937, 'An upgrading of cider-apple orchards has been energetically pressed forward by the cider-manufacturers of Hereford, at least one of which provides young trees of selected strains from their own nurseries to farmers willing to plant new orchards'.[71] These were not scattered around the landscape, on a wide variety of soils, as many of the earlier ones had been, but were instead located 'mainly on close-textured heavy red loams derived from the red marls of the Old Red Sandstone', which provided ideal conditions for apple growing. Similar initiatives were undertaken by companies in other counties, including Coates (established in 1925) in Somerset, while in Devon, the Devon Cidermakers' Federation distributed apple trees free to growers between 1933 and 1936, at the rate of a tree for every ton of apples sent to the factories.[72] But Herefordshire, the real heart of industrial cider production, led the way.

The extent of entirely new plantings should not be exaggerated, however, and the rise in the overall area of orchards in the west stalled around 1910 and then began a long, slow decline. The boom years for cider making were short lived. From a peak in 1884, when around 33 million gallons of cider were drunk in Britain, consumption fell slowly and erratically to around 17 million by 1920. Output then roughly stabilised, but only began to recover to previous levels from the 1960s.[73] Much cider was still made on, and most cider apples were still grown on, farms, low levels of investment discouraging new plantings. Up until the First World War, farm production still accounted, in most years, for the majority of cider consumed in England. Even in the 1930s, a 'considerable quantity of cider' was still made on farms, even if the 'general tendency' was by now to sell the crop to one of the commercial manufacturers.[74] On some farms, production, aimed at a local (and to an extent a tourist) market, was actually modernised during the inter-war years. According to one commentator, while 'The major proportion of the cider-apple crop is consigned to the larger factories … a number of farmers are now making cider on up-to-date lines'.[75] Only in the 1940s and 50s did farmhouse production really decline, to around 5 per cent of total production.

With the cider factories now in part supplied by more productive, modern orchards – and with demand for cider significantly lower than at the start of the century – the area of orchards began to dwindle.[76] In the three main cider counties, Devon, Herefordshire and Somerset, the orchard area fell from around 80,000 acres (*c.* 32,375 hectares) in 1910 to a little over 65,000 (*c.* 26,300 hectares) by 1935. The fall would have been even greater if the decline in cider orchards had not, to some extent, been accompanied by an expansion in those planted with fruit for dessert and culinary use. Manning in 1936 described how a number of new orchards of dessert apples – Worcester Pearmain, Cox's Orange, Allington Pippin, Laxton's Superb, Lord Lambourne and Ellison's Orange – had been established over the previous years in the south and east of Devon, although problems with scab (caused by the fungus, *Venturia inaequalis*) had necessitated high applications of potash and an intensive spraying programme.[77] By the 1930s, only 60 per cent of the orchards in Herefordshire were thought to be devoted to cider apples.[78] The decline in the area of cider orchards was thus proportionately greater than the overall fall of the orchard acreage; indeed, by 1936 there were only 67,540 acres (27,333 hectares) of cider orchards in the whole of England. Decline continued thereafter: by 1948 the national figure had dropped to 50,000 acres (20,234 hectares).[79]

There was, moreover, a widespread belief that the condition of the old cider orchards was deteriorating. In the words of one observer, writing in 1936, 'Unfortunately the cider orchards in the West, once well cared for, suffered from neglect for many years before the beginning of the present century' and had not been much improved since.[80] Stamp in the following year described those in Somerset and Devon, in particular, as being 'for the most part small, old, neglected'.[81] Many were already in a state of advanced decay, Stamp noting that in some 'only a few old trees may remain in an acre of what is really pasture'.[82] As we shall see, the orchard acreage dwindled even more rapidly in the western cider counties in the post-war years. But West Country orchards, and especially what we think of as the 'traditional' cider orchards of the region, had been in decline for decades. And many, as we have seen – the 'close' orchards of Devon, the arable orchards of Herefordshire – had never really conformed closely to our idealised image of what such orchards should be.

Notes

1   W. Page (ed.), *Victoria History of the County of York, North Riding*, Volume 1 (London, 1914), 545.

2   J.T. Barber, *A Tour through South Wales and Monmouthshire* (London, 1803), 211.

3   Cornwall Record Office, P64/3/1.

4   H.P.R. Finberg, *Tavistock Abbey: a Study in the Social and Economic History of Devon* (Cambridge, 1951).

5   N. Alcock, An East Devon Manor in the Later Middle Ages, Part 1: 1374–1420, the Manor Farm, *Devonshire Association Transactions* 102 (1970), 141–87.

6   M. Gee, *The Devon Orchards Book* (Wellington, 2018), 30.

7   Devon Record Office, AR/2/508, 1383.

8   T.L. Stoate, *A Survey of West Country Manors, 1525: the lands of Cecily, Marchioness of Dorset, Lady Harington and Bonville in Cornwall, Devon, Dorset, Somerset, Wiltshire* (Bristol, 1979).

9   Gee, *Devon Orchards*, 41.

10 J. Beale, *Herefordshire Orchards, a Pattern for All England, Written in an Epistolary Address to Samuel Hartlib, Esq.* (London, 1656), 5.

11 Devon Record Office, 123M/L897.

12 Devon Record Office, 123M/L1488.

13 Devon Record Office, 123M/L1106.

14 J. Thirsk, The South-West Midlands. In J. Thirsk (ed.), *The Agrarian History of England and Wales,* Volume 5.1, *1640–1750: Regional Farming Systems,* 159–96, at 166; G. Harrison, The South-West. In Thirsk (ed.), *Agrarian History of England and Wales,* Volume 5.1, 358–92, at 382.

15 Gee, *Devon Orchards*, 45–46.

16 Beale, *Herefordshire Orchards*, 5.

17 J. Norden, *The Surveyor's Dialogue* (London, 1607), 201.

18 T. Nourse, *Campania Felix; or, the Benefits and Improvement of Husbandry* (London, 1700), 28.

19 Shropshire Record Office, 2028/1/5/31; Somerset Record Office, DD\X\RMN/3, 1577.

20 Shropshire Record Office, 11/96.

21 Shropshire Record Office, 11/456, 11/560–61 and 11/565–66.

22 Shropshire Record Office, 11/497.

23 T. Rudge, *General View of the Agriculture of the County of Gloucester* (London, 1807), 197 and 213.

24 The digital copies of the tithe maps and apportionments provided online by The Genealogist were used in these and all subsequent calculations.

25 Devon Record Office, 48/2/4.

26 Dorset Record Office, D/PIT/T652.

27 Dorset Record Office, D/SHA/CH675.

28 Dorset Record Office, D/FFO/12/69.

29 A. Black, *Black's Guide to the Counties of Herefordshire and Monmouthshire,* 7th edn (Edinburgh 1880), 7.

30 W. Marshall, *The Rural Economy of Gloucestershire, Including Its Dairy; Together with the Dairy Management of North Wiltshire; and the Management of Orchards and Fruit Liquor in Herefordshire,* Volume 2 (London, 1796), 205–6.

31 T. Davis, *General View of the Agriculture of Wiltshire* (London, 1811), 82–83.

32 W. Pitt, *General View of the Agriculture of the County of Stafford* (London, 1796), 88.

33 Harrison, The South-West, 366.

34 D.H. Robinson, *Fream's Elements of Agriculture* (London, 1949), 195–96.

35 W. Pitt, *General View of the Agriculture of the County of Staffordshire* (London, 1808), 89.

36 Herefordshire Council, Herefordshire through time, https://htt.herefordshire. gov.uk/herefordshires-past/the-post-medieval-period/agriculture-and-industry/ herefordshire-industry/brewing-and-malting, accessed 1 August 2021.

37 Norden, *Surveyor's Dialogue,* 208.

38 J. Hatcher, *The History of the British Coal Industry, Volume 1: Before 1700: Towards the Age of Coal* (1993), 68.

39 J.M. Ducumb, *General View of the Agriculture of the County of Hereford* (1805), 141; *House of Commons Journal,* 47, 13 February (1792), 328–30.

40 T. Williamson, G. Barnes and T. Pillatt, *Trees in England: Management and Disease since 1600* (Hatfield, 2017), 32–33.

41 Quoted in Gee, *Devon Orchards Book,* 38.

42 Marshall, *Rural Economy of Gloucestershire,* Volume 2, 237; J. Sinclair, *The Code of Agriculture* (London, 1818), 313.

43 Marshall, *Rural Economy of Gloucestershire,* Volume 2, 235.

44 J. Clarke, *General View of the Agriculture of the County of Hereford* (London, 1794), 36.

45 Marshall, *Rural Economy of Gloucestershire,* Volume 2, 251–52.

46 Sinclair, *Code of Agriculture,* 313; Marshall, *Rural Economy of Gloucestershire,* Volume 2, 253.

47 Marshall, *Rural Economy of Gloucestershire,* Volume 2, 224.

48 The National Archives, Kew, 30/46/1/6, 'Travel Diary: Journey from Babworth to Oxford and back', July 1793, The Ven. John Eyre, Archdeacon of Nottingham.

49 C. Vancouver, *General View of the Agriculture of Devon (*London, 1808), 238.

50 W. Marshall, *The Rural Economy of the West of England,* Volume 1 (London, 1805), 213–14; J. Sinclair, *The Code of Agriculture* (London, 1818), 311.

51 Sinclair, *Code of Agriculture,* 313.

52 Marshall, *Rural Economy of the West of England,* Volume 1, 216.

53 C. Hassell, *General View of the Agriculture of the County of Monmouth* (London, 1815), 57.

54 W. Pitt, *General View of the Agriculture of the County of Worcester* (London, 1810), 149.

55 Pitt, *Worcester,* 150–52.

56 Pitt, *Worcester,* 149.

57 The National Archives, Kew, E134/43 Eliz/East18.

58 R. Butler, Social and Economic History. In W. Page (ed.), *Victoria History of the County of Gloucestershire,* Volume 2 (London, 1907), 127–72, at 193.

59 Deakins Jam and Fruit, http://www.deakin.broadwaymanor.co.uk/deakin/naunton-field-jam-factory.htm, accessed 1 August 2021.

60 L. Stamp, *The Land of Britain: Its Use and Misuse* (London, 1948), 119, 121.

61 Stamp, *Land of Britain: Its Use and Misuse,* 119–21; Report on the Orchard and Fruit Plantations of Worcestershire, Worcestershire County Council, 1900, Worcestershire Record Office, 13575/1/5.

62 Worcestershire Record Office, 705/273/7775/27ii.

63 Worcestershire Record Office, 705/1037/9520/17i and ii.

64 Stamp, *Land of Britain: Its Use and Misuse,* 119.

65 Worcestershire Record Office, 705/273/7775/27ii.

66 The National Archives, Kew, MAF 266/87.

67 W. Minchington, The British Cider Industry Since 1880. In H. Pohl (ed.), *Competition and Cooperation of Enterprises on National and International Markets* (Stuttgart, 1997), 125–40, at 126; L.P. Wilkinson, *Bulmers of Hereford: a Century of Cider Making* (Newton Abbot, 1987); E.F. Bulmer, *Early Days of Cider Making* (Hereford, 1937).

68 W.H.R. Cutler, Agriculture. In W. Page (ed.), *Victoria History of the County of Hereford*, Volume 1 (London, 1908), 407–29, at 428.

69 B.T.P. Barker, Long Ashton Research Station, 1903–1953, *Journal of Horticultural Science* 28 (1953), 149–51.

70 Stamp, *Land of Britain: Its Use and Misuse*, 119.

71 Stamp, *Land of Britain: Its Use and Misuse*, 119.

72 D. Manning, Commercial Horticulture in Devon, *Scientific Horticulture* 7 (1939), 143–49, at 148.

73 Minchington, British Cider Industry.

74 Minchington, British Cider Industry, 127.

75 Manning, Commercial Horticulture in Devon, 148.

76 Stamp, *Land of Britain: Its Use and Misuse*, 119–21.

77 Manning, Commercial Horticulture in Devon, 148.

78 Stamp, *Land of Britain: Its Use and Misuse*, 119.

79 Minchington, British Cider Industry, 138.

80 Anon., Cider Developments in the West, *Journal of the Ministry of Agriculture* 43 (1936–37), 213–15, at 214.

81 Stamp, *Land of Britain: Its Use and Misuse*, 121.

82 Stamp, *Land of Britain: Its Use and Misuse*, 114.

CHAPTER 5

The orchard countries: south-east England

The history of orchards in the south-east of England – a region which we define here, for convenience, as the counties of Kent, Middlesex, Surrey and Sussex, together with the southern portions of Essex, Hertfordshire, Bedfordshire and Buckinghamshire – is rather different from that in the west. Cider making was never a major activity here, although by no means unknown. Orchards were primarily geared towards the cultivation of dessert or culinary varieties of apples, and of plums and cherries. In the period before the mid-nineteenth century, across much of the region, the majority of orchards were small, serving domestic needs and producing a limited surplus for local sale, with some specialised producers supplying the principal market towns. But already by the seventeenth century, some localities had come to specialise in commercial production, if only on a limited scale. This was especially the case in Kent and parts of Hertfordshire, encouraged by environmental conditions but, above all, by the proximity of London. The character of fruit growing was, however, transformed after *c*. 1850 by a range of factors that should by now be familiar, especially the expansion of urban markets in other parts of England and the growth of the rail network. The period between *c*. 1850 and *c*. 1950 was here, as elsewhere, the 'orchard century', in which the area planted with fruit trees expanded significantly in most of the districts in which the industry was already important, while several entirely new areas of commercial production emerged.

Kent: commercial production before 1800

FIGURE 27. A typical example of a Kent cherry orchard, grazed by sheep.

Kent, the 'Garden of England', has long been famed for its orchards. It was particularly famous for its red cooking cherries, of which more than 20 different varieties were being grown by the nineteenth century (Figure 27).[1] William Bullein, writing about red cherries in his *Government of Health,* of 1595, was already able to describe how 'In the country of Kent be growing great plenty of this fruite'.[2] But Kent also produced plums and pears and, in particular, apples, and has given its name to a large number of old varieties, including Kentish Fillbasket, Maid of Kent, Kentish Pippin and Beauty of Kent. Indeed,

as early as 1597, John Gerard described how 'Kent doth abound with apples of most sorts'.[3] Throughout the sixteenth and seventeenth centuries, the county's pre-eminence in the cultivation of both kinds of fruit was repeatedly asserted. Lambarde, writing in 1576, stated that: '... as for orchards of apples and gardeins of cherries, and those of the most delicious and exquisite kindes that can be, no part of the realm (that I know) hath them, either in such quantitie and number, or with such arte and industrie, set and planted'.[4] Three decades later, John Norden confidently stated, in his *Surveyors Dialogue*, how 'above all others, I thinke, the Kentishman be most apt and industrious, in planting orchards with Pippins and Cherries, especially neere the Thames, about Feversham and Sittingburne'.[5] Kent was also famous, by the eighteenth century, for its 'cobnuts', or filberts, which were grown in particular in the area around Maidstone, where, as Halsted described in the 1790s, there were 'many plantations of filberts, which turn out to good account, the fruit of them being sent to the London markets'.[6]

The same writer also emphasised the large apple orchards in the Maidstone area, and how 'a great quantity of cyder is made from them'. Writing nearly two centuries earlier, John Norden, in 1607, thought that Kent, along with the West Country, was a cider-making area and one where, as in the west, many of the apple trees were planted in hedges rather than orchards. But the scale of production was, he believed, limited by the sale of much of the apple crop to London, and cider was only important in the 'inland', or interior, parts of the county.[7] In the early modern period, much of Kent was given over to pasture farming, and, with the exception of the narrow strip of calcareous ground on and below the chalk escarpment of the North Downs, the soils were mainly acidic in character and poorly suited to the production of malting barley. Such circumstances may, as in western England, have encouraged cider making, especially around Maidstone, where several wealthy individuals were described in their wills as 'cider merchants' in the eighteenth century, including William Stone of Maidstone, who died in 1751; John Ashdowne of Tonbridge, whose will was proved in 1793; and Henry Allen of Gillingham, who died in 1786.[8] But the use of the term 'merchant' suggests that they marketed cider produced on local farms rather than making it themselves, and there is, perhaps, an implied contrast in the description of the last of these men as 'brewer and cider merchant'. Cider was thus of some importance, but it never attained the dominance that it did in the west, presumably because Kent itself produced some malt and was bounded by counties that did likewise. Indeed, large-scale brewing of beer was carried out in the county from an early date: the Shepherd Neame Brewery in Faversham was founded as early as 1698, and brewing had taken place on the site since at least 1570.[9] Many early commentators, we should also note, suggest that Kentish cider was of poor quality and only produced on an irregular basis.[10] Production appears to have dwindled in the course of the nineteenth century, when cider from the west of England became more freely available.

The mid-Kent area, around Maidstone, was one of the most important of Kent's orchard districts. Culinary and dessert apples, pears, plums and – as

Halsted notes – cobnuts, or filberts were all grown there. Commercial production of the latter required careful pruning: rather than being coppiced, the individual poles growing on a stool were cut, almost like a mass of separate, diminutive pollards. This was skilled work, which was often handed down within families living in Maidstone itself and in the surrounding villages.[11] All these different fruit grew well on the fine, warm, limey soils overlying the sandstone of the Kentish Rag. But equally important was the fact that the crop could be taken with relative ease to the London markets via the Thames and the Medway, the latter being navigable all the way to Maidstone by 'large Hoys, of Fifty to Sixty Tuns Burthen, the Tide flowing quite up to the Town', according to Daniel Defoe in 1722.[12]

Defoe also described how around Maidstone were 'the largest cherry orchards … in any part of England … and the best of them which supply the whole city of London come from hence'.[13] But the main area associated with cherries – and the second main orchard area in Kent – lay farther to the north, close to the coast, between Faversham and Chatham. Other kinds of fruit were also cultivated here, but cherries were always the main produce. They flourished on the deep, rich loams overlying the sands of the Thanet Formation and, in places, the chalk, and early writers were unanimous in identifying this as the place where commercial fruit growing first began in England. It was probably Lambarde, in his *Perambulation of Kent,* of 1576, who first discussed the activities of Richard Harris, Henry VIII's fruiterer, who in 1533 obtained 105 acres (42 hectares) from the King at Tenham, or Teynham, a village lying between Faversham and Sittingbourne, 'and with great care, good choice, and no small labour cost, brought plantes from beyond the seas, and furnished this ground with them, so beautifully, as they not onely stand in most right lines, but seem to be of one sorte, shape and fashion, as if they had been drawen thorrow one mould, or wrought by one and the same patterne'.[14] More details are supplied by the anonymous author of the *Fruiterer's Secret,* of 1604, who described how Harris had:

> Fetched … out of the Lowe Countries, Cherrie grafts, & Peare grafts, of diverse sortes: Then took a piece of ground belonging to the King in the parish of Tenham in Kent, being about the quantities of seven score acres; whereof he made an Orchard, planting therein all these foraigne grafts. Which Orchard is, and hath been from time to time, the chiefe Mother of all other orchards for those kindes of fruite in Kent, and of other divers places.[15]

The emphasis of such writers on the activities of Richard Harris in the genesis of the north Kent orchards almost certainly simplifies a more complex and longer history. Such were the numbers and extent of orchards in the area within a generation of Harris's time that specialised production must already have existed on some scale before he embarked on his activities. In 1637 Camden described how 30 parishes in the area around Faversham were 'replenished with Cherie-gardens, and Orchards, beautifully disposed in direct lines'.[16] The principal explanation for the importance of the north Kent orchards lies not in the actions of a single individual but in geography – in the combination of deep, well-drained loams and easy access to the London markets. The towns of Chatham, Sittingbourne and Faversham all lay on navigable inlets from the Thames estuary, which itself provided a highway to the capital. The importance of the London market is emphasised by many writers. John Norden in 1607, for example, described how 'Neere London, and the Thames side, the fruite is vented in Kinde, not only to the fruiterers in gros, but by the country wives in markets.'[17] And location, perhaps more than soils, explains the emergence of Kent's third early orchard area, in the far north-west of the county, close to the capital. By the end of the eighteenth century, the parishes of Erith and Plumstead were famous for their cherries, while Sutton-at-Hone, Wilmington and St Mary and St Paul Cray were all areas of intensive market gardening and fruit growing.[18]

Orchards, it should perhaps be emphasised, were not restricted in the seventeenth and eighteenth centuries to these three main districts of Kent. They could be found attached to farms almost everywhere in the county. But these localities, benefitting from particular circumstances of geography, stand out as being especially important. It is unclear how far back in time their origins can be traced – they may have already emerged, in less distinct form, in the Middle Ages. But it seems probable that they mainly developed as London expanded rapidly in the early modern period, its population rising from around 50,000 in the 1520s, to more than 200,000 in 1600, reaching over half a million by the end of the seventeenth century.

Sheer numbers of people were not the only factor encouraging the early development of commercial fruit growing. London was also an immensely wealthy city. It had a rich merchant oligarchy, was the place where parliament sat, and was ringed by royal palaces. By the end of the seventeenth century, it was the centre of fashion, and already the London 'season' was developing, attracting the social elite of the nation. Tradespeople grew rich servicing such a market. Not surprisingly, Kentish landlords sometimes planted extensively on their home farms, and they actively encouraged the maintenance or expansion of orchards on the holdings of their tenants, especially in the late seventeenth and early eighteenth centuries, when prices for more conventional agricultural produce were relatively low (the same period also saw a steady expansion of hop growing in Kent, again mainly to supply the London market). Orchard land in the seventeenth century commanded around twice the rent of ordinary farmland.[19] Leases from Edenbridge, Leigh, Offham and elsewhere include clauses insisting that tenants plant new fruit trees to replace old ones in their orchards or even, in one case, stipulating that as a condition of their tenancy they should plant as many fruit trees as the landlord directed.[20]

The expansion of fruit growing in Kent seems to have slowed, and may even have gone into reverse, in the second half of the eighteenth century. In part this was because, as agriculture moved out of depression, crop production now made better economic sense, at least on the better soils of the county. But it was also because of the continued expansion of hop growing, which was a less precarious activity, less susceptible to the vagaries of the weather. Hasted, writing about the county's orchards in the 1790s, noted that there were 'great numbers of them everywhere, but not so much as formerly', due to their replacement by hop grounds.[21] At Harrietsham in 1769, a parcel of land was described as 'formerly planted with fruit trees and now with ashen trees planted for hop poles…'.[22]

Most early Kent orchards appear to have contained tall trees, spaced at intervals of around 30 feet (*c.* 9 metres), standing in permanent grass that was mown or grazed by livestock. But, echoing in more muted form the diversity already noted for the West Country, other, more intensive kinds seem to have existed. Cobbet described in the 1820s how, in some of the mid-Kent orchards, the apple trees were planted 'very thickly, and, of course, they are small', suggesting something akin to the 'close' orchards of Devon.[23] Some of the orchards near the north Kent coast were apparently similar. In May 1819 Anne Lister, of Shibden Hall, in west Yorkshire, commented in her diary on the 'beautiful orchards' between Rochester and Canterbury, 'the trees in rows 5 or 6 yards ascended about 3 feet in height from the bottom, whitewashed to prevent moss' (*c.* 4.5 or 5.5 metres, *c.* 1 metre).[24] By the mid-nineteenth century, some, again particularly in mid-Kent, contained cultivated ground planted with vegetables, including potatoes; others were combined orchards and hop grounds, although the hop plants, which helped shelter the young fruit trees, were often removed as the trees matured.[25] Whatever their precise form, the extent of Kentish orchards in the period before the mid-nineteenth century should not be exaggerated. Although there were some large commercial enterprises, mainly planted by gentlemen enthusiasts, for the most part orchards were small, covering a few acres each, and they were generally located, as was normal practice, beside the farm. While already an important part of the local economy, in other words, the orchards were much like those commonly found throughout England, only slightly larger and rather denser on the ground. Even in 1840, the total area of orchards in the county was probably less than 11,000 acres (*c.* 4,450 hectares), around 1.5 per cent of the land area. The great age of the Kentish orchards was yet to come.

Kent: the age of expansion, 1850–1950

In Kent, as in many other parts of England, the second half of the nineteenth century saw a phenomenal expansion in the scale of fruit growing and in the area of land occupied by orchards. The reasons for this have already been noted: large-scale industrialisation and urbanisation, rapid population growth, rising disposable incomes and the advent of the railways, together with the emergence of new food processing industries and, from the late 1870s, the onset of agricultural depression, which obliged or encouraged farmers to diversify into new forms of production. But growth was initially slow in Kent. Indeed, the period between *c.* 1850 and 1870 was, perhaps, more one of shifts in the character of the fruit planted than of any great increase in the area devoted to orchards. In many districts, apples were replaced by plums and cherries, which could now be transported to distant markets before they rotted or, in the case of plums, to London jam factories.[26] The construction of the London to Brighton rail line, with a branch line to Shoreham, in 1836, and of the South Eastern Railway from London to Dover, in 1837, greatly facilitated the transport of fruit, and in August 1840 the *Maidstone Gazette* could report that cherry prices had improved significantly in the county because of the 'great quantity sent by railway to Liverpool, Manchester and other manufacturing places'.[27]

FIGURE 28. An old apple orchard at East Farleigh, near Maidstone, Kent, featuring large, 'bush'- pruned 'veteran' trees.

Even growers located away from rail lines could benefit from their construction, those close to London taking advantage of the increased prices being paid at Covent Garden due to the establishment of the rail links with the Midlands and the north.[28]

The area devoted to orchards in Kent in 1872, around 11,000 acres (*c.* 4,450 hectares), was perhaps only marginally greater than it had been in 1840.[29] But this figure had almost doubled by the mid-1890s, and by 1906 it had reached 28,770 acres (11,640 hectares).[30] Most of this growth was associated with the rise of large commercial orchards, although farm orchards continued to be important and were now managed with a new intensity. In the mid-Kent area, around Maidstone, expansion was particularly rapid, and orchards spread into the adjacent parts of the Weald, with the development of many large 'fruit holdings' which benefitted from the good rail links to London. An advertisement for a local property which appeared in the *South Eastern Gazette* for 1873 drew attention to 'the facilities afforded by the railway for the obtaining of manure and for the conveyance of fruit and other produce to the London market'.[31] Apples continued to be the main fruit grown in the district, but plums and damsons, and to an extent cherries, were cultivated on an increasing scale (Figure 28). By the end of the century, jam was being produced by local companies, including the Mid-Kent Jam Factory, established in the village of Hadlow in 1892.[32] The fruit-growing areas in the north-west of the county also experienced significant expansion, benefitting from the proximity of London, its rising population and its food processing factories. Here some particularly large, specialised fruit growers had emerged by the end of the century, some cultivating 500 acres (*c.* 200 hectares) or more.[33] One was Thomas Wood, who in 1874 established his own jam factory at Swanley – beside the railway line. By 1912 it was allegedly producing 3,500 tons of jam, 850 tons of candied peel and 10,000 bottles of bottled fruit each year.[34] Expansion was, perhaps, less marked in north Kent, in the old cherry-growing areas around Sittingbourne, although there was some increase in the area of plum orchards. Here as elsewhere in Kent, fruit farms and orchards of all sizes could be found in close proximity. As one

FIGURE 29. Ploughing in a Kent orchard, *c.* 1900. In the nineteenth and early twentieth centuries, many of the county's orchards were under-planted with vegetables, soft fruit or, occasionally, other crops.

observer put it in 1908, 'every class of grower and of plantation is found, from the ordinary farmer with the old grass orchard, to the specialised fruit-grower having possibly 500 to 1,000 acres of fruit in mixed plantations'.[35]

The reference to 'old grass orchard' and 'mixed plantations' reflects the fact that there were now significant variations in the character of management of Kentish orchards. Mowing for hay had now largely ceased, and while grazing with sheep continued, especially in the northern orchards close to the Thames marshes, it was at a reduced intensity, with much supplementary feed for the livestock being supplied in the form of oilcake or grain; in many orchards, poultry were now kept instead. But by the end of the nineteenth century, many orchards – and especially the new, larger commercial examples – were interplanted with strawberries, blackcurrants, gooseberries and raspberries destined for the London market, and the practice of planting vegetable crops between the trees now seems to have become common (Figure 29). Moreover, in the case of apples, pears and plums, the old, vigorous standard trees were already, by 1900, being replaced by half-standard, pyramid or dwarf bush trees, particularly on the larger commercial holdings, although standards were still widely employed.[36] By this time, the orchards of Kent were often very intensively managed, with substantial inputs of both labour and materials. The trees – in the large commercial orchards especially – were regularly sprayed, a 'laborious, but eventually economic, process'. They were also intensively manured:

> The kinds made use of include London manure, fish refuse, rags, shoddy and wool waste, soot, bone-meal and various "artificial" manures such as superphosphate, nitrate of soda, kainite and sulphate of ammonia.[37]

All in all, contemporary descriptions imply a capital- and labour-intensive industry somewhat at variance with our usual romanticised, pastoral images of orchards in the 'Garden of England'. Not only did London provide the manure and fertilisers on which the industry depended, it also provided the seasonal workforce that the fruit harvest required, with working-class families flocking to the orchards, as they did to the hop fields, for a cheap 'holiday'.[38] But returns on the necessary investment in labour and materials, as elsewhere, could be precarious. Crops could be decimated by unseasonal frosts, and while 'on the one hand the crop may be insufficient to cover the cost of its growth … on the other hand in an abundant season the markets will sometimes be so glutted that the fruit will not realise the expense of picking and is left to rot'.[39]

The area occupied by orchards in Kent at the start of the twentieth century – around 28,000 acres (*c.* 10,900 hectares) – was already considerable,

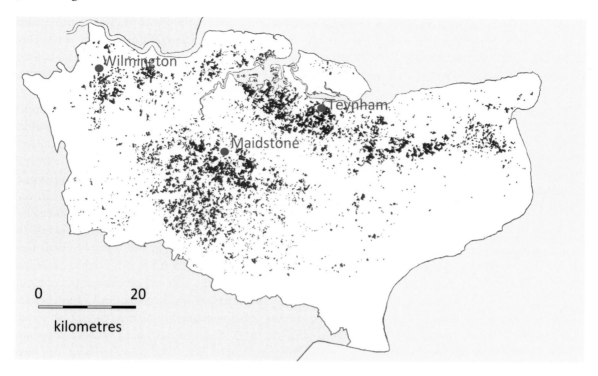

0

20

kilometres

representing around 3 per cent of the county's area and significantly more than this, of course, in those districts where fruit production was concentrated. But it continued to grow, reaching over 60,000 acres (24,000 hectares) by 1930, more than 6 per cent of the total land area.[40] Orchards increased in numbers in all the districts in which they were already abundant and now spread into new areas (Figure 30). The most important was that part of the county lying to the east of Canterbury, in parishes like Ash and Staple, where development had formerly been held back by their distance from rail lines.[41] Commercial orchards here had been 'made possible by the development of motor transport after the war of 1914–1918'.[42] Yet there were also some places where orchards declined, most notably in the north-west of the county, where many were uprooted to make way for London's expanding suburbs, although a significant number survived and new pockets of activity emerged in the area. Moreover, there are some signs that by the 1930s, orchards were being managed rather less intensively than at the start of the century, probably because the proximity of London and the expansion of its satellite towns meant that wage rates were, compared with many rural areas, fairly high. Whereas at the start of the twentieth century a high proportion of the orchards in Kent were interplanted with soft fruit or vegetables, by the 1930s, grass orchards grazed by sheep were the rule, and it was estimated that these accounted for around 90 per cent of the examples in the county.[43] Much of the fruit grown in the county was still consumed in London, often sold in the wholesale markets at Covent Garden and Spitalfields, but some went to local jam factories and an

FIGURE 30. The distribution of orchards in Kent in the 1930s, as recorded by the Land Utilisation Survey. (Places named are ones referred to in the text.)

even higher proportion than formerly was now taken by rail to more distant destinations. The crop produced by the Chambers family in the 1920s, who farmed near Maidstone, for example, was purchased by wholesalers from as far away as Leeds, Liverpool and Manchester.[44] Kent was, by the outbreak of the Second World War, the premier fruit-producing county in England, with orchards occupying no less than 70,000 acres (*c.* 32,000 hectares), or 7.5 per cent of its total land area. Around half of the nation's cherries were grown there.[45]

In the neighbouring county of Sussex, commercial orchards never developed to the extent that they did in Kent. In the middle decades of the nineteenth century, there were significant concentrations of orchards in the High Weald, especially around Tilehurst, Rotherfield and Lower Beeding, forming an extension of the fruit-growing area of mid-Kent.[46] But elsewhere the landscape was characterised by a scatter of small farmhouse orchards. With the onset of the agricultural depression, the area devoted to fruit growing increased significantly, with new concentrations of activity emerging on the coastal plain and in the central and north-eastern parts of the county.[47] Nevertheless, at the outbreak of the Second World War, orchards accounted for less than 0.7 per cent of Sussex's land area.[48] The contrast with Kent is in part explained by environmental circumstances and in part by the county's distance from London: where concentrations of orchards were to be found, they were usually a consequence of both pockets of favourable soils and the presence of rail lines. In the Weald, for example, Briault noted in 1942 how 'The larger orchards frequently occur in conjunction with nurseries and many of these groupings appear to relate to the railways'.[49]

The west Hertfordshire cherry district

The orchards of Kent still loom large in the popular imagination. Less well known is the fruit-growing district lying to the north-west of London, in west Hertfordshire and the adjoining parts of Buckinghamshire, and especially between the towns of Chesham, Watford, St Albans and Berkhamsted. Here, on the dipslope of the Chiltern Hills, an important fruit-growing industry – noted, like that of north Kent, for its cherries, but also producing apples and some pears – seems to have been developing by the end of the seventeenth century, and continued to be of some importance into the twentieth.

The Chiltern Hills comprise a steep chalk escarpment which extends all the way from the Goring Gap, in Oxfordshire, through the south of Buckinghamshire, to the Hitchin Gap, in Hertfordshire. To the south and east of the escarpment, the ground falls away almost imperceptibly, as a gentle dipslope, which in west Hertfordshire and the neighbouring areas of Buckinghamshire is cut at particularly wide intervals by steep-sided valleys, some containing rivers (the Wye, the Misbourne, the Gade, the Chess and the Bulbourne) but others being dry. In these valleys, the underlying chalk is exposed. But on the gently sloping tablelands between, it is masked by relatively thin layers of rather later deposits: the sandy, stony clays of the clay-with-flints and the clays, silts and gravels of the Lambeth Group. These environmental circumstances, combined with modest but dependable rainfall, made the district ideal for growing fruit, and especially cherries, with their shallow roots. The surface silts and clays were sufficiently water retentive to prevent summer droughts, but they lay thinly enough over the porous chalk to prevent waterlogging. They were a classic example of Hoare's ideal fruit-growing country, 'in the neighbourhood of chalk'; that is, where chalk was obscured by thin layers of water-retentive drift. [50] Indeed, so well suited were the local soils for cherries that gean, or wild cherry (the undomesticated version of *Prunus avium*) grew abundantly in the local woods, thus providing a convenient source of rootstocks. [51] The area possessed other features which encouraged the early development of orchards. It was, for the most part, characterised by relatively small farms. And while extensive areas of common land survived into the nineteenth century where the surface drift was most sandy and acidic, most of the open fields had (as in Kent) disappeared at an early date, and, indeed, much of the land had always comprised hedged fields in individual occupancy. Farmers were thus able to plant however much land as they desired as orchards. But above all, the district lay within easy reach of London – between 20 and 30 miles (32 and 48 kilometres) away by road.

By the end of the seventeenth century, the area was already famous for its black dessert cherries, as distinct from the red morello cooking cherries which characterised the Kentish industry. William Ellis, an agricultural writer who lived at Little Gaddesden, described in 1742 how 'the County of Hartfordshire does certainly more abound in Plantations of the common Black Cherry Tree, than any other in England, and in particular the western parts where I now live, is as famous for the black, as Kent is for the red or Flemish Cherry'. [52] A number of varieties were grown, some of which were local to the area, including the May-Duke, or Archduke, which probably originated on the Buckinghamshire side of the county boundary, and the Caroon, also known as the Hertfordshire Black or the Mazzard. Ellis was fulsome in his praise of the latter:

> Oh! How rich a Fruit is this Black Kerroon Cherry, eaten in a Morning tasting, off the Tree: which, for its noble, pleasant Taste, and laxative, antiscorbutic Quality, is most delicious. [53]

More than a century later, in 1864, Clutterbuck described how the 'Carron' and the 'small Hertfordshire Black' were the mainstays of the local industry. [54]

The cherries were not all sent to the London markets; nor were they all eaten raw. At the height of the summer glut they were consumed in vast numbers locally, often cooked into pasties, sometimes described as 'cherry bumpers', the production and consumption of which continued well into the nineteenth century. In 1832 William Hone described how these were 'highly esteemed for their delicious flavour' by the local people:

> Entertainments called "the pasty feasts," in which the above mentioned "niceties" shine conspicuous, are always duly observed, and constitute a seasonal attraction "for all ages," but more particularly for the "juveniles", whose laughter-teeming visages, begrimed with the exuberant juice, present unmistakeable evidence of their "having a finger in the pie".[55]

Nevertheless, the importance of cherries should not be exaggerated. Many of the local orchards appear to have been dominated by apples, although in a county famed for the quality of its barley, little or no cider appears to have been produced.[56]

The development of orchards in west Hertfordshire is less well documented than it is in Kent. The industry perhaps emerged in part as a response to the agricultural depression of the late seventeenth and early eighteenth centuries. This was a mainly arable district, and for small farmers orchards may here have been a particularly useful form of diversification at a time of low cereal prices. William Ellis suggested that cherries, in particular, were an attractive crop for such people because they were usually harvested between the hay and the grain harvests, when labour was abundant and cheap.[57] Arthur Young described, in the *General View of the Agriculture of the County of Hertfordshire*, how:

> In the south-west corner of the county … there are many orchards; apples and cherries are their principal produce. Every farm has an orchard; but the larger the farm the smaller the orchard. Orchards are found chiefly in farms of from 20 to 50 acres. The apples are most profitable; but cherries very beneficial to the poor, in the quantity of employment which they require in gathering the crop, for which the poor are paid from 4d to 8d per dozen pounds.[58]

Later commentators noted that although the cherry crop was profitable, it was 'very often destroyed in a single night by an untimely frost'.[59] The fruit was usually sold on the trees to dealers, realising between 12 shillings and 16 shillings per 'ped', or basket, each holding 'about four dozen pounds' (c. 22 kilograms).[60]

By the time that maps became reliable and abundant in the area, in the middle and later decades of the eighteenth century, orchards already took up a higher percentage of the land area than the 0.5–1 per cent typical of farmhouse production – although not very much more. Farms shown on eighteenth-century maps of Great Gaddesden, Hemel Hempstead and Redbourne, for example, had between 1.4 and 3 per cent of their land devoted to orchards. One in Wheathampstead – Heron's Farm, surveyed in 1768 – had as much as 3.5 per cent.[61] But, as in parts of the West Country in the same period, the extent of orchards may under-estimate the scale of production, for west Hertfordshire was another area in which apples and other fruit were regularly planted in hedges. Norden in 1607 believed the practice was then

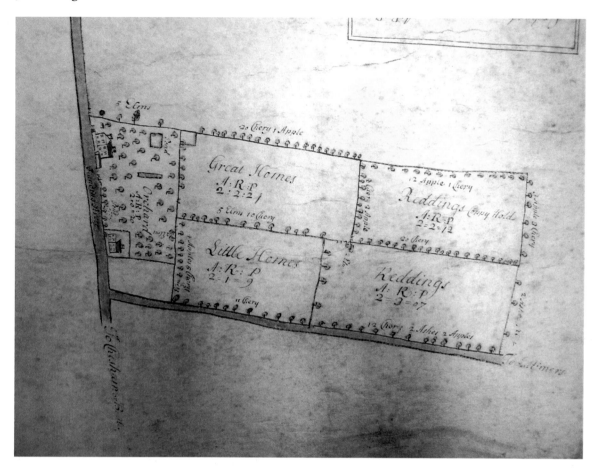

in decline in the district, but it was evidently still continuing over a century later, for William Ellis described hedgerow fruit trees as a typical, indeed normal, feature of the local landscape. [62] An undated map of *c.* 1700 of a small farm in Flaunden, close to the boundary between Hertfordshire and Buckinghamshire, shows that orchards made up only 2 of its 56 acres (0.8 of its 23 hectares), but, unusually, the surveyor recorded the different kinds of tree growing in the hedges. These, in addition to 27 oaks, 18 elms, 9 ash and 15 'asps' (aspen), included 59 apple trees and no fewer than 165 cherry trees (Figure 31). [63] This is roughly equivalent to another 3 acres (1.2 hectares) of orchard composed of well-spaced standard trees. But the practice of hedgerow planting seems to have gradually declined through the later eighteenth and early nineteenth centuries, and there was no compensating increase in the area devoted to orchards, in spite of the continuing growth of nearby London. The tithe maps and apportionments drawn up in the late 1830s and early 1840s do not always systematically record orchards in this area, but parcels of land so named account for between 1.5 and 3 per cent of the land area in parishes like King's Langley, Abbots Langley or Sarratt. [64]

FIGURE 31. A map of a farm at Flaunden, west Hertfordshire, surveyed around 1700, showing the local custom of growing apple trees and cherry trees in hedgerows. The other parts of the farm, not shown here, had hedges which were similarly planted. Hertfordshire Archives and Local Studies, D/EX905/P1.

Most were small, with an average area of less than 1.5 acres (0.6 hectares), and only a few examples extended over more than 5 acres (2 hectares). Fruit growing remained a sideline, albeit an important one in the economies of the smaller farms.

It might be thought that all this would have changed with the arrival of the railways, mirroring the great expansion seen in Kent. Indeed, the main line from London to Birmingham and Manchester was built right through the heart of the district in the late 1830s. But instead there was stagnation. As Clutterbuck put it in 1846: 'It does not seem that these orchards have been extended of late years, in spite of the access to the Manufacturing Districts affected by the introduction of railways'.[65] The Second Edition Ordnance Survey 6-inch maps, surveyed around 1900, suggest that orchards covered much the same area as they had done in *c.* 1840. It is not entirely clear why the industry failed to grow, but the explanation may lie in the character of the wider local economy. In Kent, as we have suggested, the proximity of London and the relatively high wage levels this produced led to a decline in the intensity with which orchards were managed in the first three decades of the twentieth century. In south-west Hertfordshire, fruit growing was more seriously affected, and at an earlier date, by similar but more local developments. Paper mills had been an important part of the local economy since the early eighteenth century but proliferated in the course of the nineteenth. John Dickinson acquired mills on the river Gade at Apsley, near Hemel Hempstead, in 1809 and the nearby Nash Mills in 1811.[66] By 1826 he had established additional works farther downstream, at Home Park in Kings Langley, and in 1830 he opened another farther to the south, at Croxley.[67] He was joined by other producers, and by the 1870s paper mills were closely spaced along the valleys of the west Hertfordshire rivers.[68] By the end of the nineteenth century, this was one of the more industrialised areas of south-east England outside of London, and there was acute competition for labour. This both raised local wage levels and reduced the supply of the seasonal workers which commercial orchards required.[69] In these circumstances, the failure of the district's orchards to grow significantly is unsurprising.

There were, it should be emphasised, some exceptions to this general picture of stasis. There were a few places where the orchard acreage grew significantly. One was the town of Berkhamsted. Here the firm of Lanes was established by Henry Lane sometime around 1777, but it was greatly expanded under John Edward Lane from the 1840s.[70] Like a number of contemporary businesses, it was both a commercial nursery (famous for, among other things, marketing the successful cooking apple 'Lane's Prince Albert') and a fruit-growing enterprise. By the time of his death, in 1889, Lane was renting 142 acres (57 hectares) from the Ashridge estate, of which around half comprised nursery grounds and around 2 acres (0.8 hectares) were orchard.[71] But he also owned, amongst a portfolio of other properties, a further 13 acres (5 hectares) of orchard, 'planted with trees (now in full growth)'.[72] From 1889 the company was run by Frederick Quincy Lane, who further expanded the orchard side of the business.[73] By 1902 the company reputedly had a total of 20,000 apple, pear, plum and cherry trees growing on 60 acres (24 hectares) of land, as well as 15 acres (6 hectares) devoted to cobnuts. Most of the fruit was, by this stage, being sent to Manchester and neighbouring industrial towns – the orchards were only a short distance from Berkhamsted station, on the direct line to the north-west of England.[74]

Large fruit producers like this were, however, relatively unusual in the area. For the most part, fruit growing in west Hertfordshire remained the business of small farmers and smallholders. Typical of the latter, perhaps, was the Stone family of Croxley Green, between Watford and Rickmansworth. Walter Stone took a lease on 12 acres (5 hectares) of orchards, meadow and arable in August 1893.[75] The lease contained a number of clauses relating to the orchard, including an instruction to:

> Keep all trees properly pruned and when necessary substitute and plant young trees of good varieties. These should be properly planted, manured, protected, staked and screened from damage by cattle or wind.[76]

The orchard included apples, pears and plums, but it mainly grew cherries. Like many such diminutive enterprises, the orchard was one part of a small portfolio of businesses. Under Walter Stone's two sons, a coal delivery and goods service was developed, initially using horses and carts but from 1929 a small lorry. The business continued into the post-war years, but the tenancy was eventually surrendered in 1960. At this point, to judge from the Ordnance Survey 1:25,000 maps, orchards were still numerous in the area, with only a slight decline since the start of the century, in spite of the inexorable growth in the suburbs of 'Metroland'.

The 'Prune' orchards of Buckinghamshire and Bedfordshire

In Kent and Hertfordshire, the development of commercial fruit growing was initially stimulated by the proximity of London, with further growth in the former county encouraged by the arrival of the railways. In the Vale of Aylesbury, in Buckinghamshire, and in the adjacent parts of south-west Bedfordshire, in contrast, the emergence of a local industry devoted to the cultivation of 'Aylesbury Prunes' seems to have been a more direct consequence of the development of the rail network. The name of the fruit is slightly misleading, as these were not 'prunes' in the normal sense, of dried plums, but a type of damson. Aylesbury Prunes were small, dark plums which if picked early were suitable for cooking, but if left on the tree until late in the season could be treated as a dessert variety. They may, in fact, have originated in Berkshire, but had probably been grown on a small scale in local orchards for decades. From the late 1840s, however, they began to be planted on a commercial scale in the villages lying in a band roughly 3 miles (5 kilometres) in width, extending for some 12 miles (*c.* 19 kilometres) from Weston Turville, near Aylesbury, Buckinghamshire, in the south-west to Totternhoe, near Dunstable, Bedfordshire, in the north-east.[77]

The soils lying at the foot of the Chiltern escarpment – calcareous loams and deep, calcareous clays overlying chalk – were ideal for the cultivation of plums. But much of the land lay in unenclosed open fields until well into the nineteenth century (Totternhoe was the last village in Bedfordshire to be enclosed, under an award of 1891). More importantly, the area lay at a distance from London and other large urban markets, too far for perishable fruit like plums to be transported by road. This situation was transformed by the construction of the London to Birmingham rail line, which passed more or less through the centre of the district, in 1838. Within a few decades, there were vast numbers of orchards in the area, especially in the villages of Totternhoe, Billington, Eggington, Slapton and Eaton Bray; in the latter parish alone there were around 100 separate orchards by *c.* 1880, amounting in all to around 50 hectares of land.[78]

Surviving records make clear the close association of the rail line and the orchards. Most of the fruit was purchased by local middlemen and taken, packed in baskets, or 'skips', to the stations at Cheddington or Stanbridge, in Bedfordshire; much seems to have been destined for industrial towns like Bolton, in Lancashire.[79] The plums, as was often the practice, were auctioned on the tree. One sales catalogue from 1911, relating to orchards in Stanbridge, Eaton Bray, Northall and Cheddington, describes how trees excluded from the sale would be 'marked by the usual hay, straw or whitewash band'.[80] Most of the orchards seem to have been laid to grass. In some, sheep were allowed to graze, but in many, the owners raised flocks of the famous Aylesbury ducks. There does not appear to be any truth in the local tradition that the 'prunes' were used to make dye for military uniforms.

The orchards in the area did not only grow 'prunes', it should be emphasised, but also other kinds of plum and damson. One sale catalogue, produced when outlying portions of the Ashridge estate were placed on the market in 1923, described several farms as having 'enclosures of Orchard Land planted with Prune and Damson trees in full bearing'. Some of the properties described were medium-sized or even large farms on which orchards were a minor if important arm of the business. Ivinghoe Aston Farm, for example, was described as an 'important stock and fruit farm' covering 490 acres (*c.* 200 hectares), of which *c.* 2.5 per cent was orchard land. But some were smallholdings, covering between 7 and 13 acres (*c.* 3 and *c.* 5 hectares), most or all of which were devoted to fruit.[81] Whatever their precise character, the local orchards continued to flourish through the first half of the twentieth century – the Ordnance Survey 1:25,000 maps, prepared shortly after the Second World War, suggest that at that time they covered an area even greater than in 1900 – but then they went into a steady decline. A number of orchards remain, but generally in varying degrees of dereliction. Many comprise thin scatters of ageing plum trees in what are now essentially pasture fields (Figure 32).

Other orchard districts

A number of other important orchard districts developed in south-east England. In particular, on the loamy soils of the Thames floodplain and terrace gravels in west Middlesex, and in the adjacent parts of south Buckinghamshire, orchards and market gardens supplying London were already a notable feature of the landscape by the eighteenth century. They expanded significantly after 1800 as the growth of the metropolis

FIGURE 32. The remains of one of the 'Aylesbury Prune' orchards at Eaton Bray, south Bedfordshire. No longer cropped or managed, the orchard is rapidly becoming a large pasture field.

obliterated the orchards in Fulham, Hammersmith and Twickenham, which had formerly provided much of its fruit. But they grew even more rapidly following the construction of the Great Western rail line in 1838 and, in particular, the spread of the various London and South Western suburban lines through the district in the 1850s and 60s. In Harmondsworth, there were already 100 acres (40 hectares) of orchard when the parish was surveyed in 1839; by the end of the century, there were 1,000 acres (400 hectares).[82] Feltham, Hillington, Isleworth, West Drayton, and East Bedfont all had extensive areas of orchard by the 1860s, and there were significant quantities in many adjacent parishes, including those such as Iver, lying just across the county boundary in south Buckinghamshire.[83] Apples were a major product, and, because there were a number of nurseries as well as market gardens in the area – the great company of Veitch's had nursery grounds at both Feltham and Langley – several varieties developed in the nineteenth or early twentieth century bear the names of local parishes, including Feltham Beauty and Hounslow Wonder.[84] But plums were also widely grown, and cherries were a major crop, especially in Harlington, although they seem to have declined in importance during the early twentieth century.[85]

Middleton in 1923 described how most of the orchards in the district were either entirely composed of apples or contained 'apples, plums and pears all mixed together without any ordered arrangement'.[86] Most were underplanted, usually with soft fruit but sometimes with rhubarb or cut flowers: 'one large orchard, near Harlington, is entirely undercropped with peonies'.[87] By this stage, however – mirroring a pattern we have already seen in north-west Kent – the area occupied by orchards was beginning to fall, as a consequence of the inexorable westward expansion of the city they served and of the development of the resources or facilities it required. By 1940, according to Stamp, the west Middlesex orchards were 'rapidly disappearing under the rising tide of housing and as a result of gravel working, the construction of reservoirs and, latterly, the construction of Heathrow airport'.[88] By the time the Ordnance Survey

1:25,000 maps were produced, in the immediate aftermath of the Second World War, orchards had almost entirely disappeared from the district.

Smaller concentrations of activity emerged elsewhere in London's orbit. Some developed early but then stagnated or disappeared, replaced by housing or superseded by other forms of production required by the capital. In the Lea valley around Cheshunt, for example, orchards were already numerous by the middle decades of the nineteenth century (78 are shown on the tithe map of Cheshunt alone).[89] Growth continued until the 1920s, to judge from the evidence of the successive Ordnance Survey maps, but was then reversed as orchards were replaced by glasshouses and housing. South Essex, beside the Thames, presents a particularly complex picture. Here the nineteenth century saw the growth of a major market gardening industry, of which orchards formed one part.[90] This first emerged in the immediate vicinity of London and along the band of light, well-drained soils which runs beside the Thames from Rainham to Stanford-le-Hope and Grays Thurrock: the latter parish had more than a fifth of its land area devoted to market gardens and orchards by 1870.[91] Indeed, as early as 1777, a property in Grays Thurrock called 'Ripleys, otherwise Notts, otherwise Stodies Farm' was placed on the market with a 'Great Orchard' and a 'Little Orchard', which together extended over no less than 18 acres (*c.* 7 hectares).[92] Both market gardens and orchards developed apace with the onset of the agricultural depression from the 1870s, and orchards in particular expanded rapidly eastwards, towards the mouth of the Thames, in the vicinity of Vange and Basildon and around Southend. Some of the fruit went by water to London, much was taken there by rail via the London, Tilbury and Southend line, opened in 1856. But a significant proportion was consumed locally, as Southend developed as a significant holiday resort. Here, on the freely draining, slightly acidic soils, cherries were a major crop, as they were on the similar soils on the opposite side of the estuary, in north Kent. There was already a noticeable concentration of orchards here by 1900, but expansion was particularly rapid over the following quarter century, although slowing by the 1930s, as the steady growth of Southend and surrounding settlements saw the replacement of many examples by housing.

Of particular note are the large orchards which were planted at Hadleigh, beside the Thames, a few kilometres to the west of Southend, which were associated with the Salvation Army's Home Farm Colony, established in 1891 on 900 acres (364 hectares) of land with the aim of providing 'employment (and food and lodgings in return for his labour) to any man who is willing to work, irrespective of nationality or creed'.[93] The colony had 20 hectares of orchards (rising to 30 by the 1930s), a farm and extensive market gardens, as well as a brickworks. There was a jetty from which produce could be taken by barge to London. As Rider Haggard described, the 'colonists' would be trained in useful manual work and then 'sent out to situations, or as emigrants to Canada. About 400 of such men pass through the Colony each year'.[94]

Conclusion

South-east England has a distinctive orchard history which marks it out clearly from the areas in the west of England, which we examined in the previous chapter. Cider was never a major object of production, even in Kent, but extensive areas of orchards developed from an early date in places with suitable soils and good access to London. By the middle of the nineteenth century, the capital was surrounded by districts well placed to supply it with fruit. In many of these, significant further expansion occurred during the 'orchard century', the railways providing easier access not only to London, but also to more distant markets, while agricultural depression encouraged farmers to diversify into new forms of production. In others, however, urban and industrial growth served to gradually supress or destroy local fruit growing. South-east England thus has a varied and complicated orchard history, but also an immensely important one. By the early decades of the twentieth century, as we have seen, Kent was the most important fruit-producing county in England, far outstripping its nearest rivals.

Notes

1   L. Dudley Stamp, *The Land of Britain: Its Use and Misuse* (London, 1948), 118.
2   W. Bullein, *The Government of Health* (London, 1959), 59.
3   J. Gerard, *The Herball, or General Histories of Plantes* (London, 1597), 1275.
4   W. Lambarde, *A Perambulation of Kent; Conyeining the Description, Hystorie, and Customes of the Shyre* (London, 1576), 8.
5   J. Norden, *The Surveyor's Dialogue* (London, 1607), 209.
6   E. Halsted, *The History and Topographical Survey of the County of Kent*, second edn, Volume 1 (London, 1797), 267.
7   Norden, *Surveyor's Dialogue*, 209.
8   The National Archives, Kew, 11/1627/175, 11/1227/137 and 11/114/162.
9   J. Homer, *Brewing in Kent* (Stroud, 2016).
10 W. Marshall, *The Rural Economy of Gloucestershire, Including Its Dairy; Together with the Dairy Management of North Wiltshire; and the Management of Orchards and Fruit Liquor in Herefordshire*, Volume 2 (London, 1789), 239–40.
11 C.W. Sabin, Agriculture. In W. Page (ed.), *Victoria History of the County of Kent* (London, 1908), 457–71, at 468.
12 D. Defoe, *A Tour Through This Whole Island of Great Britain* (London, 1722), 33.
13 Defoe, *Tour*, 33.
14 Lambarde, *Perambulation of Kent*, 246.
15 Anon., *The Fruiterer's Secret* (London, 1604), unpaginated introduction.
16 W. Camden, *Britain, or a Chorographical Description of the Most Flourishing Kingdomes, England, Scotland and Ireland* (London, 1637), 334.
17 Norden, *Surveyor's* Dialogue, 209.
18 D. Harvey, Fruit Growing in Kent in the Nineteenth Century, *Archaeologia Cantiana* 79 (1964), 95–108, at 104.
19 G. Mingay, Agriculture. In A. Armstrong (ed.), *The Economy of Kent, 1640–1913* (Woodbridge, 1996), 51–84, at 62.

20 Kent Archives, U908/T59/1, U908/T17/1 and U908/T234/1.

21 E. Hasted, *The History and Topographical Survey of the County of Kent,* Volume 1 (London, 1797), 266.

22 Kent Archives, EK/U2298/T7.

23 W. Cobbett, *Rural Rides* (London, 1830), 58 and 217.

24 West Yorkshire archives, Calderdale, SH:7/ML/E/3/0019.

25 Mingay, Agriculture, 71.

26 Harvey, Fruit Growing in Kent, 96–97.

27 *Maidstone Gazette,* 11 August 1840.

28 Harvey, Fruit Growing in Kent, 97.

29 Harvey, Fruit Growing in Kent, 97.

30 Parliamentary Papers, Board of Agriculture and Fisheries, Agricultural Statistics for 1895 and 1906.

31 *South Eastern Gazette,* 26 May 1863.

32 The National Archives, Kew, BT 34//859/36656.

33 W.E. Bear, Flower and Fruit Farming in England – Part 3, *Journal of the Royal Agricultural Society of England,* 3rd series 10 (1899), 46.

34 P. Kropotkin, *Fields, Factories and Workshops* (London, 1899), 216.

35 Sabin, Agriculture, 467.

36 Sabin, Agriculture, 467.

37 Sabin, Agriculture, 468.

38 Stamp, *Land of Britain: Its Use and Misuse,* 109.

39 Sabin, Agriculture, 468.

40 Parliamentary Papers, Board of Agriculture and Fisheries, Agricultural Statistics.

41 L. Dudley Stamp, *The Land of Britain, Part 85: Kent* (London, 1936), 602–3.

42 Stamp, *Land of Britain: Its Use and Misuse,* 118.

43 Stamp, *Land of Britain: Its Use and Misuse,* 118.

44 Kent Archives, U1383 B4/1.

45 Stamp, *Land of Britain: Its Use and Misuse,* 114–18.

46 B. Short, P. May, G. Vine and A.-M. Bur, *Apples and Orchards in Sussex* (Lewes, 2012), 92–94.

47 Short *et al., Apples and Orchards in Sussex,* 102–10.

48 Parliamentary Papers, Board of Agriculture and Fisheries, Agricultural Statistics for 1939.

49 E.W.H. Briault, *The Land of Britain, Parts 83 and 84: Sussex (East and West)* (London, 1942), 520.

50 A.H. Hoare, *The English Grass Orchard and the Principles of Fruit Growing* (London, 1928), 37.

51 W. Ellis, *The Timber Tree Improved* (London, 1738), 66.

52 Ellis, *Timber Tree Improved,* 65.

53 Ellis, *Timber Tree Improved,* 130.

54 J. Clutterbuck, *Agricultural Notes on Hertfordshire* (London, 1864), 14.

55 W. Hone, *The Year Book of Daily Recreation and Information* (London, 1832), 1203.

56 A. Young, *General View of the Agriculture of Hertfordshire* (London, 1804), 143.

57 W. Ellis, *Chiltern and Vale Farming* (London, 1733), 141–42.

58 Young, *Agriculture of Hertfordshire,* 143.

59 Clutterbuck, *Agricultural Notes,* 14.

60 Clutterbuck, *Agricultural Notes*, 14.

61 Hertfordshire Archives and Local Studies, 15597, AH 681, D/EV R2 and AH/2772.

62 J. Norden, *The Surveyor's Dialogue* (London, 1608), 209; Ellis, *Timber Tree Improved*, 64.

63 Hertfordshire Archives and Local Studies, DE/X905/P1.

64 Hertfordshire Archives and Local Studies, D/P64/27/1–27/4, DSA4/63/1–32 and DSA4/92/1–6.

65 Clutterbuck, *Agricultural Notes*, 14.

66 A.J. Ward, *The Early History of Papermaking at Frogmore Mill and Two Waters Mill, Hertfordshire* (Berkhamsted, 2003); W. Branch Johnson, *Industrial Archaeology of Hertfordshire* (Newton Abbot, 1977), 55–61.

67 J. Evans, *The Endless Web* (London, 1954).

68 M. Stanyon, Papermaking. In D. Short (ed.), *An Historical Atlas of Hertfordshire* (Hatfield, 2011), 80–81.

69 J.P. Moore, The Impact of Agricultural Depression and Landownership Change on the County of Hertfordshire, c. 1870–1914. Unpublished PhD thesis, University of Hertfordshire, 2010, 60–61.

70 *Berkhampsted Review*, August 1974, Dacorum Heritage Centre archives, not catalogued.

71 Dacorum Heritage Centre, BK 3906.360.9.

72 *Buckinghamshire Herald*, March 1890.

73 Hertfordshire Archives and Local Studies, DE/Ls/B5l7.

74 *Berkhampsted Review*, July 1902, Dacorum Heritage Centre archives, 1116.04.

75 M. Pomfret, *Stone's Orchard, Croxley Green* (Croxley Green, n.d.).

76 Pomfret, *Stone's Orchard*, 8.

77 M. Farnell, The Neglected Aylesbury Prune, *Buckinghamshire and Bedfordshire Countryside*, March 1972, 14–16.

78 G. Barnes and T. Williamson, *The Orchards of Eastern England* (Hatfield, 2021), 57.

79 Farnell, Aylesbury Prune, 15.

80 Bedfordshire Record Office, BML 10/7/12.

81 Hertfordshire Archives and Local Studies, DE/By/B1.

82 T.F.T. Baker, J.S. Cockburn and R.B. Pugh (eds), *Victoria History of the County of Middlesex*, Volume 4 (London, 1971), 12–13.

83 S. Reynolds, *Victoria History of the County of Middlesex*, Volume 3 (London, 1962), 115, 117, 198, 259; Baker *et al.*, *Victoria History*, Volume 4, 75.

84 J. Morgan and A. Richards, *The New Book of Apples* (London, 2002), 212 and 225.

85 Reynolds, *Victoria History of Middlesex*, Volume 3, 259; C.H. Middleton, The Orchards of Middlesex, *Journal of the Ministry of Agriculture* 29 (1922–23), 269–75, at 272.

86 Middleton, The Orchards of Middlesex, 270.

87 Middleton, The Orchards of Middlesex, 273.

88 Stamp, *Land of Britain: Its Use and Misuse*, 116.

89 Hertfordshire Archives and Local Studies, DSA4/30/2.

90 J. Pam, Essex Agriculture: Landowners' and Farmers' Responses to Economic Change, 1850–1914. Unpublished PhD thesis, University of London, 2004, 138–40.

91 Pam, Essex Agriculture, 138.

92 Essex Record Office, D/DU 218/5.

93 G. Parhill and G. Cook, Hadleigh Salvation Army Farm: A Vision Reborn (Hadleigh, 2008); H. Rider Haggard, *Rural England,* Volume 2 (London, 1906), 493–504.

94 H. Rider Haggard, *Regeneration: Being an Account of the Social Work of the Salvation Army in Great Britain* (London, 1910), 196.

CHAPTER 6

The orchard countries:
East Anglia and the Fens

Before 1850

Most people probably do not associate East Anglia – which we here define rather broadly, to include Huntingdonshire, north Essex and east Hertfordshire, as well as Norfolk, Suffolk and Cambridgeshire – with orchards and fruit growing. But even in the late nineteenth century, some parts of the Fenlands could already boast densities of orchards comparable to those of Herefordshire or Devon. By the end of the 'orchard century', overall densities in both Essex and Cambridgeshire were similar to those in the West Country, with Suffolk and Norfolk not far behind. But while, to a significant extent, the orchard history of the eastern counties is short and recent – a phenomenal expansion in the late nineteenth and first half of the twentieth century – this late flourishing of fruit growing had ancient roots.

Farm orchards were numerous in the region from an early date, especially in the old-enclosed parts of Norfolk, Suffolk, Essex and Hertfordshire, where farms were scattered widely across the landscape, standing in the midst of their properties, rather than being closely clustered in villages, hemmed in by open fields. But even in the latter districts, in Cambridgeshire and the old county of Huntingdonshire, they were common enough. Indeed, only on the chalk escarpment of the 'East Anglian Heights' or on the dry, sandy soils of Breckland or along the Suffolk coast, were they thin on the ground. This was because – largely for environmental reasons – farms were fewer in these districts, each covered a large area, and most were occupied by individuals whose focus was on large-scale grain production and who had little inclination to waste time on fruit trees, which anyway did poorly on these dry soils. Tuddenham, in west Suffolk, a parish extending across more than a thousand arid hectares, contained only a single small orchard in *c.* 1900, to judge from the evidence of the Ordnance Survey maps. A survey of the manor drawn up in 1766 describes in some detail 15 separate farms, only one of which had an orchard.[1] With these notable exceptions, small farm orchards were thick on the ground, and, as elsewhere in England, the cultivation and consumption of fruit was deeply woven into the fabric of everyday life and shaped local food traditions. The apple called the Norfolk Beefing, recorded in a fruit list from Mannington Hall, the home of the Walpole family, in 1698, was thus used to make 'biffens'. The apples were baked whole and gradually flattened and dried, either domestically or in commercial bread ovens, especially those of the Norwich bakers.[2] Various other fruit varieties had been developed in the region by the start of the nineteenth century, including the apples Winter Majetin, Winter Broaden, Dr Harvey and Jolly Miller, and the plum Willingham Gage. But the importance of orchard fruit did not extend to a regional predilection for cider. In a region famed for the quality of its malting barley, beer was always the alcoholic drink of choice.

That is not to say that cider was never produced in the region. As we shall see, it was manufactured on an industrial scale in Norfolk from the late nineteenth century onward. Even before this it was produced at many country houses, as at Hamels in east Hertfordshire in the early decades of the eighteenth century (in 1718 the new 'apple mill room' there was boarded with 'feather edged elm boards').[3] It was made by farmers in some districts, in certain periods. In 1790 Nathaniel Kent, in his survey of Norfolk agriculture, asserted that cider was never made in the county.[4] Yet in 1845 White's *Directory* could describe how, in south Norfolk, 'many of the farmers make cider for their own consumption, and some little for sale'.[5] And from as early as 1722, it was produced commercially by Clement Chevallier, who came from Jersey and settled at Aspall Hall, just north of Debenham, in Suffolk.

A friend later described how Chevallier, 'coming out of a Cyder country, amongst other improvements of his estate he has been a great planter of Apples, many of them of the sorts in use for Making of Cyder in Jersey & has had a large Mill for that use brought from Hence & has I believe been at a great expense for becoming a large dealer in it'.[6] The stone milling trough, brought all the way from the Îles de Chausey, off the coast of Normandy, still survives, along with other equipment, in the 'cyder house', which he constructed (by converting an earlier barn) to house it. Production rose rapidly, reaching no less than 7,827 gallons a year by 1731, Chevallier marketing his produce widely across north central Suffolk – both to inns and to private individuals – and serving some customers as far afield as Norwich and Ipswich.[7] There is, however, little doubt that cider making on this kind of scale was unusual in the eastern counties at the time. In Chevallier's own words, 'from the year 1728 to 1740, I made, & sold, more Cyder than any Person in the Neighbourhood could have imagined'.[8] But his very success suggests that cider was not an unfamiliar drink in Suffolk in the early eighteenth century.

Although, soon after his arrival at Aspall, Chevallier planted a range of cider varieties brought from his homeland, his cider was mainly made using apples from trees already growing in the orchard at Aspall Hall or purchased in large quantities from local farms. A second planting, made at Aspall in the 1730s, comprised ordinary English dessert and culinary varieties, such as Golden Pippin, Golden Pearmain, Golden Reinette and Nonpareil.[9] This was in line with wider local practice. When cider was produced in the eastern counties, either on a domestic or a commercial scale, ordinary eating or cooking varieties were the main ingredient, with specialised cider apples being added in only small quantities, if at all.

East Anglia was, in medieval and early modern times, a populous and relatively wealthy region, with a number of large towns. At the end of the seventeenth century, Norwich was still the second largest city in the country, with a population approaching 30,000.[10] Not surprisingly, such markets encouraged a degree of early commercial production, especially within or on the edge of the main urban centres. In 1662 Thomas Fuller thought it impossible to tell whether Norwich was 'a city in an orchard or an orchard in a city', so full was it of fruit trees.[11] Some were growing in private gardens and orchards, but others on the commercial smallholdings which were an important feature of the city from an early date, such as the property comprising 'an orchard, a little house and a small piece of land' in St Stephens, described in a grant of 1466.[12] But small commercial enterprises also developed in satellite villages and even in more remote locations if soils were particularly suitable and reasonable transport links existed. The cultivation of cherries, in particular, seems to have become closely associated with particular parishes. William Bullein, in his *Government of Health* of 1595, acknowledged the primacy of Kent in the cultivation of cherries but added: 'So are there in a towne neare unto Norwich called Ketreinham [Ketteringham], this fruite is colde and moyst in the first degrée'.[13] Stowmarket in Suffolk was also famous for its cherries; the area around Sudbury was famed for the cherry known as the Polstead Black, after the eponymous village;[14] and White's *Directory* for 1845 described how the village of Marham, in west Norfolk was also known *as* 'Cherry Marham' because it was 'formerly noted for its great abundance of cherries and walnuts'.[15] Some degree of specialised commercial production thus existed in East Anglia from an early date. But the only extensive district in which, before the nineteenth century, fruit production had come to form a major part of the economy was the Fenland of Cambridgeshire and west Norfolk.

William Gooch, writing in his *General View of the Agriculture of the County of Cambridge,* of 1811, described how at 'Ely, Soham, Wisbech &c' there were 'many large gardens, producing so abundantly of vegetables and common kinds of fruit, as to supply not only the neighbouring towns but counties, the produce being sent to a great distance, to Lynn, &c. &c. by water, and by land, affording employ for many hands, labourers, retailers, carriers, &c. &c.'. He added that orchards were 'numerous and large in the same districts as the gardens; the chief growth, apples and cherries; Soham is remarkable for the latter'.[16] The main concentration of orchards was in the north Fens, around the Cambridgeshire town of Wisbech and extending over the county boundary into west Norfolk. The scale of production, while clearly impressive to Gooch, should not be exaggerated. Even in the late 1830s and 40s, when the tithe maps were surveyed, orchards still occupied only a relatively small area of land, although it should be noted that in only a few local parishes were they systematically recorded as a land-use category. Elsewhere, their presence can only be inferred from the names given to particular parcels of land. In Wisbech St Peter, the term 'orchard' appears no fewer than 22 times in the 'name and description of land and premises' of the tithe apportionment.[17] The plots in question were, however, small – only two covered more than 3 acres – and they amounted in all to only 43 acres (*c.* 17 hectares), around 0.6 per cent of the parish area. In the nearby Norfolk parishes of Emneth and Outwell (1841), there were 33 parcels named 'orchard', covering around 1 per cent of the parish area.[18] In all these places, land otherwise described might have been planted with fruit trees, however, and in those where 'orchard' was employed as a land-use category, the number and area were rather higher. In Walsoken, for example, no fewer than 47 parcels are so described, a total of 100 acres (*c.* 40 hectares), or 2.2 per cent of the parish area.[19] A commercial industry thus existed in the district by the early nineteenth century, but it was on a small scale by later standards.

On the face of it, the damp Fenlands seem an odd place in which to find commercial fruit growing. As noted earlier, orchards did best where light, sandy clays or loams overlay some freely draining substrate, such as sandstone or chalk. Here, in contrast, estuarine silts and clays gave rise to strong loams without underlying permeable rocks, and the entire area lies at or below sea level. Fruit growing was, however, possible because of the complex system of artificial drainage. Water levels could be kept low because of the dense network of drainage ditches, connected by mechanical pumps to the arterial channels. A major encouragement to fruit growing was the fact that Wisbech was an important inland port on the river Nene. Fruit could be loaded into small ships, taken down the river, and then along the coast, as far as the coalfields of north-east England. At this stage, the chief produce of the Fen orchards was probably apples. The tithe apportionments indicate that many orchards were under grass, but some of the larger examples are described as 'arable', suggesting that they were already being interplanted with soft fruit, vegetables or other crops, as was to be the usual local practice by the end of the century.

While the silts of the northern Fenland made good orchard land, the peats which characterised its central and southern portions were too damp, acidic and unstable for fruit trees. However, a number of 'islands' of higher ground existed, where clays overlay the freely draining Lower Greensand. By the end of the nineteenth century, orchards were numerous here, and Gooch's reference to Ely and Soham seems to suggest that the same had been true at its start. In fact, even in the years around 1840, to judge from the evidence of the tithe maps, the industry was poorly developed, no more than a sideline. The 1843 apportionment for Ely, for example, describes only 20 plots as 'orchard', although here, once again, fruit trees may have been a prominent feature of the many more which were categorised as 'Garden &c'. All in all, commercial fruit growing in East Anglia, even in the Fens, was still in its infancy in the middle decades of the nineteenth century.

The 'orchard century': before the Great War

It was thus only in the period after *c.* 1850 that commercial fruit growing in the eastern counties really developed apace, fuelled by a constellation of influences that should by now be familiar to readers: the growth of urban markets, the spread of the rail network, the emergence of new food processing industries and – in the last decades of the nineteenth century – agricultural depression. The orchards in the northern Fens around Wisbech grew rapidly. By 1900 there were more than 7 square kilometres of orchards within 5 kilometres of the centre of the town, covering around 9 per cent of the land area. The industry had initially depended on water transport to distribute its produce, but the largest markets lay in the Midlands and north-west England. The opening of the railway line from Wisbech to Peterborough, in 1850, accordingly saw a rapid growth in orchards, many planted by large companies like that owned by the Crockett family.[20] The opening of the line to March, and onwards to Cambridge, around the same time allowed access to southern markets, while transportation was further facilitated by the Wisbech and Upwell Tramway, opened in 1883, which was mainly intended for the movement of agricultural produce, including orchard fruit.[21] The orchards grew some plums but were still mainly devoted to apples, especially cooking varieties, such as Bramley's Seedling. By the end of the century, much of the crop went to the canning factory of the Wisbech Fruit Preserving Company Ltd, which opened in the town in 1890 (Figure 33).

The orchards farther south, on the Fen 'islands', now became a major part of the agricultural economy, and expansion was also rapid in the nearby villages on the southern margins of the Fens. By 1900 orchards accounted for over 9 per cent of the land area in Histon and Cottenham; in Impington, the figure was nearly 12 per cent. Growth was stimulated both by the arrival of the railways – especially the completion in 1847 of the line from Cambridge to Huntingdon, which passed through the middle of the district – but also by the emergence of a local processing industry.[22] The Chivers jam company, based in Histon, was established in 1873 but expanded massively a few years later with the completion of the Victoria Works, located, as was typical, beside the railway line. Plums had already been important in the local orchards, but the market provided by the factory further encouraged their cultivation.

The orchards of the north Fens, and on the Fen edge and islands farther south, were sometimes laid to grass, but more usually soft fruit, vegetables or even flowers were cultivated between the trees. Typical, perhaps, was an example near Ely, which was advertised for sale in 1890:

> Planted with a choice selection of apple, pear, plum, and other trees in full profit and bearing. And as undergrowth with gooseberry and current bushes. Which produce large quantities of Fruit for the London and Manchester markets.[23]

In the south of Cambridgeshire, on the calcareous loams and clays lying at the foot of the chalk escarpment of the East Anglian Heights, a third great orchard area had developed by the close of the nineteenth century. It was focused on the parishes of Great Eversden, Little Eversden, Melbourn and Meldreth, where,

by the time the Second Edition 6-inch Ordnance Survey maps were made, around 1900, orchards accounted for 3.7 per cent, 8.7 per cent, 3.4 per cent and 8.75 per cent of the land area, respectively. There are signs that the local villages were already making a good living from fruit growing at the start of the nineteenth century, although as yet only in small farm orchards – in part, perhaps, because many parishes still lay unenclosed and surrounded by commons and arable open fields (Meldreth was not enclosed until 1820, Melbourn as late as 1840).[24] There are certainly a number of early references to large local nurseries which seem to have specialised in fruit trees. One in Melbourn, put up for sale in 1826, contained more than a thousand fruit trees, mainly plums and apples.[25] The stock of another, in nearby Bassingbourne, auctioned off in 1839, consisted of:

> 2000 Thrifty, dwarf and standard apple and pear trees. In sorts from 5 to 15 years old. The trees will be sold in half rows about one hundred in a lot; they were selected with great care by the late proprietor of the nursery, and we strongly recommend for early fruiting.[26]

But here, once again, it seems to have been the arrival of the railways which really stimulated a fruit-growing industry in an area well suited to the

FIGURE 33. An orchard of Bramley's Seedings apple trees at Upwell, Norfolk, with the 'bush'-pruned, open-centred trees characteristic of the older commercial orchards in the East Anglian Fens.

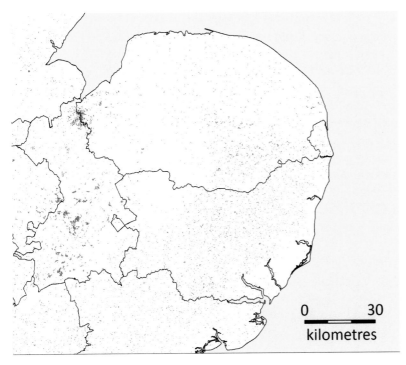

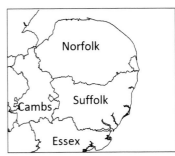

FIGURE 34. The distribution of orchards in eastern England, *c.* 1900, based on the Second Edition Ordnance Survey 6-inch maps. Note the concentrations of commercial orchards on the Norfolk–Cambridgeshire border, around Wisbech, in the northern Fenland; in central Cambridgeshire, on the fen edge around Histon; and in the south of the county, at the foot of the chalk escarpment of the 'East Anglian Heights'. Elsewhere, the thin scatter is mainly made up of domestic and farmhouse orchards. Such orchards were fewer on the lighter land, especially on the heathy soils of coastal Suffolk and on the arid 'Breckland' of south-west Norfolk and north-west Suffolk.

cultivation of fruit, especially plums. The line from Cambridge, via Audley End and Bishop's Stortford, to London was opened in 1845, while that running through the heart of the district, from Cambridge to London, via Royston and Hitchin, was opened in 1852.

By the start of the First World War, Cambridgeshire was, without doubt, the premier fruit-growing county in eastern England, benefitting not only from suitable soils, but also from a climate characterised by the warm, dry summers required for the commercial production of both plums and dessert and culinary apples (Figure 34). Elsewhere in the eastern counties, most orchards were still farm orchards, although more and more examples of commercial enterprises were now emerging in areas suitable for fruit growing. Many were associated with small farms and smallholdings, but some larger farmers, and even substantial landowners, established extensive fruit farms in an attempt to boost the income from the land in the face of the continuing poor prices for more conventional agricultural produce. In 1907 the Cubitt family, owners of the Honing estate, in north-east Norfolk, planted an area of 10 hectares immediately to the south of their park with fruit trees, which was steadily augmented over the following decade and a half to more than 55 hectares.[27] Localised clusters of orchards continued to develop in the vicinity of many of the larger towns and, in particular, in and around the parish of Tiptree, to the south-west of Colchester. In 1885 Arthur Charles Wilkin, farmer and fruit grower, established the Britannia Fruit Preserving Company in the village, initially processing some 50 tons of fruit each summer with a plant comprising a portable engine, four copper pans and a fruit pulper.[28] By 1905 more than 200 tons of fruit were being grown by the family each year, of which half was made into jam in a new factory, '… lighted by electricity, and served by light trolleys running on tramways, which are laid throughout the building'.[29] The company initially benefitted from the presence of the Kelvedon railway station, some 6 kilometres to the northwest of their farm, on the main line to London.[30] But in 1904 the Kelvedon and Tollesbury Light Railway was opened between Kelvedon and Tollesbury, running right past the factory, which was provided with its own sidings. The company, which made much of its claims to provide good-quality products, both soft fruit and top fruit, 'freshly gathered fruit and no adulteration',[31] produced much of its own fruit, and by 1906 had acquired over 800 acres (323 hectares) of land in the surrounding area, especially in the villages of Tiptree, Tollesbury and Goldhanger. By 1926 Wilkin and Sons owned 1,000 acres (405 hectares) of land and employed 440 regular workers (Figure 35).[32]

Elsewhere in East Anglia food processing companies, located close to rail lines, often had a less obvious impact on land-use patterns in their immediate hinterlands, instead drawing their supplies from – and stimulating production across – rather wider areas. Two cider-making businesses – Routs and Gaymers – were established in the Norfolk village of Banham in the middle of the nineteenth century. The former remained there, and remained small, but in 1896, William Gaymer (1842–1936) established a new, purpose-built factory beside the railway station at Attleborough, some 5 miles (8 kilometres) to the north, at a cost of nearly £6,000 (Figure 36).[33] The business expanded steadily, in 1906 acquiring a depot near Bishopsgate railway station in London. In addition, commercial cider production was revived at Aspall following a period in which it had largely been made for domestic consumption: slowly in the early years of the century but more rapidly after the construction of the Mid Suffolk Light Railway in 1908, which had a station a little over a kilometre to the north of Aspall Hall.[34],[35] By 1914 around 7,000 gallons were being produced each year, the company paying the costs of transportation 'to any station GER [Great Eastern Railway] or MSLR [Mid Suffolk Light Railway]'.[36]

The Orchard century: the inter-war years

The growth in East Anglia's orchard acreage accelerated through the 1920s and 30s, with expansion now fuelled not only by expanding markets, reliable transport infrastructure and continuing agricultural depression, but also by the proliferation of smallholdings, especially following the passing of the Land Settlement (Facilities) Act, in 1919. In Norfolk alone, there were, by 1946, no fewer than 1,896 county council smallholdings, covering 31,928 acres (12,921 hectares), many of which included an orchard.[37] Commercial orchards of all kinds were most numerous, as we would expect, where areas of suitable soils existed close to rail lines. Growth was, for example, rapid on the loams of east Norfolk, although in part this was because of the purchase, in 1919, of the Burlingham estate by

Norfolk County Council and its conversion to smallholdings. In spite of the growing importance of road transport through the 1920s and 30s, rail lines continued to structure the geography of fruit growing, not least because some of the principal rail companies went to considerable lengths to attract or retain customers. The sales particulars for a large fruit farm at Great Hormead, in north-east Hertfordshire, drawn up in 1945, described how 'the vendor has been in the habit of sending his fruit to Spitalfields, the Boro' and Covent Garden Markets. During the last two seasons the Railway Company has collected the fruit from the orchards, put it on the rail and delivered to the markets.'[38]

The orchards at Great Hormead were extensive, covering nearly 40 acres (16 hectares) and producing 9,000 bushels of apples and about 65 tons of plums each year. But much larger businesses had by now developed in many places. Of particular note was that of the Seabrook family, who began to grow fruit on a commercial scale in Boreham, in Essex, in the 1880s, but whose business expanded rapidly in the inter-war years. By the 1950s, they had 1,150 acres (465 hectares) of orchard in the parishes of Boreham, Hatfield Peverell and Terling.[39] Like Lanes of Berkhamstead (above, pp. 97–8), the company operated as a nursery business as well as being a commercial fruit grower, and it introduced many new varieties, of apple especially. William Seabrook published *Modern Fruit Packing for the Market* in 1922, *Modern Fruit Growing* in 1933 and *Fruit Production in Private Gardens* in 1942.[40]

One large-scale enterprise calls for particular comment, as it became the subject of a national scandal. In 1929 the businessman John Alexander Whitehead purchased part of the Cockayne Hatley estate, located on the claylands of Bedfordshire, on the county boundary with Cambridgeshire, and by 1931 had planted 2,000 Cox's Orange Pippin trees grafted on dwarfing rootstocks.[41] Keen to expand his business more rapidly, Whitehead set up his Cox's Orange Pippin Orchard company and sought financial input from numerous small investors, or 'treeholders', as they were called. In return for their money, these individuals became owners of a number of trees and received the profits from the fruit eventually produced, minus cultivation and other costs. More than 2,000 people – many of them women – signed up, attracted by Whitehead's patriotic claims and the benefit of being able to visit and enjoy the orchards and the grounds of Cockayne Hadley Hall.[42] But the business rapidly degenerated into a pyramid selling scheme, with individuals rewarded for recruiting additional investors. By 1939 more than 2.5 million trees had been planted and more than 200 people were employed in the orchards, but the business made increasing losses and Whitehead siphoned off some of the money raised into other ventures.[43] In 1940 he wrote to the 'treeholders', falsely claiming that the War Agricultural Committee was demanding that part of the orchards should be planted with potatoes and that they would need to pay a part of the costs of cultivation (at an estimated rate of £1 5 shillings per 100 trees).[44] His accountant reported him to the authorities, and although Whitehead escaped imprisonment, he was obliged to return £1,000 that he had taken out

Attleborough. Messrs. Gaymer & Sons, Cyder Works.

FIGURE 35. The orchards
of Wilkins and Sons at
Tiptree, Essex.

of the business. Short of capital, he mortgaged parts of the estate and, following a particularly bad harvest, in 1946, sold the orchards to the Co-operative Wholesale Society.[45]

While the inter-war period saw an increase in the area planted with orchards throughout East Anglia, Cambridgeshire remained the premier fruit-growing county. Already by 1910, it had 5,867 acres (2,274 hectares) of commercial orchards, accounting for around 1.1 per cent of its land area, compared with 2,042 acres (826 hectares), or 0.21 per cent of the land area, in the case of Suffolk and 7,989 (3,233 hectares), or 0.43 per cent, in the case of Norfolk – much of which was made up of orchards in the far west of the county, an extension of the Cambridgeshire fruit-growing district centred on Wisbech.[46] By 1939 Norfolk had 9,368 acres (3,791 hectares) under fruit and Suffolk 4,484 acres (1,815 hectares), but Cambridgeshire could now boast no less than 10,173 acres (4,117 hectares).[47] Expansion was rapid in all of the county's main fruit-growing districts. In the 1930s the orchards in the Wisbech area grew apples and some plums, with about 40 per cent underplanted with gooseberries.[48] On the southern Fen edge and islands, in villages like Cottenham and Willingham, the emphasis was on plums, mainly destined for 'the Histon jam and fruit-preserving factory of Messrs. Chivers … though considerable quantities are consumed locally in the Cambridge market'.[49] Some also went by train to the Midlands and the north.[50] In south Cambridgeshire, orchards also continued to flourish, again mainly producing plums and some apples. In Haslingfield, there had been around 7 hectares of orchards in 1840, rising to 24 hectares by the time the Second Edition 6-inch map was surveyed, in 1901. By the 1940s this figure had leapt to 59 hectares, around 6 per cent of the parish area.[51]

In many Cambridgeshire orchards, as in previous decades, not only soft fruit, but also other crops, were cultivated between the trees. Pettit described in 1941 how the area around Cottenham was 'remarkable for the intensive production of soft fruits, and of cutting flowers and vegetables'.[52] In some orchards, as at Willingham, in 1934, even arable crops, such as sugar beet, were grown.[53] Arable and underplanted orchards were by now common in other eastern counties. Typical was an example at Rayleigh, in Essex, which in 1924 contained 1,000 trees – apple, pear, plum, damson, greengage, medlar, quince and filbert – all interplanted with black and red currants, gooseberries and raspberries.[54] In some cases, however, cropping of this kind only continued until the trees matured and shaded out the ground below, and a significant number of orchards in the region were always laid to grass and often used to run poultry (an advertisement for a 'freehold grass orchard' in Nayland, Suffolk, in 1937 included a note that 'The fowl house is not included in the sale'). However else they might be used, the inter-war orchards of eastern England, like those in Kent, were very intensively managed and regularly sprayed. Most of the larger commercial orchards now contained a relatively limited range of fruit varieties, often grafted on dwarfing or semi-dwarfing rootstocks, which were planted in continuous blocks or mixed only with pollinators. The particulars drawn up

FIGURE 36. An old
postcard showing the
Gaymer's Cider factory,
erected in 1897 beside
the railway line at
Attleborough, Norfolk.

when French's Farm, in Hadleigh, Suffolk, was put up for sale in 1984 describe how the principal plantings, from the 1930s and 40s, comprised five varieties of apple (Cox's Orange Pippin with Emneth Early pollinators, Worcester Pearmain, Tydeman's Early Worcester and Laxton's Superb) three of pear and two of plum, in orchards extending over some 50 hectares.[55]

As in the period before 1914, the market provided by local processing industries fuelled expansion as much as the great conurbations lying at the end of rail lines. The continuing importance of the Chivers jam factory at Histon has already been noted: the firm expanded steadily, and by the 1920s the main processing buildings, fruit stores and ancillary plant sprawled over an area of more than 7.5 hectares. By 1931 some 3,000 people were employed there and Chivers was the largest canner of fruits and vegetables in the country.[56] Much of the fruit required came from the 3,000 acres (1,200 hectares) of orchard and fruit ground owned by the Chivers family itself (out of a total farmed estate of 7,000 acres (2,800 hectares).[57] But most was supplied by local growers. Wilkin and Sons at Tiptree likewise continued to provide a ready market for Essex fruit growers, as did the Elsenham Jam Company, founded in 1890 in the village of that name in the north-west of Essex.[58] Aspalls cider company continued to flourish, still mainly using normal dessert or culinary varieties of apple, some now brought all the way from the Cambridgeshire orchards, although the surviving account books record that some cider-making varieties, such as Madelleine and Bedam, were purchased from the orchards of Charles Townshend at Fordham, near Ely.[59] The company's output was, however, dwarfed by that of Gaymers, at Attleborough, in Norfolk, who were producing around 1.5 million gallons *per annum* in 1930 and 2.4 million in 1940. In 1933 the company began to plant orchards beside the factory, which by 1946 extended over more than 17 hectares.[60] These contained a wide range of apples, some of which were cider varieties from the west of England, but these only supplied a small proportion of the fruit required by the company (indeed, they may have been planted in part for their symbolic importance, as a form of advertising; in years when the quality of the fruit was good, some was sold, through the Norfolk Fruit Growers co-operative, based at Wroxham).[61] As a document drawn up in 1966 described, 'Gaymer's take thousands of tons of apples per annum from East Anglian growers and thereby provide a very useful outlet for some of the surplus apple crop'. The company used 'mixed varieties of dessert and cooking apples, and in this respect differs from the West County cyder manufacturers', with their dependence on specialised cider varieties.[62]

The post-war years

The advent of the Second World War brought a halt to the expansion of orchards in the eastern counties, but only a few neglected, overgrown or derelict examples were actually grubbed out, to make way for arable crops now so much in demand because of the enemy blockade. The government was concerned about supplies of vitamin C, and the region mainly produced fruit for eating, rather than apples to be used in the production of cider. Indeed, the war was in many ways a good period for local growers. True, there were labour shortages and difficulties in acquiring equipment, but as one Essex grower later recalled:

> On the other hand there was no trouble selling the fruit, and we got the control price for all the grades. 16/8d for ordinary varieties, £1 13s 4d for Cox's. It did not seem very much but we got it for all apples regardless of quality and this made it a good price....[63]

When the war ended, the orchard area in the eastern counties began to increase once more, but with growth now occurring in new places. In Cambridgeshire, there was almost no expansion in the immediate post-war years, followed by a decline through the early 1950s, and in Norfolk only modest growth, again followed by slight decline. But in Suffolk, the area under fruit trees rose steadily, from 1,852 acres (750 hectares) in 1945 to 2,630 (*c.* 1,000) in 1950, reaching 2,920 (*c.* 1,180) in 1955, while in Essex, it increased in the same period from 3,717 acres (*c.* 1500 hectares) to 4,915 (*c.* 1,990), reaching 5,428 (*c.* 2,196 hectares) by 1955, with particularly dramatic growth on the loamy soils in the north-east of the county, in the area extending from Colchester north to the Stour and eastward to the sea. The shift in geographical emphasis was not lost on observers, especially the expansion in Essex, with Norbury, for example, remarking in 1952 that 'In recent years there has been a large expansion of acreage in Essex, which county is particularly suited for growing dessert apples where low rainfall conditions are desirable for growing Cox and other dessert apples'.[64]

Although small producers continued to be important in the eastern counties through the 1940s and 50s, much of this final expansion in the orchard acreage was associated with large commercial businesses. Over a quarter of the Suffolk fruit acreage by the late 1950s, for example, was made up of just seven large firms.[65] In most new orchards, apples and plums were now grown on very dwarfing rootstocks, the trees cropped for 20–25 years, then grubbed up and replaced. In the post-war decades, moreover, the practice of planting soft fruit or vegetable in orchards declined. The ground between the trees was often now managed as bare earth or, from the 1960s, as grass kept short with mowers towed by tractors, and with only the area around the base of the trees comprising bare ground, sprayed with herbicide. Such orchards are today a particularly prominent feature of the Fenland landscape around Wisbech (Figure 37).[66] But grass orchards, especially ones doubling as poultry farms, also continued to exist, especially on older or smaller enterprises.

Conclusion

East Anglia has a long history of fruit growing, but, being remote from London and a region of beer rather than cider drinking, its orchards were limited in extent before the nineteenth century. It did have its own cider-making tradition and, in the form of the Chevalliers of Aspall, a notable instance of early

production for the market. There were also localised pockets of early commercial fruit growing and, by the eighteenth century, a measure of regional specialisation in the Fens. But, to a greater extent than the regions discussed in the previous chapters, East Anglia's orchard heritage is largely a product of the 'orchard century', from the 1850s to the 1950s. A phenomenal expansion of commercial fruit growing was fuelled by a constellation of economic and agrarian factors but, above all, by improved transport systems and the emergence of food processing industries. Cambridgeshire, and adjoining parts of Norfolk, were the prime fruit-growing counties, but a late surge in activity ensured that by the 1950s they were rivalled, in terms of the area occupied by orchards, by Essex and Suffolk. By this stage, East Anglia had become one of the most important fruit-growing regions of England, at least in terms of dessert and culinary apples, and plums.

FIGURE 37. A modern, intensively managed orchard near Wisbech, Cambridgeshire. Note the low-growing trees on dwarfing rootstock, the bare earth around their bases and the strips of mown grass, all typical features of orchards from the later twentieth century.

Notes

1   Suffolk Record Office, Bury St Edmunds branch, 507/1/48.
2   M. Askay and T. Williamson, *Orchard Recipes from Eastern England* (Lowestoft, 2020), 66–67.
3   A. Rowe (ed.), *Garden Making and the Freeman Family: a Memoir of Hamels 1713–1733* (Hertford, 2001), 6 and 87.
4   N. Kent, *General View of the Agriculture of the County of Norfolk* (London, 1796), 63.

5   W. White, *History, Gazetteer and Directory of Norfolk* (Sheffield, 1845), 37.

6   Private Collection: Aspall archive, DC Box 1/2.

7   Private Collection: Aspall archive, DC Box 1/2, 4 and 5.

8   Private Collection: Aspall archive, DC Box 3/1.

9   Private Collection: Aspall archive, DC Box 2/1, folio 84.

10 P. Corfield, From Second City to Regional Capital. In C. Rawcliffe and R. Wilson (eds), *Norwich Since 1550* (London, 2004), 139–65, at 142.

11 T. Fuller, *The History of the Worthies of England* (London, 1662), 274.

12 Norfolk Record Office, DCN 45/37/13.

13 W. Bullein, *The Government of Health* (London, 1595), fol. LXXXIII.

14 E. Kent, *Sylvan Rambles, or a Companion to the Park and Shrubbery* (London, 1825), 384; T. Gissing, Polstead Cherries, *The Phytologist* 2 (1857–58), 326.

15 W. White, *A History, Gazeteer and Directory of Norfolk* (Sheffield, 1845), 620.

16 W. Gooch, *General View of the Agriculture of the County of Cambridge* (London, 1811), 195–96.

17 The National Archives, Kew, IR 29 and 30/4/90.

18 Norfolk Record Office, DE/TA 10.

19 Norfolk Record Office, DE/TA 33.

20 L. Stamp, *The Land of Britain: Its Use and Misuse* (London, 1948), 115.

21 P. Paye, *The Wisbech and Upwell Tramway* (Tarrant Hinton, 2009); The National Archives, Kew, RAIL 491/831.

22 T. Kirby, Railways. In T. Kirby and S. Oosthuizen (eds), *An Atlas of Cambridgeshire and Huntingdonshire History* (Cambridge, 2000).

23 Cambridgeshire Record Office, 283/SP 597(ii).

24 W.E. Tate and M. Turner, *A Domesday of English Enclosure Acts and Awards* (Reading 1978), 72–75 and 142–43.

25 Cambridge Record Office, 296/B 693.

26 Cambridge Record Office, 296/B 727.

27 Private archive.

28 *The Lady*, 11 April 1985.

29 *Essex Weekly News*, 2 December 1904.

30 Information sheets, Tiptree Heritage Centre; Wilkins and Sons website, 'History': https://web.archive.org/web/20141112223240/http://www.tiptree.com/goto.php?ref=y&sess=+A5E5147191D51+F18435A52+9+B581D1058+E+357+9+25F1D1758&id=14, accessed 30 March 2020.

31 *Ibid.*

32 Harvest Home at Tiptree, company brochure, 1926; Tiptree Heritage Centre.

33 Norfolk Record Office, GAY 1/6/47–57.

34 P. Paye, *The Mid-Suffolk Light Railway* (Upper Bucklebury, 1986).

35 Private Collection: Aspall archive, DC Box 12/2.

36 Private Collection: Aspall archive, DC Box 12/4.

37 H. Upcher, Norfolk Farming, *Transactions of the Norfolk and Norwich Naturalists Society* 16 (1946), 37–105, at 105.

38 Hertfordshire Archives and Local Studies, D/231 254.

39 N.V. Scarfe, *The Land of Britain: Essex* (London, 1936); P. Wormwell, *Essex Farming, 1900–2000* (Colchester, 1999), 203–4.

40 W. Seabrook, *Modern Fruit Growing* (London, 1933); W. Seabrook, *Fruit Production in Private Gardens* (London, 1942).

41 A. Crossley, *Apple Years at Cockayne Hatley: the History of Coxes Orange Pippin Orchards ("COPO")* (Cockayne Hatley, 1999), 6.

42 Bedfordshire Record Office, X604/32 and X604/33/2–4.

43 Bedfordshire Record Office, X604/34/18, 21, 22, 25.

44 Bedfordshire Record Office, X604/34/35.

45 Bedfordshire Record Office, X604/34/77; Crossley, *Apple Years*, 38–39.

46 Parliamentary Papers, Board of Agriculture and Fisheries, Agricultural Statistics for 1910.

47 J.E.G. Mosby, *The Land of Britain: Norfolk* (London, 1938), 183.

48 Stamp, *Land of Britain: Its Use and Misuse*, 115.

49 Stamp, *Land of Britain: Its Use and Misuse*, 115.

50 G.H.N. Petitt, *The Land of Britain: Cambridgeshire and the Isle of Ely* (London, 1941), 399.

51 Ordnance Survey 1:25,000, Sheet 52/45, revision of 1938–1947.

52 Petitt, *Cambridgeshire and the Isle of Ely*, 399.

53 Cambridgeshire Record Office, K515/L/2069.

54 Essex Record Office, D/DTo/E200.

55 Suffolk Record Office, Bury St Edmunds branch, HE 503/11/449.

56 *Proceedings of the Institute of Mechanical Engineers* 121 (1931), 72.

57 *Journal of the Royal Agricultural Society* 92 (1861), 142–51.

58 Bishop's Stortford Council Website, History, Sir Walter Gilbey: http://www.stortfordhistory.co.uk/guide2/sir-walter-gilbey/, accessed 20 May 2020; Essex Record Office, D/DBi T1–27, E1, T/P 68/12/3.

59 Private Collection: Aspall archive, DC Box 12/7 and 12/8.

60 Norfolk Record Office, GAY 1/2/2–7 and GAY 1/6/56.

61 Transcript of oral history interview with Roy Woods, Gaymer's orchard manager 1975–88; Attleborough Heritage Centre.

62 Norfolk Record Office, GAY 1/5/20.

63 Essex Record Office, C139.

64 C.P. Norbury, Modern Developments in Fruit Growing, *Journal of the Royal Society of Arts,* 100, 4881 (1952), 719–34, at 720.

65 Suffolk Record Office, Ipswich branch, HD 285/2/5.

66 Oral history interview with Andrew Tamms, Crapes Fruit Farm, Aldham, Essex, September 2020.

CHAPTER 7

The recent history of orchards

The long decline of commercial orchards

Contrary to what is sometimes suggested, the decline of commercial orchards in England began in the 1950s, long before Britain became a member of the European Economic Union in 1972 (Figure 38). Before accession, fears had been expressed in many quarters about the likely impact of large-scale imports of fruit, from close neighbours in Europe, on indigenous growers. But fruit had long been imported into England, and often in large quantities. In 1911, 1926, 1932, 1933 and 1934, poor apple harvests had, for example, driven the West Country cider factories to supplement local supplies with fruit from France. Indeed, even in the later eighteenth and nineteenth centuries, apples had been imported on a considerable scale from across the Channel, except during the period of the Napoleonic Wars, shortly after the end of which one observer described how he had 'passed through Covent Garden, and seen upwards of 1000 casks of apples that have been imported from France, and not less than an equal quantity heaped together in warehouses near Fleet Market, containing in the whole not less than 40,000 bushels'.[1] The scale of imports from Europe increased when customs duty on fruit was lowered in 1838, and following the repeal of the Corn Laws, in 1846, there was a steady growth in the quantity of American apples being imported, much to the consternation of English growers. The famous Conference Pear was so named because it was first exhibited at the pear conference held by the Royal Horticultural Society in 1888, at Chiswick, to discuss the threat faced by commercial growers from imported American and Canadian fruit.[2]

Various tariffs were imposed and withdrawn over the years, as in 1932, when significant import duties were levied on European and American fruit, although not on that coming from New Zealand, Australia, Canada or other parts of the Empire.[3] The problem of imports seems to have intensified significantly, however, in the immediate post-war period, and many commentators echoed the views of Leslie H. Clark of the Essex Farmers Union, expressed in 1948, that the guaranteed prices imposed during the Second World War had 'removed the price incentive to grow, grade and pack to the best possible standard.'

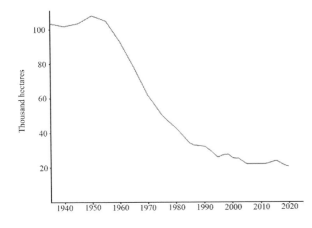

FIGURE 38. A graph showing the decline of the national orchard area in the post-war period. The figures include only commercial orchards, on holdings of 1 acre (c. 0.4 hectares) or more. Source: the Agricultural Census.

'With control fixed well below the price that the consumer was prepared to pay we have experienced the inevitable result of second rate fruit making the same price as good fruit'. Foreign competitors, he argued, had focused on quality – on 'good growing and packing which had not been applied to anything like the same extent in this country'.[4] Consumers preferred these good-quality imports, and prices for home-grown fruit were depressed by the 'effects of large quantities of poor quality, badly graded stuff coming onto the market in glut years from scrub orchards.'

The close supervision of food production which had developed during wartime continued in peacetime, and the Ministry of Agriculture worked hard to improve the appeal and quality of British fruit, and especially British apples, although with limited success. In 1962 an article in *British Farmer* warned that:

> World markets face a surplus of high grade apples and pears. Under these conditions there is no room for low grade fruit, which can bring loss to those who incur the expense of marketing, and depresses the price of better grades. It is purchased by certain retailers who buy it cheaply and sell dearly foisting it on to the public under the label "English Apples", thus bringing our fruit into disrepute.[5]

Foreign competition was thus already a problem to English growers before 1972, and accession did not end imports of fruit from elsewhere in the world, which were facilitated from the late 1980s by improvements in packaging and in the growth of container trade. Although by removing tariffs, joining Europe lowered the cost of fruit grown by the UK's close neighbours and thus further increased the scale of imports, it was other effects of the Common Agricultural Policy that contributed more to the decline in commercial orchards, in particular by ensuring that more money could be made from the land they occupied by growing arable crops. The system of subsidies also ensured that across Europe as a whole an unsustainable level of fruit surpluses developed or, as an article in *The Times* put it, 'the EU intervention scheme subsidises growers in other European countries for producing a glut of apples that nobody wants…'.[6] By the late 1980s, this had led to systematic efforts to reduce the number of orchards by providing grants for their removal.[7] In 1995 a Ministry of Agriculture, Fisheries and Food (MAFF) press release described how 'English apple growers are delighted with the latest figure from Brussels showing that the target of between 10 per cent and 15 per cent of the European Union apple orchards will be grubbed (30,000 hectares) leading to a significant reduction in European apples', and claimed that applications had already been received to grub out 14 per cent of the national area.[8] At both the national and the European levels, problems of overproduction were exacerbated by improvements in yields from modern orchards planted with dwarfing or semi-dwarfing rootstocks, intensively fertilised and sprayed with high levels of herbicide and pesticide. DDT (dichlorodiphenyltrichloroethane) now gave much more effective protection against capsid and apple blossom weevil, while new synthetic phosphorous sprays provided an effective way of controlling red spider mite.[9] In 1982 The Apple and Pear Development Council estimated that old apple orchards produced 7 tonnes of fruit per hectare, whereas a new orchard would produce 20 tonnes.[10]

Yet it should be emphasised that the reduction in the area occupied by orchards in England that began in the 1950s was also the consequence of factors which were largely unrelated to the scale of foreign imports or to government policies either at the national or the European level. Compared with many other branches of agriculture, fruit growing remained reliant on significant inputs of seasonal and casual labour, including individuals trained in pruning, and in many parts of England this became harder to obtain as the economy of rural areas became more diversified. Fruit picking had traditionally been women's work, but more and more women were now in full-time employment (Figure 39). Also important were structural changes in the wholesale and retail sectors, which had an impact in particular on the smaller growers. The number of independent greengrocers in the UK fell by 90 per cent between the mid-1960s and the mid-2000s, with a concomitant decline in wholesale

FIGURE 39. Harvesting in the orchards of Wilkin and Sons of Tiptree, Essex, in the 1930s. Commercial orchards depended on a sizeable body of casual workers, most of whom were women.

fruiterers, as the large supermarket chains steadily increased their market share.[11] A number of growers moved into the 'pick your own' (PYO) market in the 1970s and 80s, but this became less popular through the 1990s.

One way in which successive governments, both before and after 1972, tried to improve the efficiency of the fruit-growing industry, and the appeal of its products to consumers, was to reduce the range of varieties being marketed, a policy also driven by concerns about the greater susceptibility of some of the older varieties to disease. In 1944 MAF published a 'Primary List' of apples recommended for planting in new orchards, which included only Bramley's Seedling, Cox's Orange Pippin, Edward VII, Grenadier, Laxton's Superb, Miller's Seedling and Worcester Pearmain; Laxton's Fortune and Lord Lambourne were also under consideration, pending the results of field trials. These varieties, nearly half of which had been introduced since 1900 and the majority since 1850, were considered 'sufficient for most districts', although it was conceded that in some areas 'other varieties are known to succeed and, in consequence, the nursery trade will arrange for the propagation of trees of the following varieties: Allington Pippin, Beauty of Bath, Blenheim Orange, Charles Ross, Early Victoria, Ellison's Orange, James Grieve, Lane's Prince Albert, Lord Derby, Monarch and Newton Wonder'.[12] Government attempts to reduce the range of fruit cultivated commercially continued through the 1970s and into the 1980s. In 1982 MAFF informed fruit growers that:

> For the English fruit industry to survive it is vital that the number of varieties is reduced as a matter of urgency. Certainly the multiplicity of dessert varieties marketed during the September–December period is severely depressing prices. Fewer varieties, with improved continuity of supply, can be backed by increased promotion.

> It is fashionable for some farm shops to offer a wide range of marginally commercial varieties. This, however, we believe to be counter-productive. The good, well run farm shop or PYO unit, providing good commercial varieties, at full retail prices, is the best ambassador the English fruit industry can have.[13]

Cox's Orange Pippin, Discovery and Bramley's Seedling were now the officially preferred apples, Conference and Comice were the recommended pears, and the only second-choice varieties suggested were the apples Crispin, Spartan and Idared, and even these were to be planted with caution. Research was continuing into the viability of other varieties, but these were few in number – Golden Delicious, Worcester Pearmain, Tydeman's Early and Egremont Russet. 'Growers are strongly urged to consider grubbing varieties not listed above'.[14]

In terms of landscape and the environment, however, the most important development in the second half of the twentieth century and the early decades of the twenty-first was not the reduction in the range of fruit cultivated, but the decline in the number and extent of orchards, which can only be described as catastrophic. Overall the area occupied by commercial orchards in England plummeted after the 1950s, falling from 108,600 hectares in 1950 to

61,700 hectares in 1970, and reaching less than 30,000 by 2010. It is still falling, albeit now at a slower rate.

The fate of 'traditional' orchards

The decline of commercial fruit growing in England needs to be distinguished from the slow attrition of 'traditional' orchards, comprising tall trees on vigorous rootstocks, of the kind considered of particular significance for biodiversity. These include small farm orchards, most of the older cider orchards in western England, and a proportion of the older commercial examples elsewhere, together with many of those associated with country houses and institutions. Orchards like this had begun to disappear from the landscape long before the start of the wider decline in the orchard acreage just described. Even in the inter-war years, small farm orchards were being criticised by agricultural advisers and others as relics of a bygone age. They were located beside the farmhouse, rather than on the best site available for the production of top fruit; their tall trees were hard to spray; and, since these orchards represented at best a minor income stream in the farm business, their owners were unlikely to invest in the spraying tackle, packing sheds or other plant deemed necessary for commercial success. Stamp described them in 1948 as 'casual' orchards, 'generally left to look after themselves except for an occasional pruning', and in which 'any control of pests is the exception and spraying is almost unknown'.[15] He was particularly concerned about their location:

> It is really only within the last two or three decades – particularly since about 1930 – that we have begun to understand scientifically the soil requirements of different species of orchard tree and also to realise that the most important factor of all is the climatic one of freedom from spring frosts. It is not too much to say that the bulk of British orchards, if not badly sited, do not occupy the best sites available.[16]

Such concerns were heightened by the sharp spring frosts of 1929, 1935, 1938, 1941 and 1945, which wiped out the fruit crop in many small orchards.[17]

As farms grew larger through the middle and later decades of the twentieth century, and as they began to focus on a more limited range of activities – arable or livestock, dairying or fattening – farm orchards were increasingly neglected by owners who simply lacked the time or the inclination to pick and sell the small surplus they produced. Moreover, with fresh fruit easily available, all year round, in local greengrocers or supermarkets, they were less concerned to maintain them for their own personal use. There was thus little incentive to replace old trees as they died. Orchards degenerated into gardens or paddocks. Others were simply grubbed out and incorporated into the adjacent fields, something which was particularly likely to happen when one farm was absorbed by another and one of the farmhouses was sold off as superfluous to requirements. Indeed, the British government provided grants for grubbing out derelict orchards from the 1940s, with 'derelict' being defined as those which, 'on an average of the past four or five years', were 'no longer capable of bearing a crop worth marketing'.[18]

These included some commercial examples but were mainly farm and small cider orchards. Grant aid schemes went through various permutations with, in particular, a more generous rate of support being introduced in 1971.[19]

As with other aspects of post-war food production, cash incentives were accompanied by a barrage of advice. In 1961 MAFF asked farmers, rhetorically:

> Is your orchard an asset or a liability? There is no doubt that quite a number of orchards – the smaller ones in particular – are likely to be an embarrassment to the owner rather than a source of gain…. In these days of fierce competition only the quality product can hope to find a paying market…. What can be done with these worn out orchards, those orchards which are so small that they do not warrant the expenditure on spraying tackle and equipment for grading and packing? What can be done with those mis-sited orchards where frost claims the crop three years out of four? What can be done to clear the rubbishy samples of fruit which not only clutter up the market but – worse – depress the price of first class sendings? There can only be one answer – grub out and put the land to more profitable use.[20]

By this time, as we have seen, large commercial orchards were also in decline, and wider moves to reduce the national orchard acreage were underway, but old farm orchards were vulnerable in additional ways. Many fell victim to 'infilling' – they represented valuable building land within village 'envelopes' where development was permitted by planners. One of the few negative consequences of the 1947 Town and Country Planning Act was that, by reducing the scope for suburban sprawl, it encouraged higher densities of houses in those areas which *were* zoned for residential development.[21]

The extent to which 'traditional' farm orchards have been lost across England is hard to estimate, in part because of problems of definition. But a recent study in the counties of Norfolk, Suffolk, Hertfordshire, Essex, Cambridgeshire and Bedfordshire, which examined the sites of around 8,300 orchards shown on Ordnance Survey 6-inch maps from the first decade of the twentieth century (the vast majority of which were attached to farmhouses) suggests that only *c.* 8 per cent survive in recognisable form.[22] Some additional farmhouse orchards were planted in the course of the twentieth century, but they were few in number and were often planted with half-standard trees rather than the tall specimens characteristic of 'traditional' orchards.

In western England, many old cider orchards occupied, as we have repeatedly noted, an ambivalent, intermediate position between 'farm' and 'commercial' types. They formed a substantial but not a primary source of income for many farmers, the fruit by the middle decades of the twentieth century often being sold to one of the major cider-producing firms. As we have seen, many such orchards were already in a declining or derelict condition before the Second World War, and they continued to deteriorate after it. In 1936 there had been 67,000 acres (27,114 hectares) of cider orchards in the western counties, but by 1957 this had fallen to 40,927 acres (16,562 hectares) – bucking the overall national trend of expansion – and by 1965, to 28,001 acres (11,331 hectares).[23] In fact, the decline of 'traditional' cider orchards was even greater than these figures suggest because the pre-war tendency for the production of cider apples to be concentrated in large, modern orchards continued with a new intensity. As an internal MAFF memo from 1960 put it:

> Farm cider orchards being grubbed up are counterbalanced by the increase in orchards run more commercially in Hereford, though not in Somerset or Devon. These new orchards are often more intensive using bush or smaller root stocks. Overall, the new orchards are more than replacing the grubbed up orchards in cropping potential.[24]

This process continued through the following decades, fuelled by the significant increase in the consumption of cider nationally which occurred between the 1960s and the 1990s, encouraged by the energetic advertising campaigns mounted by Bulmers, Gaymers and Taunton Cider, and by the new availability of the drink in draught form.[25]

The concentration of industrial cider production in the Hereford area probably explains why, while the area of orchards in Devon declined by nearly 54 per cent between 1945 and 1965, and that in Somerset by 45 per cent, in Herefordshire it fell by only 32 per cent. Moreover, while in 1965 (the first year such information was recorded in government statistics) around 41 per cent of orchards in Devon were considered 'commercial' rather than essentially domestic in character, and 54 per cent of those in Somerset, in Herefordshire the figure was nearly 70 per cent. Over the next 10 years, while there was some further contraction in Herefordshire, the area of orchards in the other two counties virtually collapsed, falling from 4,333 acres (1,753 hectares) to 1,785 acres (722 hectares) in Somerset and from 4,249 acres (1,720 hectares) to a tiny 658 acres (266 hectares) in Devon.[26] Gee has described how, in the latter county, 'orchards for domestic use or small scale cider making' had become an irrelevance. 'Keeping the orchard only made sense if you had an established market, determined by inertia rather than by business reasons. The result was benign neglect or destruction. Smaller fruit farms disappeared. Cider making was static. There was little planting.'[27]

Cider orchards continued to exist in the west of England, but many were now modern and intensive in character, comprising highly productive, low-growing trees with a limited life span. Surviving examples of 'traditional' orchards, in contrast, continued to deteriorate, with trees not being replaced and scrub invading. An assessment of such orchards in Somerset, carried out in 2007, concluded that of the 2,741 known examples, nearly two thirds were in a 'poor' condition, because they had few young trees, had invasive scrub or had been subject to a measure of replanting. In 2014 a further survey of 148 sample orchards concluded that 70 per cent were now in 'poor' condition.[28]

Other kinds of orchard comprising tall trees growing in permanent grassland also experienced a steady decline in the second half of the twentieth century. Large psychiatric hospitals, and residential institutions such as children's homes, gradually abandoned the practice of growing their own food. Farm and garden work was increasingly seen as exploitative rather than rewarding or therapeutic. Money could, moreover, be made by selling off the land formerly used for

such activities, and in 1958 the Ministry of Health advised all hospital boards
to dispose of food-producing facilities on the grounds that 'advances in medical
treatment and improvements in the supply of clean milk and vegetables have
reduced the need for hospitals to have their own farms'.[29] Some institutions
continued to produce a proportion of the food consumed by residents into the
1970s, but not after this, and orchards tended to be neglected or cleared away
before farms and gardens were. Moreover, through the following two decades,
large residential institutions, and especially psychiatric hospitals, began to be
closed down, to be replaced (to an extent) with smaller units of care. They
were either converted into flats or demolished and their sites built on. In a
few cases, surviving orchards were retained and conserved as a 'feature' of new
developments, as, for example, when the Three Counties Hospital, at Arlesley,
in Bedfordshire, was redeveloped as Fairfields, in the 1990s. But in most cases,
orchards were simply lost. Of course, in a number of places both large residential institutions and the orchards attached to them have survived, and in some
cases the latter are now carefully preserved. But for the most part, in the second
half of the twentieth century, institutional orchards went the same way as old
cider orchards and small farm orchards.

Nor did old garden orchards fare much better. As we have already noted,
the 1940s and 50s saw a rash of demolitions of country houses; many more
were converted to new institutional uses or into flats, their orchards seldom
surviving. Even where such places remained in private hands, orchards were
often neglected, as owners reduced their gardening staff and increasingly purchased what fruit they required from local shops, like everyone else. And while
small collections of fruit trees were maintained in innumerable small gardens
in towns, suburbs and countryside alike, the kinds of true orchards planted in
the grounds of large middle-class houses tended to disappear. People had less
interest in making jam or apple pie, fewer could employ a gardener, and many
examples, once again, fell victim to 'infilling', meaning they were sold off from
the house and built on. The same fate befell many market gardens with old
orchards attached in suburban or suburbanising areas.

Reaction: the rise of heritage orchards

The loss of old farm and cider orchards, and the associated loss of old fruit
varieties, was part and parcel of the wider 'modernisation' of British agriculture, which continued through the 1950s, 60s and 70s, but which by the latter
decade was facing mounting opposition. The ploughing of ancient pastures,
the removal of hedges to create ever larger arable fields, the filling in of ponds
and the draining of wetlands – to say nothing of the liberal use of insecticides
and herbicides – may have saved the nation from post-war food shortages,
but they also led to drastic reductions in biodiversity and had appalling effects
on the appearance of the countryside, especially in arable farming districts.
Books like Marion Shoard's *The Theft of the Countryside* and Richard Mabey's

The Common Ground, both published in 1980, were immensely popular and influential, and in 1982 a new organisation was established, Common Ground, with an agenda which focused not only on wildlife conservation, but also on the 'widening gaps between nature and culture, between the special and the commonplace, increasing detachment from decision making' experienced by local communities.[30] The conservation of old orchards fitted in well with such concerns, and in 1988 the organisation began its 'Save Our Orchards' campaign, 'intuitively recognising the richness of culture and nature held in the traditional tall tree orchard'.[31] Orchards were seen, not only as important for biodiversity, but as a manifestation of 'local distinctiveness':

> Orchards are more than formal collections of fruit trees, they are a manifestation of our long relationship with fruit cultivation in different localities. They vary from place to place in the kinds of fruit, the varieties, size and disposition of trees, the domestic animals that are grazed beneath them, the soft fruits, flowers and other crops grown around them, the ways and times of pruning, grafting, picking and planting'.[32]

Much attention was focused on the disappearance of old local fruit varieties and their replacement by a restricted range of 'types favoured for their keeping qualities, regular cropping and appearance, rather than taste'.[33] Common Ground accordingly organised the first 'Apple Day', in October 1990. Innumerable such events are now regularly held by fruit and orchard enthusiasts all over the country, at which members of the public can have the varieties of fruit growing in their garden or orchard identified. The organisation also produced a rash of books and advice notes, stimulating not only the publication of many further books on fruit and orchards, but also, more importantly, the establishment of a wide variety of county and regional organisations and initiatives which have worked hard to conserve old orchards, to plant new ones, and in general to raise awareness of our fruit and orchard heritage.

Not surprisingly, such developments have been especially prominent in the old cider counties of western England and include the Gloucestershire Orchards Trust, started in 2001, and the Wiltshire Traditional Orchards Project, established in 2008. Devon has several such groups: Orchard Link, covering south Devon; Orchards Live, covering the north of the county; and Exeter Apples. The Three Counties Orchard Project, which embraced seven areas within Worcestershire, Herefordshire and Gloucestershire, ran from 2014 to 2018 and trained volunteers in practical orchard skills as well as restoring 34 orchards; while the Herefordshire Orchards Evaluation project developed techniques for estimating the value of individual orchards in social and environmental terms. As Fenella Tyler, Chair of the National Association of Cider Makers stated, 'For the first time, the cider industry can properly demonstrate that the nation's orchards are worth so much more than their value to farmers alone'.[34] The project was managed by The Bulmer Foundation and its findings published in 2012. Local authorities in the west of England have also played an important role. Somerset County Council for a time offered grants for orchard conservation; Cornwall County Council did likewise, and in the mid-1990s commissioned local nurseries to propagate more than 60 old varieties traditionally grown in the county. But the eastern half of the country has also seen much activity, with county orchard groups being set up in Suffolk, Cambridgeshire, Bedfordshire and elsewhere, and above all with the establishment, in 2003, of the East of England Apples and Orchards Project. A range of national organisations with a wider conservation remit have also become interested in traditional orchards over the past few decades, most notably the People's Trust for Endangered Species, which established the Orchard Network as a 'partnership of organisations working together for the conservation of orchards across the British Isles'. In 2006 'Traditional orchards' were included in the UK Biodiversity Action Plan list, and they were again included in the revised list of 2011, because of their importance for wildlife.[35]

One effect of this burgeoning interest has been the planting, from the 1980s, of numerous new 'heritage' orchards, some established mainly with the preservation of old fruit varieties in mind, some principally designed for wildlife conservation, many in order to achieve both aims. Some are private initiatives, others are 'community' orchards, established by local groups, councils or other organisations, including county wildlife trusts (Figure 40). These groups have also worked, in many cases, to preserve existing orchards. In Hertfordshire, for example, Tewin Orchard was donated to the Hertfordshire and Middlesex Wildlife Trust in 1984 and, together with the adjacent area of woodland, is maintained as a nature reserve. The previous year, some 25 kilometres to the south-west, Stone's orchard in Croxley Green – one of the last of the west Hertfordshire orchards – was given to Three Rivers District Council and, from the early 1990s, developed as a public open space by the parish council.[36] Indeed, wherever heritage organisations, such as the National Trust, or local authorities managing country parks or similar facilities, have inherited old orchards, they have – over the past four decades – often conserved and augmented them, as, for example, at Mowlsbury, in Bedfordshire. But where private owners are indifferent or hostile, even the oldest or most biologically interesting of orchards remains vulnerable. The 1967 Forestry Act specifically excluded orchards from felling regulations, although in rare cases specific examples have been conserved with the use of Tree Preservation Orders.

Over the past few decades, orchards have thus acquired new roles. Their importance for sustaining biodiversity and as elements in our cultural landscape has become widely recognised. New examples have accordingly been planted and some old ones re-purposed. But we would not want to give the impression that the fate of orchards is entirely enmeshed in conservation

FIGURE 40. A private orchard of 'heritage' varieties, planted a few years ago by Paul Read, a prominent enthusiast, near Thrandeston, north Suffolk.

and nostalgia. There are signs that the national decline in *commercial* orchards has slowed over the past few decades and in some areas reversed. In Devon, their area has recovered slightly from its low point of 385 hectares, in the 1980s, more than doubling between 1985 and 2000 and since then hovering around the 800 hectare figure.[37] In Herefordshire, too, a recovery has occurred. In 1995 there were a little over 3,000 hectares of commercial orchard, but today the figure is around 5,000.[38] These changes are largely a consequence of the buoyancy of the market for cider and the continuing policies of large manufacturers like Bulmers or Thatchers, who offer contracts guaranteeing to purchase the fruit from new orchards for two or three decades. But such orchards, while not as intensively sprayed or as inimical to wildlife as those of the recent past, are nevertheless planted with trees on dwarfing rootstocks (MM106 or M111) at high densities (300–400 trees per acre), very different from the cider orchards of the past. Yet even the latter have, in some cases, benefitted from a renewed interest in farm-house, craft and artisan cider production, something encouraged by the fact that those businesses producing less than 7,000 litres per annum are exempt from paying excise duty – thus providing a useful path of diversification or a minor source of profit for small farmers and giving them a reason for conserving their old orchards.[39] Elsewhere in England similar initiatives have been made, using old orchards to supply fruit juice to local customers. All this said, in most parts of the country the planting of new orchards or the conservation of old ones is motivated largely by an interest in nature and heritage, and in many cases the fruit they produce is not even fully harvested.

While a commercial fruit-growing industry continues to exist in England, it is a shadow of what it was half a century ago, and the number of orchards which we might loosely describe as 'traditional' continues to dwindle, in spite of the best efforts of many owners and enthusiasts. Why this matters, and how much it matters, are issues to which we will return in Chapters 9 and 10.

Notes

1 W. Salisbury, *Hints Addressed to Proprietors of Orchards* (London, 1816), 110.
2 Waugh, *Rivers Nursery*, 103–5.
3 *B. Short*, P. May, G. Vine and A.-M. Bur, *Apples and Orchards in Sussex* (Lewes, 2012), 108.
4 Essex Record Office, D/F 152/7/1.
5 The National Archives, Kew, MAF 302/39.
6 The National Archives, Kew, MAF 456/38.
7 The National Archives, Kew, MAF 456/37.
8 The National Archives, Kew, MAF 456/38.
9 Norbury, Modern Developments in Fruit Growing, 726.
10 The National Archives, Kew, MAF 302/154.
11 D. Shapley and C. Powell, *A Brief History of Fresh Produce's Role in the UK Supermarket Revolution* (London, 2014), 8.
12 The National Archives, Kew, MAF 43/54.

13 The National Archives, Kew, MAF 302/154.

14 The National Archives, Kew, MAF 302/154.

15 L. Dudley Stamp, *The Land of Britain: Its Use and Misuse* (London, 1948), 108.

16 Stamp, *Land of Britain: Its Use and Misuse,* 109.

17 Norbury, Modern Developments, 727.

18 The National Archives, Kew, MAF 55/51 and MAF 187/11.

19 The National Archives, Kew, MAF 183/389.

20 The National Archives, Kew, MAF 302/39.

21 T. Williamson, *An Environmental History of Wildlife in England, 1650–1950* (London, 2013), 184–85.

22 G. Barnes and T. Williamson, *The Orchards of Eastern England: History, Ecology, Place* (Hatfield, 2021), 165–67.

23 The National Archives, Kew, MAF 266/87.

24 The National Archives, Kew, MAF 266/64.

25 W. Minchington, The British Cider Industry Since 1880. In H. Pohl (ed.), *Competition and Cooperation of Enterprises on National and International Markets* (Stuttgart, 1997), 125–40, at 132.

26 UK Agricultural Statistics, https://www.gov.uk/government/statistical-data-sets/structure-of-the-agricultural-industry-in-england-and-the-uk-at-june, accessed 1 September 2020.

27 M. Gee, *The Devon Orchards Book* (Wellington, 2018), 79.

28 H. Robertson, D. Marshall, E. Slingsby and G. Newman, *Economic, Biodiversity, Resource Protection and Social Value of Orchards: a Study of Six Orchards by the Herefordshire Orchards Community Evaluation Project*, Natural England Research Report NECR090 (Peterborough, 2012), http://publications.naturalengland.org.uk/publication/1289011.

29 Hansard, Volume 586, April 1958: https://hansard.parliament.uk/Commons/1958-04-22/debates/ff751ea9-ba17-411c-9132-48d87b9702d4/Hospitals(Farms).

30 M. Shoard, *The Theft of the Countryside* (London, 1980); R. Mabey, *The Common Ground: a Place for Nature in Britain's Future* (London, 1980); S. Clifford, Save Our Orchards: One Insight into the First Two Decades of a Campaign. In I.D. Rotherham (ed.), *Orchards and Groves: Their History, Ecology, Culture and Archaeology* (Sheffield, 2008), 32–42, at 32.

31 Clifford, Save Our Orchards, 33.

32 A. King and S. Clifford, The Apple, the Orchard, the Cultural Landscape. In S. Clifford and A. King (eds), *Local Distinctiveness: Place, Particularity and Identity* (London, 1993), 37–46, at 43.

33 N. Sinden, Orchard and Place. In Common Ground, *Orchards: a Guide to Local Conservation* (London, 1989), 5–11, at 9.

34 Robertson *et al.*, *Resource Protection and Social Values.*

35 Joint Nature Conservation Committee, UK BAP Priority Habitat Descriptions, 'Orchards' (2011), https://hub.jncc.gov.uk/assets/2829ce47-1ca5-41e7-bc1a-871c1ccob3ae#UKBAP-BAPHabitats-56-TraditionalOrchards.pdf.

36 M. Pomfret, *Stone's Orchard, Croxley Green* (Croxley Green, n.d.).

37 UK Agricultural Statistics, https://www.gov.uk/government/statistical-data-sets/structure-of-the-agricultural-industry-in-england-and-the-uk-at-june, accessed 1 June 2021.

38 UK Agricultural Statistics, https://www.gov.uk/government/statistical-data-sets/structure-of-the-agricultural-industry-in-england-and-the-uk-at-june, accessed 1 June 2021.

39 Gee, *Devon Orchards Book*, 101–13; L. Copas, *A Somerset Pomona: the Cider Apples of Somerset* (Wimbourne, 2001), 15.

CHAPTER 8

Studying old orchards

Because orchards have been somewhat neglected by landscape historians in the past, there is no published guide to how their history should be investigated, comparable to (for example) that provided by Oliver Rackham for studying ancient woodland in a chapter in his landmark *Trees and Woodlands in the British Landscape,* of 1976.[1] The need for such guidance is pressing, given the tendency, already noted, for people to confuse and conflate orchards of very different kinds and ages – and especially the old and 'traditional' with the commercial and derelict. The brief notes that follow are not, it should be emphasised, intended only for investigating (or identifying) orchards of the former type. The approaches described can be applied to orchards of all kinds and origins, for all in their different ways form parts of the historic landscape. And it should also be emphasised that our concern here is primarily with understanding the history of particular orchards, as habitats and places, and not with how we might investigate the more general history of fruit cultivation in an area or region.

What kind of orchard is it? First thoughts

It is good practice to begin by making an initial, provisional assessment of what kind of orchard we might be dealing with: whether it is a 'traditional' farmhouse orchard or an old commercial enterprise, for example. This initial step can be harder than we might expect. As we have emphasised, the lines between notional categories of orchard can be blurred and fuzzy, and in some cases the character or purpose of an orchard can shift over time. We might easily assume that the orchard which stands in the former grounds of Shenley mental hospital in south Hertfordshire, demolished in the 1990s, was a typical 'institutional' example, planted when the hospital itself was established in 1934. But it in fact began life as a private orchard in the grounds of the country house, Porters Park, which the hospital replaced, while much of the current planting is associated with a third incarnation, as a community orchard managed by a local trust.[2]

Such complications aside, the relationship of an old orchard to a residence or institution, or the lack of a relationship, is usually a good indication of its character, and often of its date. Examples close to country houses or institutions like children's homes or mental hospitals are, in most cases, directly associated with them and are usually located near to the remains of, or site of, the kitchen gardens. Examples close to farms, however, are slightly more complicated. If the orchard seems large for the farmhouse, and especially if other orchards existed or still exist nearby, then it probably represents (at least in its present form) a commercial enterprise of nineteenth- or twentieth-century date. Conversely, if it covers only a small area, perhaps half an acre or less, it is more likely to represent a traditional domestic orchard, although here, too, some caution is required and other possibilities need to be entertained before the site is investigated. The immigration of the middle class into rural areas, in retirement or as commuters, has a long history, and many apparently 'traditional' orchards in the Home Counties especially were planted by Edwardian businessmen to complement their timbered homes and Arts and Crafts gardens, or even by commuters in the 1960s and 70s, the original orchard having been removed by some previous owner. In the world of orchards, things are not always what they seem.

In most areas, orchards located away from residences, out in the fields, will be commercial enterprises, mainly dating to the 'orchard century', that is, between *c.* 1850 and 1950, especially if they cover significant areas, in excess of 3 acres (*c.* 1.2 hectares). In some districts, however, scattered orchards can have older origins, most notably in Herefordshire, where they were already being remarked upon at the start of the nineteenth century (above, p. 72). Not all commercial enterprises were isolated, however. An old orchard beside a late-nineteenth- or twentieth-century house or bungalow often signals the fact that it is part of a former smallholding.

When dealing with commercial orchards, it is always worth considering what factors may have encouraged fruit production at this particular location. Often, as we have seen, it was the character of the environment, and it is always worth examining briefly the soil maps for the local area – one rather simplified version of which is conveniently available online (http://www.landis.org.uk/soilscapes/). But as we have also seen, access to a market was also important, and proximity to a rail line sometimes trumped environmental considerations. In 1922 the Tamm family– to take but one example – purchased 16 acres (*c.* 6.5 hectares) at Aldham, near Colchester in Essex, to plant with fruit trees, choosing the site not on account of the suitability of its soils (which varied from poorly draining clay to stony sand), but because the land lay only two kilometres from Marks Tey station, on the main line to London, easily reached by horse and cart.[3]

Maps and documents

When researching the origin and development of a particular orchard, it is always best to begin with the Ordnance Survey maps from the nineteenth and twentieth centuries. The earliest maps produced by this body – the unpublished 2 inch to 1 mile draft, held at the British Library, in London (and also available on their website), and the 1-inch maps from the middle of the nineteenth century – do not systematically depict orchards. But the various editions and revisions of the 6-inch and 25-inch surveys, published from the mid-nineteenth century onwards (the precise date varying from region to region), record them with care, down to an area of less than 0.1 of an acre (0.04 of a hectare). These maps are now all available online, together with other Ordnance Survey maps, via the National Library of Scotland's (NLS) excellent website (https://maps. nls.uk/os/). Only if the earliest of the 6-inch or 25-inch maps shows that the orchard in question was already present is it necessary to consult earlier maps, which will mainly be available at the county record office.

It is best to begin with the Second Edition 6-inch (1:10,560) or 25-inch (1:2,500) OS maps, published at various dates between 1880 and 1913, as these are provided by the NLS in the form of a seamless scrollable and zoomable layer, continuous across the entire country, which has an 'underlay' of modern aerial photography that can be revealed using a slide bar. This makes it extraordinarily easy to find the site you are interested in. In addition, the Second Edition maps represent orchards in a highly schematic and immediately recognisable manner, with tree symbols arranged in an artificially regular grid (Figure 41). They are thus slightly easier to identify than on the earlier, First Edition maps, where an attempt was made to show the position of all trees above sapling size in the landscape, something which occasionally makes it difficult to distinguish orchards from other forms of planting. Once it has been confirmed that the orchard was in existence at the time that the Second Edition was surveyed, the NLS website allows you to access the individual sheets of the First Edition and thus to ascertain whether the orchard was already present when this map was made, usually around two decades earlier. As with the Second Edition, it took many decades to map the entire country, so that while some areas were surveyed as early as the 1860s, others had to wait until the early 1890s. During this period various changes were made to the conventions used for mapping. In particular, the earlier First Edition maps, but not the later ones, show allotments and market gardens as networks of closely spaced, parallel lines. In some cases these were also quite densely filled with fruit trees, for the same plots of land may be treated by the Second Edition maps as 'orchard'. The line between a vegetable garden containing some fruit trees and an orchard underplanted with vegetables was always a fine one (Figure 41).

The NLS website also allows you to access, as images of individual sheets, all the various revisions of the 6-inch and 25-inch maps produced *after* the publication of the Second Edition, in the first half of the twentieth century, as well as all the 1:25,000 (2 ½-inch) maps surveyed in the 1940s, 50s and 60s (although the latter are also supplied on the website in the form of a continuous scrollable layer). If the orchard being studied was already planted when the Second Edition was surveyed, these maps can be used to chart its subsequent development – stasis, expansion or contraction. If it does not appear on the Second Edition, the revised versions can be employed to provide some indication of when, approximately, it was planted. Unfortunately, there are some problems with these sources, and they need to be used with caution. The various revisions of the 6-inch and 25-inch maps adopted the same convention for showing orchards as the Second Edition, but not all areas were re-mapped with the same frequency. In areas in which the landscape was changing rapidly – especially

FIGURE 41. The depiction on old Ordnance Survey maps of the orchards in Haddenham, Buckinghamshire. Top: First Edition 6-inch, 1878, on which an attempt is made to show orchard trees individually and realistically, and, as is usual on the earlier examples of such maps, kitchen and market gardens are represented by shading made up of close-set, parallel lines. Centre: Second Edition 6-inch, 1898, in which orchards are depicted more clearly and schematically, as grids of identical tree symbols. Bottom: 1:25,000 (2.5-inch), *c.* 1950, in which orchards are shown by grids of dots but the scale of the map precludes depiction of the smaller examples.

urban or industrial districts – revisions might be numerous, but for some rural areas, only one may have been made during the whole of the period before the Second World War.[4] Moreover, in the 1930s and 40s, the Ordnance Survey often made only selected revisions before re-publication, and it is unclear whether these included details of orchards. There are particular issues with the 1:25,000 (2 ½-inch) Ordnance Survey maps. These show orchards as dense grids of dots but were surveyed at too small a scale to include some of the smaller domestic examples (Figure 41). More importantly, rather than being the result of a comprehensive, new survey of the nation, they were compiled from earlier surveys and revisions made at 1:10,560 (6-inch) scale, updated using aerial photographs. As a result:

> The 1:25,000 maps reflect quite different sources of information from different dates, often on the same sheet, reflecting their terminology as a 'Provisional edition'. For more populated areas where the larger-scale National Grid survey had taken place, the latest, more detailed six-inch to the mile mapping could be used, photographically reducing detail down to 1:25,000. For other areas, the best available source mapping could be decades earlier, supplemented by less detailed map sources, including Second World War bomb-damage surveys, and military and road mapping in the 1940s.[5]

There are a number of more general problems, which relate to all Ordnance Survey maps, including the First and Second Editions of the 6-inch and 25-inch maps. It is, for example, unclear whether the surveyors routinely depicted newly planted orchards and, if not, how mature the trees needed to be before they were recorded. An orchard absent from a Second Edition map of, say, 1902 might, in fact, have already been present in the form of very young trees; at its first appearance, on the next revision of, say, 1923, it might have been more than a quarter of a century old. In addition, a few orchards seem to have been omitted because surveyors classified them as something else. This is a particular problem with orchards associated with large country houses, which are sometimes simply treated as part of the adjacent kitchen garden. There are, in fact, many minor omissions and anomalies, where orchards known to have been planted at a particular time fail to appear on one or even two subsequent Ordnance Survey maps for no very obvious reason.

The Ordnance Survey maps, for all their reassuring impression of objectivity and comprehensiveness, need to be treated – like all maps – with a measure of caution, and in particular are not to be entirely trusted as *negative* evidence. But for the most part, they provide reliable information about an orchard's origins and subsequent development. Their evidence can, moreover, be supplemented with two other twentieth-century sources. One is the Land Utilisation Survey, a nation-wide survey of land use carried out in the 1930s by groups of local volunteers under the overall direction of the geographer L. Dudley Stamp, which is now accessible online.[6] Unfortunately, many of the sheets (especially the earliest) place orchards in a single, undifferentiated category with domestic gardens and market gardens, but for large and isolated examples this may not matter much.[7] Another is the remarkable series of vertical aerial photographs taken by the RAF in the immediate aftermath of the Second World War, particularly useful for identifying the larger orchards. Some of these are available online, either from the Google Earth 'historic' section or, in some cases, from websites hosted by county record offices.

The various sources just discussed usually allow us to establish the approximate planting date for an orchard which originated in the period after the late nineteenth century, and to chart how such an orchard, or one subsequently planted, changed in size or shape over the following decades. To discover the antiquity of an orchard already present on the First Edition Ordnance Survey 6-inch maps, our first port of call will be the tithe maps, usually surveyed around 1840 – assuming that the parish in question possesses one, which is usually the case outside some Midland districts. Tithe maps, and their associated apportionments, can be viewed at the county record office and, in some cases, on websites which they host; they are also available online, for a price, from a private provider. They were drawn up under the terms of the 1836 Tithe Commutation Act to convert the tithes owed to the incumbent (or a lay impropriator) into a fixed rental charge, a process which involved a survey of land ownership and land use within the parish in question.[8] Each land parcel is numbered on the map, and the associated schedule, or 'apportionment', lists its owner, occupier, area, land use and often the name by which it was known. Unfortunately, the precise way in which orchards were treated by the tithe commissioners varies considerably from place to place and, to an extent, from region to region.

In those parts of the country where orchards had long been of particular economic importance – Devon, Herefordshire and other western cider counties and parts of Kent and Hertfordshire, for example – 'orchard' is often employed as a category in the land use or, as it is termed, 'State of Cultivation' column. Indeed, in western counties, where this was standard practice, a distinction is often made between 'arable orchards' and ones laid to grass; on occasions the latter may be subdivided into 'meadow orchards' and 'pasture orchards'. But in many places, orchards were not treated as representing a specific form of land use. Particular parcels of land might be named as 'Orchard', 'Home Orchard', 'Cherry Orchard' and the like in the 'Name and Description of Premises' column, but their use is simply given as 'pasture'; 'meadow'; or, more rarely, arable. The difficulty in such cases is that not every piece of land planted with fruit trees was necessarily *named* as an orchard. Some bore some vaguer appellation or a name which referenced some dual use. In other words, if an orchard depicted on the First Edition 6-inch map is shown as a block of land with the same boundaries on the tithe map but is described as 'yard' or 'garden', it is unclear whether the orchard already existed at this point.

Moving back in time before the tithe maps, cartographic coverage becomes more uneven, and the maps themselves – mainly preserved at county record offices – more varied in their usefulness. Enclosure maps, drawn up in the

FIGURE 42. Typical representation of a small farm orchard (parcel number 12) on an early manuscript map, with fruit trees shown in elevation. Extract from a survey of an estate in Hemel Hempstead, Hertfordshire, 1730. Hertfordshire Archives and Local Studies, AH/680.

eighteenth and early nineteenth century, when open fields and common land were removed by parliamentary acts, usually take little interest in the precise character of land already enclosed. Estate maps, in contrast – that is, privately commissioned manuscript surveys of an individual's property – often record orchards as a feature of farms or in the grounds of a mansion, sometimes illustrating the trees schematically in elevation or in plan (Figure 42).[9] Many thousands of such maps survive from the seventeenth and eighteenth centuries, and a fair number from the sixteenth, but not for all parishes, and not necessarily for the part of the parish in which the orchard of interest lies.

Tracing the origins and development of particular orchards using documentary sources other than maps, especially for the period before the twentieth century, tends to be a bit hit and miss. As we have seen in earlier chapters, orchards are frequently referred to, in leases, wills, sales agreements and the like, but it is often difficult to tie such references to particular properties, and even

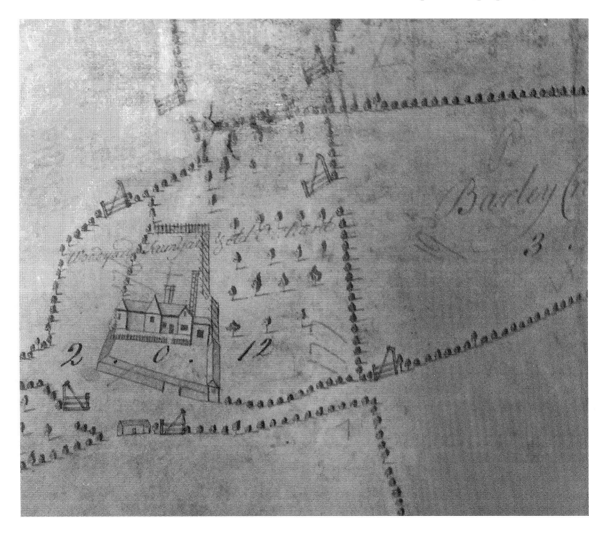

when this can be done, the orchard referred to may have been on a different site to the one that survives today. Nevertheless, it is always worth entering the name, and former names, of the property in question in the search engine of the relevant record office's catalogue – or in 'Discovery', the central online catalogue maintained by the National Archives at Kew – to see what comes up (https://discovery.nationalarchives.gov.uk/). This procedure can also throw up some useful leads which can add to the picture presented for the late nineteenth and twentieth century by the Ordnance Survey maps. Any estate agent's sales particulars relating to the property are always worth checking. They might, for example, describe an orchard as 'newly planted', while those for country houses, and even for more modest residences, occasionally give the numbers of fruit trees present, and even their varieties.

Sales contracts and leases can provide some details of who owned or occupied an orchard, but there are two documentary sources which are particularly useful for this purpose. One are the tithe maps and apportionments, already dealt with; the other, the maps and documents relating to the 1910 Finance Act. The latter established a 20 per cent tax on any increase in the value of land between the initial valuation date and the point when it was sold, necessitating a comprehensive survey and valuation of every piece of property in England.[10] The new tax was never imposed, but the archive generated by the valuation process survives. It is complex, and now divided between county record offices and the National Archives at Kew. The county record offices retain some of the working maps and papers and in some cases finished examples of the maps, but most of the latter are to be found at Kew, together with the associated Field Books. The various land parcels on the maps, which are individually updated versions of the 25-inch Ordnance Survey maps, are numbered, the Field Books giving their owner; their occupier; and, often, although not always, their use. For the history of an individual orchard, a special journey to Kew might not be justified, but it might be useful if a number of orchards are under investigation. Once the name of an owner or occupier is known, from either the tithe maps or the 1910 Finance Act maps, then it can be used to unearth other relevant material, such as lease agreements, by using the online catalogues already discussed.

Fieldwork: trees and their management

Once maps and documents have been examined, and some idea has been gained of the age and character of the orchard, it is time to examine it on the ground. Attention invariably turns first to the trees, starting with the types of fruit present. It is relatively easy to distinguish, at a glance, the main species of tree, especially when these are mature. Cherry trees, for example, generally grow tall and have a distinctively smooth and laterally fissured bark; plum trees exhibit lower growth and have bark which is smooth and dull when young but vertically fissured when old; pear trees are usually tall and with a bark divided early in life into a mesh of fissures; etc. But identification of the particular fruit *varieties* present is much more difficult. This is in part because it requires a detailed knowledge that relatively few people possess and in part because the trees need to be in fruit and, even in the case of apples alone, most older orchards contain a significant range of varieties, with very different fruiting periods. When we visit an orchard, one variety, Beauty of Bath, for example, will have finished fruiting, and the fallen apples will all have rotted or been eaten by wildlife, long before a variety such as Dumelow's Seedling is ready for identification. A proper study of an orchard requires repeat visits, something that may not always be possible.

FIGURE 43. Norfolk Beefing apples growing on a century-old tree in an orchard near Wymondham, Norfolk. Fruit identification is a difficult skill to master, but most people can soon learn to recognise the more common varieties found in their local areas.

Such a study also requires, ideally, the assistance of a good fruit identifier. This said, it is possible to learn quite quickly key indicators of some reasonably common old apple varieties, using shape, colour and taste as clues, at least of those commonly found in the local area (Figure 43). An early fruiting, relatively small, red apple with a rather bland taste and slightly woolly texture, for example, may well be the Beauty of Bath just noted. A largish, plain, green apple with a greasy skin that squeaks when rubbed will be Lane's Prince Albert. A similar green apple, but subtly striped and with patches of vivid red flush could be a number of things, but a swelling to one side of the stalk, presenting an asymmetrical profile, leaves little doubt that it is Dumelow's Seedling. Context and

timing are important. A small to medium-sized, rather hard apple, smooth and green but with large areas of deep, sometimes almost purple, red, might again be a number of things. But hanging on a tree in mid-winter, when most of the leaves have gone, in an orchard in eastern England, it is likely to be the famous Norfolk Beefing. A large, green apple, rather sour unless cooked, might again be many things, but growing on a particularly tall tree it is probably a Bramley's Seedling. Cut it open, and the presence of small, deformed pips will confirm this identification. Anyone with an interest in orchards will soon, especially by accompanying an expert, learn how to identify half a dozen or even a dozen apple varieties. It is worth noting that in most parts of England outside the West Country, more than 80 per cent of the apple trees present in orchards are probably made up of only 30 or 40 varieties, so a little knowledge, in this case, goes quite a long way.

The best approach is to take away a sample of fruit, placing each in a separate bag with a number written on it that allows you to relate the picking location to a rough plan of the site. You can then use, at leisure, one of the standard identification guides, such as Michael Clark's *Apples: a Field Guide*.[11] But better still, go to the website FruitID, which contains multiple deep-zoom images, helpful identification notes, and much more (https://www.fruitid.com/#main). When all else fails, bring the apple for identification to one of the 'apple days' organised by a local orchards group – most counties have one. This will also put you in contact with fruit enthusiasts more generally.

Of course, if you visit an orchard when there are no apples on the trees, you can do none of these things. However, some possible indications of the varieties present can, very tentatively, be made in a few cases based on the form of the tree. For example, a very tall tree is likely to be a triploid, most commonly Bramley's Seedling – especially if it also exhibits a rather smooth, unfissured bark. Blenheim Orange, more than any other tree we know, attracts the attentions of the woolly aphid (*Eriosomatinae* spp.) and in consequence displays numerous distinctive bumps on its bark, mostly between 2 and 4 centimetres in diameter. We would emphasise at this point that to be interested in orchards does not mean you need to be able to identify all the varieties of fruit trees they contain. Landscape historians and others have a different and broader agenda – to understand how and when particular orchards originated, how they were used and how they changed over time. Fruit varieties are an important part of this story, but not the totality.

We noted above the importance of making, at least, a rough plan of the trees in an orchard. This can include other information, about the spacing of the trees and about their size, condition and pattern of growth. It is often suggested that old farm and cider-apple orchards, and commercial examples established before the Second World War, are characterised by tall trees spaced at wide intervals, while recent commercial orchards tend to have low-growing trees more tightly packed together in rows, with the height of the trees controlled using dwarfing or semi-dwarfing rootstocks and rigorous pruning. As we have seen, however, this simple distinction requires some qualification, as well as further research.

In the late nineteenth century, many Kentish orchards were already planted with half-standard, pyramids or dwarf bush trees. Indeed, low-growing trees, closely spaced, had been a feature of some Devon orchards even in the eighteenth century, although their height was mainly if not entirely controlled by pruning, rather than by rootstock choice. Conversely, cherry orchards were often planted with standard trees in the 1960s and 70s, and some apple orchards from the same period have trees which, while certainly on dwarfing rootstocks, are planted in quite a widely spaced grid. There were many variations on spacing and management in the past, although how far these can be detected in surviving orchards is unclear. As we have seen (above, pp. 71–2), the early 'arable' orchards of Herefordshire had widely spaced trees, often as much as 18, 20 or even 25 yards apart (*c.* 16.5 to 23 metres). But when this form of management ceased during the nineteenth century and orchards were grassed down, closer planting was adopted.

The standard or half-standard trees, grafted on vigorous or semi-vigorous rootstocks, that are characteristic of older orchards can take a variety of forms, the consequence of variations in pruning which again remain insufficiently studied. Many old commercial orchards, and some of those attached to country houses, are planted with 'bush' trees, pruned at an early stage so that they rose from a short bole, a metre or less in height (Figures 5 and 28, above). Such a form, featuring numerous low branches, indicates that the ground around the trees was not grazed by livestock but was instead cultivated (in the case of many commercial examples) or mown (as in those associated with country houses). The old trees in cider and farmhouse orchards, in contrast, were usually managed in such a way that their branches were well out of reach of livestock. They grew tall, and had their lower branches removed. Sometimes the leading shoot was allowed to grow into a single trunk, the main, or 'scaffolding', branches coming off at irregular intervals, but often the tree was headed at a height of around 2–2.5 metres, to produce a form like a pollard.

The low-growing, closely spaced trees found in modern orchards might be pruned so that horizontal branches grew in a single plane on a framework of wires; as 'cordons', with a single, upright stem and very short laterals; or in 'spindle' forms, similar to the first but with the leader left in place, rising above the horizontal branches. They might simply be pruned as bush trees, but more closely spaced than in the old orchards just discussed, and with their height controlled less by pruning than by rootstock choice. Where commercial orchards have become derelict or have otherwise escaped replanting, trees once rigorously pruned in these various ways can survive in outgrown or even 'veteran' form (Figure 44). All such styles of pruning indicate, of course, that the ground between the trees was not grazed by sheep or cattle, but was cultivated, ploughed or mown.

Old orchards often feature examples of trees which have been toppled in a gale but have enough of their root system intact to have survived (Figure 45). In some cases, these are true 'phoenix' trees, in which the prone trunk or a lower branch has actually 'layered' – created a new rooting system. Such trees are attractive and interesting but may also be historically informative, suggesting that the orchard has not been very intensively managed since the tree fell, for otherwise it would have been removed and replaced with one capable of developing a full crown, although in domestic orchards, such a tree might simply have been retained because it was a rare or favoured variety.

Fieldwork: dating trees

Dating the fruit trees present in an orchard poses a number of problems. The age of trees is usually estimated from their circumference, measured at waist height, but the two main methods employed, developed by Alan Mitchell and John White, respectively, do not work well with fruit trees, insofar as they work at all.[12] The former suggests that, as a rough rule of thumb, most tree species growing in relatively open locations acquire an inch of girth for each year of growth. Those in woods increase their circumference at roughly half this rate, while those growing in clumps or avenues will have an increase in girth that falls between the two. Mitchell emphasised,

however, that the method does not work well with 'most small-growing trees', which put on girth at a slower rate.[13] White's method is more complicated, taking account of species, soil conditions and much else, and emphasising how growth rates will vary over time. Trees start off by putting on girth slowly, grow vigorously through middle age, but then slow down again in 'senescence', or old age, as they hollow and their crown contracts.[14] White provided a table giving expected growth rates for different kinds of tree but, unfortunately, failed to include apples, pears, plums or cherries.

As we have already emphasised, fruit trees grow fast and 'veteranise' at a relatively early age – this is one of the main reasons why orchards are so important for nature conservation. They therefore enter White's 'senescence' stage,

FIGURE 44 *(top)*. Crapes Orchard, Aldham, Essex, showing apple trees on dwarfing rootsocks, planted in the 1960s and now exhibiting 'veteran' features.

FIGURE 45 *(bottom)*. Fallen 'phoenix' apple tree in a farm orchard at Stow Bardolph, Norfolk. It is probably around 100 years old.

during which they acquire very little additional circumference each year, much earlier than most trees, usually at around 60 or 70 years of age for an apple. Ageing trees from their girths is always as much art as science, and particularly so in the case of fruit trees, but as a very rough guide, we might say that an apple tree with a girth of 750 centimetres measured today will probably have been planted in the 1960s, while one with 1 metre circumference is probably of inter-war vintage. Examples planted at the end of the nineteenth century may be around 1.2–1.5 metres. We should emphasise, however, that rates of growth can be affected by a wide range of factors, including soil type, drainage, the spacing of trees in the orchard, the vigour of rootstock type, and the character of the graft itself, with triploids generally growing faster than diploids. Bramley's Seedlings in particular can put on girth rapidly, as much as 1 metre in 50 years, and in the right conditions can reach a prodigious size. Examples planted in the inter-war period in the East Anglian Fenland can have girths of as much as 2 metres, in part because of the moist, rich soils in which they are planted. Records of girth should thus be accompanied by a note of whether the tree displays veteran features – whether, in particular, there are signs of hollowing and contraction of the crown, unlikely to be apparent in an apple tree under 60 years of age. Pear trees, so far as the evidence goes, can live longer and gain in girth more slowly than apples, although much depends on the vigour of the rootstock, while cherries and plums seldom seem to reach any very great age, and the former can attain girths of over 1 metre in 50 years. The truth of the matter is that we can only estimate age in very broad terms, but it is useful to make the attempt, if only to identify different probable phases of planting within an orchard.

Boundaries

The boundaries of an orchard are worthy of particular attention, both on maps and on the ground. The shape of the plot usually reflects the wider field pattern – whatever their age, orchards were usually planted over an existing field (or fields) or on a plot of land carved out of one. In areas of late enclosure from open fields or common land, field boundaries will tend to be straight. In areas of ancient enclosure, some at least will be more irregular, while in places where open fields were enclosed 'piecemeal' – through the gradual acquisition and subsequent hedging or fencing of bundles of arable strips – boundaries will exhibit the slight sinuosity of the strips themselves. In the area around Evesham and Pershore, in Gloucestershire, where most of the open fields disappeared in this manner in the course of the sixteenth, seventeenth and eighteenth centuries, orchards routinely have boundaries of this slightly sinuous form (see Figure 26, above). It is particularly noticeable that, when the First Edition 6-inch maps were surveyed in the late nineteenth century, many orchards in this area occupied the kinds of particularly narrow plots sometimes created by this process, where only two or three strips were amalgamated. Orchards were a convenient way of using such oddly shaped pieces of land. In south Cambridgeshire, where the open fields were mainly enclosed by parliamentary act in the early and middle decades of the nineteenth century and their late persistence may have retarded the emergence of a fruit-growing industry on soils well suited to the cultivation of plums, villages are often surrounded by an earlier penumbra of such sinuous plots. By the 1840s, many of those in parishes like Melbourn had already been planted up as orchards, and a desire to increase the land available for fruit growing may have encouraged this nibbling away of the open fields, before formal enclosure took place.

Early writers offered much advice on how an orchard should be enclosed, in part because they were keen to secure the trees and their fruit from intruders, animal or human, and in part because they wanted to provide them with shelter. Sometimes orchards were fenced, but more usually they were bounded by hedges, which needed to be 'plashed' or otherwise maintained in such a manner as to prevent cattle from entering and 'cropping the tender Twigs of the Fruit-Trees, and rubbing against their stems, and unruly People destroying the Fruit'.[15] Such hedges might be quite densely planted, with timber trees or pollards, to provide shelter. William Ellis, writing in 1754, advised planting elm, poplar, aspen or 'the Perry-Pear' for this purpose.[16] More common, in both farmhouse orchards and early commercial ones, was the planting of plums, either as free-standing rows (sometimes interspersed with other fruit or nuts) or within the boundary hedges. Growing more rapidly than the apples and pears within the orchard, they quickly afforded them a measure of protection. Given the relatively short life of plums, these trees seldom survive, but careful examination sometimes reveals concentrations of plum suckers growing in the hedges, from the original rootstocks. From the middle of the twentieth century, commercial orchards and 'fruit farms' began to be sheltered with lines of close-set, fast-growing trees, commonly poplar or hybrid willow, sometimes Italian alder (*Alnus cordata*), grey alder (*Alnus incana*) or common alder (*Alnus glutinosa*) (see Figure 3, above). Even when the orchard has been grubbed out, these often remain, now surrounding a field of arable crops.

Early orchards were, as we observed in Chapter 3, sometimes bounded not by hedges or fences, but by the wide, water-filled ditches known as moats. Either they occupied part of the central island, sharing it with the house, yards and gardens, or (more rarely) they were planted within their own moat, joined to the main one. When, in the course of the seventeenth and eighteenth centuries, moats went out of fashion and houses were rebuilt on higher and drier sites, the islands surrounded by redundant moats – even those which had formerly lacked much in the way of planting of fruit trees – might be re-purposed as the sites for orchards, even if they lay at a distance from the new residence. Early maps, and indeed the Ordnance Survey 6-inch and 25-inch maps from the late nineteenth and twentieth centuries, show numerous examples. There is, however, a fine line between a true moated site and a plot of land surrounded by deep drainage ditches, and in some parts of the country – such as the claylands of East Anglia and Essex – farms and their yards are often so bounded, and an adjoining orchard, or the site of one, likewise. In some cases, the ditches around the orchard are particularly wide and deep, not surprisingly given the poor growth that fruit trees will make in waterlogged ground, but unlike true moats, these ditches will usually be accompanied by hedges.

Odds and ends

A variety of other features are worth looking out for when surveying an old orchard, whether of 'commercial' type or associated with a farmhouse, an institution or a country house. Stools of cob nuts or filberts can sometimes be found on the edges of the orchard, usually as scattered specimens that once grew in continuous lines, or interspersed with plums or other fruit (Figure 9, above). At country houses, and in some 'institutional' orchards, these could form semi-ornamental 'nut walks' along one or more sides of the orchard. A fine example survives at Girton College, Cambridge. Occasionally in old commercial orchards, a single holly tree will occur in one of the lines of fruit trees. Some smallholders supplied material for Christmas decorations as part of their business (in 1900 James Taber Senior, of Little Braxted, in Essex, recorded in his diary how he had put mistletoe on the apple trees in his orchard).[17] One notable feature of some orchards (especially derelict commercial examples) are thickets of plum suckers, often forming continuous bands between widely spaced lines of fruit trees, which mark the locations of lost plum trees: the suckers represent the rootstock, often the myrobalan (*Prunus cerasifera*).

Some attention also needs to be paid to the ground flora. While some orchards, as we shall see, boast diverse, herb-rich grassland, many do not, due to an earlier history of spraying, ground cultivation and intensive manuring. Orchards often, in fact, contain a motley collection of plants typical of woodland edges and waste plots, together with garden escapes, but this is nevertheless of some interest in historical if not biological terms as an indication of the intensity of past disturbance, in some cases perhaps suggesting that what is now a grass orchard was formerly a cultivated one. Very occasionally, survivors from the plants grown beneath and between the trees, or from their descendants, can be found lurking in the grass. Garden asparagus has been recorded in an orchard in Essex; drooping star of Bethlehem (*Ornithogalum nutans*), widely grown as a cut flower in the middle decades of the twentieth century, has turned up in a number of East Anglian examples. But in many cases, it is hard to be sure that plants like daffodils (*Narcissus* sp.) have not simply escaped from an adjoining garden.

Orchards also need to be examined with the eye of the field archaeologist. Earthworks – 'humps and bumps' formed by various kinds of human activity in the past – occasionally occur.[18] Most will relate to the previous use of the orchard site and, in addition to any intrinsic interest they may have, are a useful

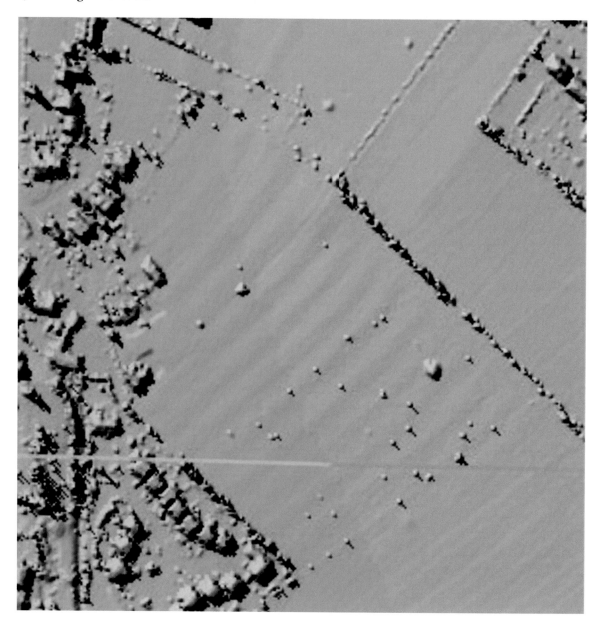

indication that the orchard in question must always have been a 'grass' orchard, because sustained cultivation would have blurred, or eliminated entirely, such archaeological traces. Quite a few examples contain 'ridge and furrow', the low ridges – usually around 7 metres across – marking the former strips in an open field. They are a notable, indeed distinguishing, feature of the surviving 'prune' orchards of south-west Bedfordshire and south Buckinghamshire, where the lines of trees are usually oriented in the same direction as the ridges (Figure 46). There can be problems, however, in distinguishing such signs of earlier cultivation from low ridges raised when the orchard was planted, to

FIGURE 46. Figure 46. LiDAR image of a derelict orchard at Eaton Bray, south Bedfordshire, showing how the lines of trees follow the alignment of the earlier 'ridge and furrow'.

FIGURE 47. Trees planted on ridges, created when the orchard was established in order to improve drainage, at Whimple, east Devon.

improve drainage for the trees themselves. Such planting ridges, while not common, are certainly not unusual. They are, for example, a notable feature of some of the old orchards on the heavy, rather poorly draining soils around Whimple, in east Devon, where the ridges have a similar width to true ridge and furrow but lack the latter's slightly sinuous profile, instead running ruler-straight and parallel with one of the orchard's boundaries (Figure 47). They can also be found in some of the orchards on the heavier soils to the south-west of Maidstone, in Kent, although here the ridges are generally narrower and later (twentieth century) in date.

A slight bank and/or ditch running across the orchard (but not extending beyond it) can indicate an earlier boundary, suggesting that the orchard may have been expanded in the past; and ponds, or depressions marking former ponds, are a common feature of many farmhouse and some early commercial orchards, reflecting the need to keep livestock or poultry adequately watered. Last, we should note that, in the right conditions, orchard trees can leave their own archaeological traces after the orchard has been destroyed, in the form of grids of dots marking planting holes, which are visible on aerial photographs. In arable fields, these will usually remain for only a few years, but at Lyveden New Bield, in Northamptonshire, the parch marks of the planting holes for the orchard established by Thomas Tresham in the late sixteenth century are still visible in the turf and provided a guide for its restoration by English Heritage in the 1990s.[19]

Examining the surviving remains of an old orchard should, where possible, be accompanied by a conversation with the owner. Where the owner used to run the orchard as a commercial concern, or where the owner's parents did, discussions can be immensely useful, providing information about where and how the fruit was marketed; how the orchard was managed in the past; and, in many cases, when the present trees were planted. Where the orchard is attached to an old farmhouse which is now a middle-class residence, however, the information may be less useful or reliable. Under successive owners, myths often grow, in particular concerning the age of the trees. Rather similar are the stories, often encountered in suburban areas, about how old fruit trees growing in neighbouring or adjacent gardens are the remains of an old orchard which existed prior to the area being 'developed' for housing, typically in the 1920s or 30s. Such tales may be given some credence by the presence nearby of an older farm or the site of a lost country house. They are easily checked, by consulting the relevant Ordnance Survey maps; are seldom true; and arise in large part from the tendency to assume that old, veteranised fruit trees are more ancient than they really are. The trees in question seem, that is, to be too old to have been planted to serve the houses with which they are associated.

Conclusion

The trick and the fun in all this is to combine these various threads of evidence to produce a convincing 'story', as so often in the study of landscape history. It is often impossible to gain a very detailed picture of how a particular orchard developed over time, or about its use, ownership and management. Knowledge of these matters rests on the chance survival of the appropriate documentary sources or on reliable oral testimony. But close analysis of maps, combined with detailed examination on the ground, can usually tell us much about the age and character of the orchard under investigation, and also – although with rather less confidence – the likely age of its constituent trees.

Notes

1   Woods as We See Them: a Guide to Fieldwork. In O. Rackham, *Trees and Woodland in the British Landscape* (London, 1976), 105–37.
2   G. Barnes and T. Williamson, *The Orchards of Eastern England: History Ecology, Place* (Hatfield, 2021), 110.
3   Barnes and Williamson, *Orchards of Eastern England*, 75.
4   R.R. Oliver, *Ordnance Survey Maps: a Concise Guide for Historians* (London, 1994).
5   National Library of Scotland, Ordnance Survey, 1:25,000 maps of Great Britain (Regular series) – 1937–1961: https://maps.nls.uk/os/25k-gb-1937-61/info1.html.

6   Vision of Britain, Land Use Maps: https://www.visionofbritain.org.uk/maps/
    series?xCenter=3160000&yCenter=3160000&scale=63360&viewScale=5805357.
    4656&mapLayer=land&subLayer=lus_stamp&title=Land%20Utilisation%
    20Survey%20of%20Britain&download=true, accessed 1 June 2020.

7   Stamp, *Land of Britain: Its Use and Misuse* (London, 1948), 113.

8   G. Beech and R. Mitchell, *Maps for Family and Local History:* The Records of
    the Tithe, Valuation Office, and National Farm Surveys of England and Wales,
    1836–1943 (London, 2004), 13–35; E.J. Evans, *Tithes: Maps, Apportionments and the
    1836 Act* (Chichester, 1993); R.J.P. Kain and R.R. Oliver, *The Tithe Maps of England
    and Wales: a Cartographic Analysis and County-by-County Catalogue* (Cambridge,
    1995).

9   A useful although now rather old introduction to such maps is provided by
    B.P. Hindle, *Maps for Local History* (London, 1989).

10 Beech and Mitchell, *Maps*, 36–68; B. Short, *Land and Society in Edwardian Britain*
    (Cambridge, 1997).

11 M. Clark, *Apples: A Field Guide*, revised edn (Tewin, 2015); R. Sanders, *The Apple
    Book* (London, 2010).

12 J. White, What Is a Veteran Tree and Where Are They All? *Quarterly Journal of
    Forestry* 91, 3 (1997), 222–26; J. White, *Estimating the Age of Large and Veteran Trees
    in Britain*, Forestry Commission Information Note 250 (Alice Holt, 1999).

13 A. Mitchell, *Collins Field Guide to the Trees of Britain and Northern Europe* (London,
    1974), 20–25.

14 See also the discussion in G. Barnes and T. Williamson, *Ancient Trees in the
    Landscape: Norfolk's Arboreal Heritage* (Oxford, 2011), 34–63.

15 W. Ellis, *The Compleat Cyderman: or, the Present Practice of Raising Plantations of
    the Best Cyder Apple and Perry Pear-Trees* (London, 1754), 16.

16 Ellis, *Compleat Cyderman*, 13.

17 Essex Record Office, D/DU 2223/2/16.

18 C. Taylor, *Fieldwork in Medieval Archaeology* (London, 1974) remains, in spite of
    its age, the best introduction.

19 C. Taylor, *The Archaeology of Gardens* (Princes Risborough, 1983), 46.

CHAPTER 9

The importance of orchards: biodiversity

Enthusiasts suggest two main reasons why old orchards should be conserved and new ones planted. The first, which we address in this chapter, is their importance for sustaining biodiversity: they are habitats for a number of important species which today have few other environments in which to survive, and they are of benefit to wildlife more generally. The second, which we discuss in the next chapter, is that they have a complex cultural importance. Orchards have been a significant part of everyday life for centuries; they can, in many districts, constitute an important part of our historical landscape; and they contain collections of old and often rare fruit varieties, developed in some cases in the very distant past.

In terms of biodiversity, it is the 'traditional orchards' which are of key importance: those defined by English Nature as 'groups of fruit and nut trees planted on vigorous rootstocks at low densities in permanent grassland; and managed in a low intensity way...', with the minimum size of an 'orchard' being taken as 'five trees with crown edges less than 20m apart'. Orchards of this kind were included in the 2006 UK Biodiversity Action Plan list, and in the revised list for 2011, of habitats considered to be of principal importance for the purpose of conserving biodiversity.[1] But such recognition was slow in coming and, as noted in the introduction, the great historical ecologist Oliver Rackham refused to engage with orchards at all. In part, earlier neglect arose in part from their evidently artificial character and in part from the fact that the principal fruit trees themselves are of non-indigenous species. But while orchards may be more highly managed and more artificial than those other semi-natural environments which all agree are worthy of conservation – heaths, meadows, ancient woods, and the like – the difference is one of degree. All were both created and sustained by particular forms of use and exploitation; all are artefacts of economic management rather than anything truly 'natural'. Moreover, as Keith Alexander in particular has emphasised, the main trees planted in orchards are closely related to indigenous species – plum to blackthorn, cultivated cherry to wild cherry and bird cherry, etc. – and many of the species particularly associated with them, such as the large fruit tree bark beetle (*Scolytus mali*), did not come to this country with the trees themselves but were already part of our native wildlife, dependent on other hosts.[2]

The most important feature of our orchard trees, as we have already emphasised, is that they grow old and 'veteranise' much more quickly than most other tree species, providing cavities and an abundance of dead wood vital for sustaining a range of organisms.[3] Apple trees begin to display such characteristics after 50 or 60 years, plums and cherries even sooner. But their importance in sustaining biodiversity is enhanced by the particular character of orchard planting. Rather than being densely crowded together, and thus casting deep shade on lower branches and trunks and on the ground surface beneath, the tall trees in a traditional orchard are quite widely spaced, producing a range of more open habitats. Orchards thus have much in common with wood pastures – that is, grazed woodland featuring ancient trees, of the kind associated with royal forests, old deer parks and wooded commons – a variety of land use that was once common but that has been in steady decline for several centuries and is now rare in most parts of England. Orchards can therefore supply a similar range of important habitats, and with some rapidity: in Alexander's words, orchards are 'an extreme form of wood-pasture'.[4] The ideal orchard, in terms of biodiversity, is one both old and still managed on broadly traditional lines, in which trees have been replaced on a regular basis so that the planting displays a varied age structure, ensuring both a range of habitats and a measure of continuity, and in which the sward is grazed, or else mown for hay (Figure 48). The long-established permanent grassland of the traditional orchard can have an importance in its own right, sustaining unusual plants and a range of fungi, while the ponds found in many old orchards, and their boundary hedges, can supply additional value. Indeed, many species are sustained by the combination of these different elements.[5]

FIGURE 48. An orchard at Mansell Lacy, Herefordshire, with widely spaced trees displaying a varied age structure, ideal for nature conservation.

Although many different kinds of organisms benefit from orchards, most scientific attention has focused on three: invertebrates, particularly saproxylic insects, meaning those directly or indirectly dependent on decaying wood; lichens; and bryophytes. All are closely associated with old wood pastures, and thus with these closely related, but usually much younger, environments.

Lichens and bryophytes

Lichens are symbiotic associations between a fungus and an algae or, in the case of certain blue–green varieties, a bacterium, and they form a large number of species. They reproduce sexually, the fungal partner producing fruiting bodies which eject spores that in some cases need to germinate and find the right algal partner in order to form a new individual, although in the case of some species spores and partner algae are ejected together. Reproduction can, however, also occur vegetatively, from fragments.[6] Lichens grow on soil and rocks but also on bark and wood, especially in the undisturbed, fairly moist yet light conditions provided by wood pastures.[7] Not surprisingly, they also flourish in old orchards, which have been described as 'amongst the most favourable sites for lichen colonisation. As well as being wind-dispersed, lichen propagules, sexual (spores) and vegetative … are carried by birds and mammals visiting orchards for their rich pickings'.[8]

Such favourable habitats are of particular importance because lichens have not fared well in England over the past two centuries. They need clean air to thrive, and in Victorian times high levels of industrial pollution and the widespread burning of coal as a domestic fuel significantly reduced the numbers of lichen species found across much of the country and encouraged the dominance in some urban areas of the dull-green variety *Lecanora conizaeoides*. Following the passing of the Clean Air Acts in 1956 and 1968, and with a reduction in the burning of coal, levels of atmospheric sulphur dioxide and other pollutants have fallen, but recolonisation of the most badly affected areas has been slow. Moreover, in rural areas, increasing levels of nitrogen in the environment, arising from the high levels of fertiliser use associated with intensive agriculture, have seen many once fairly common species decline and be replaced by yellow–orange lichens, such as *Candelariella reflexa*, *Physcia tenella* and *Xanthoria* spp., which are better adapted to conditions of eutrophication.[9]

There is no doubt that orchards are important for lichens. In all, more than 190 different species have been found in various examples across the country.[10] Surveys of seven sample orchards in north Yorkshire, all located some distance from the county's main industrial areas, recorded between 26 and 38 different species, with a total of 55 species across all seven sites. In the county as a whole, 75 lichen species have been recorded, in 23 orchards.[11] In southern England, the situation is broadly similar. Ten Hertfordshire orchards surveyed by Powell, Harris and Hicks in 2011 contained a total of 71 species, although not all were directly associated with the fruit trees; while nine Cambridgeshire orchards were found by Perrin to contain a total of 74 species, 59 of which were on the trees themselves, with individual orchards generally containing between 30 and 40 species.[12]

We should note, however, that most of the lichens recorded in these surveys were not rare or unusual species, those in Hertfordshire being considered by the researchers to be 'relatively common in a national context'.[13] There are also indications that, as in the wider environment generally, lichen populations are more diverse in orchards in the west than they are in orchards in the east of the country. An intensive survey of four orchards carried out by Natural England thus recorded a total of 44 lichen species in the orchard at Rummers Lane, Wisbech St Mary, in the Cambridgeshire Fens, but as many as 80 in one at Slew, in Devon.[14] The drier conditions of eastern England are not favourable to lichens, and, lying downwind of the industrial Midlands, the area experienced significantly higher levels of atmospheric pollution in the past than most western districts. Although conditions have now improved, orchards and other habitats are only gradually being recolonised, with the more common, less demanding lichen species leading the way.

Old orchards are also of some importance for bryophytes (a term referring to small, vascular plants, such as mosses and liverworts), at least those examples which are mainly planted with apples and pears (plum trees and, in particular, cherry trees generally carry fewer examples). This again mirrors their abundance in old wood pastures.[15] A study of five Bramley's Seedling orchards in Cambridgeshire and Hertfordshire, carried out by Whitelaw and Burton between 2009 and 2011, recorded 23 species of bryophyte; the numbers present in each orchard were variable, ranging from 10 to 21.[16] Twice this number were recorded in Rummers Lane orchard, near Wisbech, in Cambridgeshire, in a survey carried out in the early 2000s, while Stevenson and Rowntree found 40 in the royal orchards at Flitcham, in Norfolk, in 2008.[17] But in some surveys, the numbers recorded have been significantly lower. Nine orchards examined in Hertfordshire in 2017–18 contained between 12 and 20 species.[18] In this case, there is no clear pattern of difference between western and eastern orchards, with three orchards in Devon, examined by Lush and colleagues, containing between 19 and 23 different species.[19]

Variations in diversity seem, instead, to relate to the character of the orchards examined, in particular how intensively they have been managed and how recently, and to the character of the fruit trees present. Somewhat surprisingly, an orchard planted with a range of apple varieties will carry a more diverse bryophyte flora than one planted with one variety alone.[20] This probably explains the contrast, for example, between the results presented by Whitelaw and Burton, on the one hand, and Rowntree and Stevenson, on the other, the former concentrating on orchards solely devoted to the cultivation of Bramley's Seedling apples and the latter on more diverse examples.[21] The association of particular types of bryophyte with particular apple varieties can, in fact, often be observed within individual orchards, with silky wall feather moss (*Homalothecium sericeum*), for instance, being found more frequently on Blenheim Orange trees than on their neighbours in a mixed orchard. Neither the age of the individual trees, nor the antiquity of the orchard itself, appear to be major factors in generating diversity in bryophytes. A study of an orchard at Sarratt, in Hertfordshire, recorded 15 different species, even though it was only planted, as a 'heritage' collection, 30 years ago.[22]

Bryophytes clearly are a significant feature of orchards, but the figures from the various studies quoted above should be compared with the figure of 135 species of bryophyte recorded in a transect across England, embracing all types of habitat, carried out in 1997.[23] Moreover, while rare or uncommon species have been reported from some orchards, especially in the west of England, none of the 23 species recorded by Whitelaw and Burton in Cambridgeshire and Hertfordshire were deemed to be 'unexpected for the habitat or area', while those found by Stevenson and Rowntree in East Anglian orchards were considered similar to those encountered in such common habitats as 'elder scrub and sallow carr', rather than in ancient wood pastures.[24] This mirrors, to some extent, the situation with lichens, those found in orchards resembling, in the view of one group of researchers, the range associated with young secondary woodland.[25] It is, perhaps, noteworthy that a survey of the overgrown remnants of a small orchard at Sandy, in Bedfordshire, encroached upon by an adjacent area of woodland, which was carried out in 2011, recovered some lichen species of interest – including the first example of *Arthonia didyma* observed in the county – not from the fruit trees themselves but, rather, from the trees and shrubs of the invading woodland.[26] As Powell and colleagues put it, 'orchards clearly support good, diverse lichen floras and are of considerable local importance in this respect'.[27] Whether such a role, in terms of either lichens and bryophytes, could not be played equally well by other kinds of planting is, perhaps, a moot point.

FIGURE 49. The rare noble chafer (*Gnorimus nobilis*), perhaps the most impressive of the invertebrates associated with old orchards.

Invertebrates

Orchards are almost certainly more important for sustaining populations of invertebrates. Indeed, a number of rare species are more likely to be found

there than in other habitats, including the apple-tree lace bug (*Physatocheila smreczynskii*), the mistletoe marble moth (*Celypha woodiana*; Torticidiae) and, in particular, the noble chafer (*Gnorimus nobilis*) (Figure 49). The latter is a saproxylic species, that is, one that depends for its survival on the decaying debris ('wood mould') found in old trees. Its larvae develop in the moist conditions of hollowed trunks, feeding on the mould and producing distinctive faecal pellets. Although old orchards are home to a wide range of invertebrates, they are particularly important for saproxylic species, not least because their principal habitat – old grazed woodland with well-spaced, hollow trees – is now scarce in most parts of England. Indeed, in many regions, orchards provide their best chance of future survival. Blossom, fruit, foliage, bark, roots and mycorrhizal fungi, alone or in combination, sustain in varied ways a wide range of invertebrates. But dead wood is the key resource provided by old orchards.

Although there are a wide range of saproxylic organisms, especially flies (Diptera), such as *Asteia amoena* and *Sylvicola cinctus,* most scientific attention has focused on saproxylic beetles (Coleoptera), which are generally considered to have very poor mobility because they 'evolved under continuous open forest conditions – a natural high density of suitable habitat, i.e. sufficient density of hollow trees – and there was not therefore selective pressure for relatively high mobility'.[28] The relationship between insect and dead wood can take many forms. In some cases, the larvae feed on decaying wood and the adults on nectar; in others, the insect feeds not on the decaying wood itself, but on other organisms which do so.[29] More than 400 different saproxylic species have been recorded in orchards across Britain, and numbers from individual orchards can be impressive. Alexander and colleagues recorded no fewer than 73 from one at Colwall, Herefordshire, in 2009, and 89 from Rough Hill orchard at Birlingham in Worcestershire, in 2014.[30] In the study of orchard biodiversity undertaken by Lush and colleagues, referred to earlier, Broadway orchard, in Kent, was found to sustain 201 species of invertebrate, of which 79 were saproxylics, and Slew orchard, in Devon, 167, of which 40 were saproxylics.[31] Some orchards, it is true, boasted lower numbers – 117 and 19, respectively, at Luscombe, in Devon, for example – but still noteworthy compared with most other kinds of habitat.[32] Variations in the numbers recorded are the consequence of a wide range of factors, including the spacing of trees and the nature and intensity of past and present management, but of particular importance, not surprisingly, is the character of the trees, with orchards containing a significant number of large veteran examples having a greater variety of saproxylic species than orchards dominated by younger specimens.[33]

Yet orchards in this, as in other respects, are not self-contained habitats, sufficient to themselves, and the character of the surrounding landscape may also be a significant influence on the saproxylic fauna. Keith Alexander discussed the particularly rich assemblage recorded from Rough Hill orchard, in Birlingham, Worcestershire, where no fewer than 89 species of saproxylic invertebrate – both beetles and flies – were recorded in 2013, of which four had rare 'Red Data Book' status. The site had been surveyed on two previous occasions, in 2001 and 2006, and Alexander noted how 'The three datasets ... show remarkably low levels of consistency': of the 31 Rare and Scarce species recorded in the three surveys, 'just one has been found during each survey episode, Scolytus mali'.[34] While he acknowledged that this might simply reflect the fact that the surveys were each only capturing small elements of the total population present in the orchard, he thought it more likely that 'the site may be acting as a stepping stone' for species moving through the landscape; 'it may be part of a complex meta-population structure, with species continually colonising from neighbouring areas while others die out at the site level'.[35] The orchard lies within an area particularly rich in veteran trees: the important wood-pasture sites of Bredon Hill and Croome Park, which boast an abundance of saproxylic invertebrates, are located a mere 3 kilometres to the south-east and the north-west, respectively. If orchard saproxylics are looked at in this way, we might expect to find less diverse populations in areas in which old wood pastures and veteran hedgerow trees are less prominent in the landscape, such as the more intensively arable areas of eastern England, and to some extent this seems to be the case. While two of the 16 orchards examined in a recent survey in Norfolk, Suffolk, Cambridgeshire, Essex and Hertfordshire could boast more than 50 saproxylic species, for most the count was less than 30.[36] Even allowing for differences in survey methods and intensity, this suggests less diverse populations than in many western orchards, which is not surprising given that some of the eastern sites are largely surrounded by wide arable fields with sparsely timbered hedges. But this, of course, rather increases the importance of orchards in such districts for conservation. There are few alternative habitats to sustain these species.

We might note, in passing, that as well as providing a vitally important habitat for saproxylic beetles, orchards also throw some important light on their true character. In eastern England, some of the highest numbers of saproxylic beetles have been recorded from the old commercial orchards in the East Anglian Fens, characterised by particularly massive Bramley's Seedling apple trees. No fewer than 53 different species were recorded from an orchard at Marshland St James and 27 from one at White House, Walpole Highway.[37] As noted earlier, many environmental scientists emphasise the poor dispersal rate of saproxylic beetles, suggesting that habitats where they are common must have developed directly from the primaeval woodlands of remote prehistory, or at least must always have boasted significant numbers of veteran trees. But as Alexander has emphasised, this assumption has never been rigorously tested, and is 'primarily based on the very consistent association between rich saproxylic assemblages, on the one hand, and historic woodland and wood-pasture sites, on the other…'.[38] He suggested that, in reality, there is much variation in the ability of such insects to disperse across the landscape, and that some – as his study of Rough Hill orchard just noted suggests – may move relatively easily across short distances at least. In an important study, Alexander attempted to identify the least mobile species of saproxylic beetle, creating an 'Index of Ecological Continuity' which ranked them in terms of their probable dispersal ability, and that could be used to identify those places – wooded commons, old parklands – which were most likely to represent the remnants of the original, post-glacial, woodlands.[39] What is striking about the assemblages from these two Fen orchards is that between 10 and 20 per cent of their saproxylic insects feature on the list of species used to calculate the 'Index of Environmental Continuity', many with the highest rating, of '3'. The overall 'score' of that at Marshland St James is 28 – enough to place it in the 'national importance' category of sites supposedly displaying direct ecological continuity with the wildwood. This suggests that even these selected species must, in some cases, be more mobile than we assume, for when these orchards were planted, the drained Fens had been largely devoid of trees and wood pastures for centuries. The beetles must have spread through the region as the commercial orchards, planted in the eighteenth and nineteenth centuries, matured, their ageing Bramley's Seedling trees growing massive and hollow in the rich Fen soils.

Other flora and fauna

Many other varieties of flora and fauna can be found in orchards, although in most cases they are not closely or particularly associated with them. Fungi are perhaps the least researched due to the obvious problems involved in recording something which generally appears only fleetingly, although a survey of seven orchards in Herefordshire, carried out between 2007 and 2012, recorded a total of 136 species of fungi and 20 of myxomycete (slime moulds).[40] Some were associated with the old grassland, some with the trees, others with fallen wood or animal dung. They included 10 rare or scarce species, one of which was nationally threatened. Not noted in this survey, but very rare and very much an orchard specialist, is the orchard tooth fungus (*Sarcodontia crocea*), which is only found on fruit trees (Figure 50). Shaggy bracket, or shaggy polypore (*Inonotus hispidus*), is also a characteristic species of old orchards, but, as well as growing on apple trees, can be found on ash, beech and poplar.

Surveys of the grasses and wildflowers in orchards are easier to carry out but have tended to produce rather varied results, reflecting the diverse character and history of the orchards themselves. In some, such as Slew orchard, in Devon, studied by Rush and colleagues, unimproved neutral grassland of the kind classified as MG5 in the National Vegetation Classification Scheme, with a wide range of grasses and vascular plants, can be found.[41] These are usually the larger farmhouse examples, or old cider orchards in western England, which are still grazed by livestock or cut for hay. Elsewhere the ground flora is rather different. In commercial orchards that are still managed or have been recently abandoned, it is usually poorer, because of a history of intense spraying and the shading produced by dense planting. In many orchards, however, especially in eastern and south-eastern England, a diverse but rather motley collection of plants can be found that, while including species which we usually associate with hay meadows, such as oxeye daisy (*Leucanthemum vulgare*), cocksfoot (*Dactylis glomerata*) or common mouse ear (*Cerastium fontanum*), or with long-established pastures found on the relevant soil type, also includes examples typical of very different habitats.

Woodland-edge or hedgerow species, such as black horehound (*Ballota nigra*) and lords and ladies (*Arum maculatum*), can thus occur in the sward, and in old-enclosed districts, where orchards can be bounded by very old hedges, true woodland plants can be found, and even such supposed 'ancient woodland indicators' as dog's mercury (*Mercurialis perennis*), primrose (*Primula vulgaris*), bluebell (*Hyacinthoides non-scripta*) or barren strawberry (*Potentilla sterilis*). The

FIGURE 50. The rare orchard tooth fungus (*Sarcodontia crocea*), growing on an ancient apple tree in an orchard near Wymondham, Norfolk.

grassland of many orchards, however, is dominated by plants associated with roadsides, waste and cultivated ground, including plantains (*Plantago* sp.), fat hen (*Chenopodium album*), pineapple weed (*Matricaria discoidea*), prickly sow thistle (*Sonchus asper*), thyme-leaved speedwell (*Veronica serpyllifolia*) and dark mullein (*Verbascum nigrum*).[42] Daffodils (*Narcissus sp.*), drooping star of Bethlehem (*Ornithogalum nutans*) and other garden plants occur. In many cases these will have spread from adjacent areas of garden, but in old commercial orchards they may represent the descendants of plants once cultivated between the trees. This kind of previous land use is one factor giving rise to the formation of this rather random flora. Other factors include periods of intensive management and spraying, the proximity of old hedges and the presence of heavily shaded areas. But perhaps more important than all these influences are current management practices. In many old orchards, probably the overwhelming majority of examples outside the west of England, the ground beneath the trees is now mown, often on an irregular basis and with the cut grass often left to lie, rather than being used for grazing or to provide a hay crop. As a result, the sward is often lush and rank, and vigorous but relatively common plants out-compete those which benefit from the less nutrient-rich conditions produced by traditional practices.

Mention should also be made here of mistletoe (*Viscum album*), the familiar parasitic plant, which is a feature of many old orchards, especially in the west of the country (Figure 51). Apart from being important in its own right, mistletoe provides feed for the mistle thrush (*Turdus viscivorus*) and the blackcap (*Sylvia atricapilla*) and is host to half a dozen rare invertebrate species, including the mistletoe marble moth. It is much less common than it was even a few decades ago, largely because of the decline in the number of old orchards.

FIGURE 51. Mistletoe engulfing an old apple tree in an orchard at Mansell Lacy, Herefordshire. The loss of orchards is a major factor in the decline of mistletoe in England.

In terms of fauna other than saproxylic flies and insects, it would probably be fair to say that old orchards have an importance that depends, to a significant extent, on the character of the niches and habitats which exist in the wider environment. An old orchard growing in a landscape of extensive arable fields arguably has a more important role in sustaining biodiversity than one set in a more 'traditional' countryside, featuring a mixture of land-use types and an abundance of hedges and mature trees. In the former circumstance, old orchards can be havens for a wide range of mammals and – in the right conditions – amphibians that may have few other refuges in the locality.

FIGURE 52. Fieldfares in
an orchard. Fieldfares
are regular visitors to
orchards in the autumn
and early winter months,
feeding on fallen apples
and pears.

In all situations, however, they can be particularly important for birds. Rot holes in old fruit trees provide nesting sites for species, such as lesser spotted woodpecker (*Dryobates minor*), nuthatch (*Sitta europaea*), treecreeper (*Certhia familiaris*), pied flycatcher (*Ficedula hypoleuca*), little owl (*Athene noctua*) and various tits, while orchard invertebrates provide sustenance for an even greater range.[43] Indeed, it has been demonstrated that predation by birds can reduce the damage caused to the fruit crop by a number of invertebrate pests.[44] On the other hand, Bullfinches, as we have noted, have always posed a problem for fruit growers due to the damage they cause to flower buds, although less so in recent years due to the marked decline in their numbers which has occurred since the 1970s.[45] Other species, such as the house sparrow (*Passer domesticus*), are also known to feed on buds. The apples and pears rotting on the ground provide rich pickings, not least for the fieldfare (*Turdus pilaris*), which crosses into Britain in great numbers every autumn, and is frequently seen in orchards (Figure 52), while the hawfinch (*Coccothraustes coccothraustes*) feeds on plums and cherries, and will even break plum and cherry stones with its tough beak (in the seventeenth century, Thomas Browne observed that hawfinches were 'chiefly seen in summer about cherrie time').[46]

Orchards can also be a good habitat for crustaceans, although a study carried out in Norfolk in 2005 recorded only one 'rare' species, the worm slug (*Boettgerilla pallens*) (from the orchard at Redmayes Farm, Yaxham).[47] The overwhelming majority were 'frequent' and 'common' species, with a handful of ones classed as 'occasional' (two of which were found, not on the orchard floor or on the trees, but underneath an old wooden pallet!). Overall, it is unclear whether, in general terms, old orchards are of greater conservation importance than a small pasture field, mown or cut for hay and surrounded by old, well-timbered hedges. But for the conservation of certain kinds of organism – lichens, bryophytes and saproxylic insects – and for some individual species, such as mistletoe, they clearly do have a considerable significance.

The character of the habitat: the age of orchards and fruit trees

The authors are landscape historians by training, rather than ecologists, and while we can therefore contribute little to an understanding of how important orchards may be for wildlife conservation, we can, perhaps, throw some additional light on the character of orchards as habitats. The first points to be made concern the age of orchards and that of their constituent trees. Here there is something of a contrast between orchards in eastern and in western England. In Herefordshire, in particular, most surviving 'traditional' orchards are probably more than two centuries old. In the east and south-east, the proportion is much lower. Indeed, as noted earlier, only around 8 per cent of the orchards present in 1900 in the eastern counties still survive in recognisable condition, and a significant proportion of these are commercial examples, planted in the nineteenth century, rather than old farmhouse ones. Most of what people describe as 'old' orchards in eastern and to a large extent south-east England, the larger examples at least, are commercial or institutional plantings of twentieth-century date rather than old farmhouse examples, although this does not necessarily render them any less important for wildlife conservation. Of course, there are orchards in the east which are as old as those found in a county like Herefordshire. But conversely, a significant minority of old orchards in Herefordshire, and in western counties more generally, began life after 1900. Even farmhouse and cider orchards tended to come and go from the landscape over time, in part perhaps because as trees aged and pathogens like honey fungus increased, it made sense to replant on an adjacent or neighbouring site.

Even the oldest orchards cannot boast the kind of immense antiquity of many other key habitats, such as ancient woods. Nor are their individual trees as old as the coppice stools found in some of the latter, which, in the case of ash in particular, may have lived for many centuries.[48] It is true that great claims have been made for the antiquity of some apple trees. The original Bramley's Seedling tree, planted as a pip in 1810, still survives at Southwell, in Nottinghamshire, and the 'Milton Wonder', in Milton, Oxfordshire, may be of similar age.[49] But both are examples of a particular phenomenon – the trees have regenerated by throwing up new trunks in the ruins of the old – something which seems to be rare even with examples of *Malus* growing wild, and which must have been vanishingly rare when orchards were more rigorously managed, and when any collapsed trees would usually have been used as firewood and replaced. Observation, over several years, of old orchards in eastern England suggests that while apple trees begin to exhibit 'veteran' features when they are around 50 or 60 years old, they can remain healthy, and crop regularly, until they are around 100. By this stage, however, they usually have very hollow boles and are prone to gale damage, and few probably survive for much more than 125 years. Pear trees age slightly more slowly, and live rather longer – with a reasonable number perhaps making 140 years or so. Cherries mostly die before they reach their eighth or ninth decade, and plum trees seldom make more than six decades. All these estimates apply to trees planted on old-fashioned, vigorous rootstocks; those on dwarfing rootstocks are less long lived. Fruit trees thus, compared with most tree species, live fast and die young.

The rapid growth and early ageing of their constituent trees ensures that orchards often look a lot older than they really are. They seem to be part of a lost rural world, whereas many are relics of an industry brought into being by rail lines and large-scale urbanisation. The wonderful Tewin Orchard, in Hertfordshire, managed as part of a larger wildlife reserve by the Hertfordshire and Middlesex Wildlife Trust, is described in publicity material, websites and the like as a 'traditional village orchard', a description that seems reasonable given the huge size of its great spreading Bramley's (Figure 53).

FIGURE 53. Tewin Orchard, Hertfordshire, now part of a wildlife reserve managed by the Hertfordshire and Middlesex Wildlife Trust. In spite of its ancient appearance, it was planted as late as 1938.

But the orchard was planted as recently as 1933 as a business venture, by one William Stenning Hopkyns; his daughter, educated at the Slade art school in London, gave it to the trust in 1984.[50] Orchards do not, in general, have the long histories their appearance often suggests. Their futures are even shorter if they are not appropriately managed. As noted in the opening chapter, they are peculiarly fragile and ephemeral. Their trees will soon die and, if they are not replaced, a grazed orchard will rapidly become a pasture field, a fate already being suffered by many western cider orchards by the 1930s. If left entirely to their own devices, and not even grazed, an orchard will soon be invaded by scrub, which will eventually develop into secondary woodland. The fruit trees will die – of old age or because they have been outcompeted by birch, ash, oak or whatever else has invaded the site – and, while some trees may regenerate from fallen fruit, and while plum thickets may develop from the suckers arising from the rootstocks of dead plum trees, such survivors will be a minority in a tangle of vegetation that no longer resembles, even very vaguely, an orchard. Of course, to some extent such essential fragility is characteristic of many if not most of our semi-natural habitats. Heaths and downland, if not managed by grazing, will soon revert to secondary woodland; meadows, less dramatically, will lose their distinctive array of wildflowers if they cease to be mown for hay and are instead grazed by livestock. But the extent of interventions required to sustain an orchard is significantly greater.

The character of the habitat: past and present

There is a further level of complication. Some years ago, one of the authors was walking through an old and very overgrown orchard – full of veteran and in some cases collapsing trees – with a noted enthusiast, who declared: 'Now this is what I call a traditional orchard'. But it might have been better described, perhaps, as a *derelict* orchard, and the appearance of such places today may be a poor guide to how they would have been in their more managed heyday, when they were rather less wildlife-friendly places. As we have seen, in the past even the cider orchards of western England were often rather different to the 'traditional' orchard as defined by Natural England, that is, with tall trees and permanent grassland. Well into the nineteenth century, many writers described the 'typical' Devon orchard as a 'close' orchard, comprising close-set trees maintained at a height of 1.5 metres or less, and with cut grass and weeds piled around their base as a mulch against weeds. The 'typical' Herefordshire orchard was an arable field, scattered with widely spaced fruit trees. Both kinds, it is true, disappeared in the later nineteenth century, but by this time, across England as a whole, many orchards were being managed with an intensity that is often belied by their present appearance. By the start of the twentieth century, those in the south-east were already often planted with dwarf trees, spaced at intervals of 2.5–3 metres, heavily fertilised with manure and industrial waste (above, pp. 89–91). Others, both here and elsewhere in the country, contained taller trees, more widely spaced, but had cultivated ground rather than permanent pasture between and beneath them. All orchards of any size, moreover, were intensively sprayed with fungicides and insecticide, and fungi, moss and mistletoe were regularly removed. Where old commercial orchards have survived but are no longer intensively managed, and are either derelict or have been given a new purpose as community orchard or nature reserve, they may be rich in wildlife. But in many cases, this is an artefact of neglect, like the crumbling, over-mature trees with which many are populated.

It might reasonably be argued that while all this may be true of old *commercial* orchards, it is much less true of those associated with farmhouses, for it is clear, not least from the negative comments made by twentieth-century agricultural writers, that these were much less likely to have been intensively sprayed or manured. Nor, in most cases, was the ground between the trees regularly cultivated. These were, nevertheless, more managed environments than their surviving remains often suggest, and some aspects of that management must have reduced their value as wildlife habitats. It is unlikely, for example, that large quantities of windfalls would have been allowed to accumulate, to provide the kind of feast for winter birds afforded by many old orchards today. And they would certainly have contained much less dead wood. Orchards, as we have seen, were an important source of firewood in the fuel-hungry world of the past. Old limbs would have been removed, fallen branches collected: 'the prunings of the *Trees*, and *old dead Trees*', would all have been destined for the fire, rather than being left for the benefit of wildlife.[51] Indeed, numerous references suggest that, rather than being allowed to slide into hollow, unproductive senescence, ageing trees were routinely replaced. There are farming diaries which contain such entries as 'digging and cutting two useless apple trees out of the orchard'.[52] Numerous leases include clauses which allowed the lessor 'liberty of ingress, egress and regress to cut down and stub up all such old decayed trees that shall have done bearing and to cut and carry away the same', or which instructed the tenant 'when necessary [to] substitute and plant young trees of good varieties'.[53] And many contracts survive which instruct estate gardeners to 'plant new trees of the Like goodnesse in the roome of such as shall see decay'.[54]

Looked at from the perspective of the historian, orchards are thus rather peculiar habitats. They are highly artificial, they are fragile, and they only survive through regular interventions and management. Yet in most if not all cases, they were less biodiverse environments in their heyday, when they were more intensively managed and served a practical and economic function, than they are today. The ideal orchard for wildlife conservation – under-managed and under-used, littered with windfalls and fallen wood, and including a significant proportion of over-mature and decaying trees – would perhaps have struck our ancestors as a rather odd place.

Conclusion

Orchards clearly do play an important role in wildlife conservation, but they differ from other key habitats in England in one important respect. Ancient woods, wildflower meadows, ancient pastures or heathland contribute most to biodiversity when they are managed intensively along lines that perpetuate, or at least mimic, past practice. Orchards, in contrast, are most beneficial when managed less intensively than in the past. All these habitats, however, are now castigated by some conservationists as forms of 'wildlife gardening', as attempts to maintain biodiversity through the perpetuation of redundant economic and agricultural practices which are doomed to failure. To such people, the future lies in a very different approach, that of 're-wilding', in which nature supposedly flourishes as human interventions are minimised or removed altogether. There would be no place for orchards on a re-wilded nature reserve. These are important and complex issues, however, to which we shall return in the concluding chapter.

Notes

1   Joint Nature Conservation Committee, UK BAP Priority Habitat Descriptions, 'Orchards' (2011), https://hub.jncc.gov.uk/assets/2829ce47-1ca5-41e7-bc1a-871c1ccob3ae#UKBAP-BAPHabitats-56-TraditionalOrchards.pdf.

2   K. Alexander, The Special Importance of Traditional Orchards for Invertebrate Conservation, with a Case Study of the BAP Priority Species the Noble Chafer *Gnorimus nobilis*. In I.D. Rotherham (ed.), *Orchards and Groves: Their History, Ecology, Culture and Archaeology* (Sheffield, 2008), 12–18, at 13.

3   Alexander, Special Importance, 13–14.

4   Alexander, Special Importance, 13.

5   Joint Nature Conservation Committee, UK BAP Priority Habitat Descriptions, 'Orchards'..

6   C.W. Smith, *The Lichens of Britain and Ireland* (London, 2009); F. Dobson, *Lichens: an Illustrated Guide to the British and Irish Species*, fifth edn (London, 2005).

7   J.R. Laundon, *Lichens* (Princes Risborough, 1986), 17.

8   A. Henderson, Lichens in Orchards. In Rotherham (ed.), *Orchards and Groves*, 76–85, at 78.

9   Eutrophication is the enrichment of the environment by nutrients, especially compounds of nitrogen, leading to significant changes in the balance of organisms.

10   Henderson, Lichens in Orchards, 78.

11   Henderson, Lichens in Orchards, 78.

12   M. Powell, A. Harris and M. Hicks, Lichen Ecology in Traditional Hertfordshire Orchards and the Implications for Conservation, *Transactions of the Hertfordshire Natural History Society* 43, 2 (2012), 69–79; V. Perrin, Cambridgeshire Orchard Survey: Phase 2 Survey, 2006–09: Traditional Orchards Habitat (Peterborough, 2010).

13   Powell *et al.*, Lichen Ecology in Traditional Hertfordshire Orchards, 69–79, at 71–73.

14 M. Lush, H.J. Robertson, K.N.A. Alexander, V. Giavarini, E. Hewins, J. Mellings, C.R. Stevenson, M. Storey and P.F. Whitehead, *Biodiversity Studies of Six Traditional Orchards in England*. Natural England Research Reports 25 (Peterborough, 2007), 137.

15 A. Oldén and P. Halme, Grazers Increase β-diversity of Vascular Plants and Bryophytes in Wood-Pastures, *Journal of Vegetation Science* 27 (2016), 1084–93; T. Kiebacher, C. Keller, C. Scheidegger and A. Bergamini, Epiphytes in Wooded Pastures: Isolation Matters for Lichen but not for Bryophyte Species Richness, PLoS ONE 12 (2017), https://doi.org/10.1371/journal.pone.0182065.

16 M. Whitelaw and M.A.S. Burton, Diversity and Distribution of Epiphytic Bryophytes on Bramley's Seedling Trees in East of England Apple Orchards, *Global Ecology and Conservation* 4 (2015), 380–87, at 382.

17 Lush *et al.*, *Biodiversity Studies*, 138. R. Stevenson and J. Rowntree, Bryophytes in East Anglian Orchards, *Field Bryology* 99 (2009), 10–18, at 13.

18 Barnes and Williamson, *Orchards of Eastern England*, 223, based on surveys carried out by Agneta Burton and associates from the Hertfordshire Natural History Society.

19 Slews Orchard, Luscombe Farm orchard, and Colston orchard; see Lush *et al.*, *Biodiversity Studies,* 50, 60 and 106.

20 C.R. Stevenson, C. Davies and J.K. Rowntree, Biodiversity in Agricultural Landscapes: the Effect of Apple Cultivar on Epiphyte Diversity, *Ecology and Evolution* 7 (2017), 1250–58.

21 Whitelaw and Burton, Diversity and Distribution of Epiphytic Bryophytes, 382. Stevenson *et al.*, Biodiversity in Agricultural Landscapes.

22 Barnes and Williamson, *Orchards of Eastern England*, 223, based on surveys carried out by Agneta Burton and associates from the Hertfordshire Natural History Society.

23 J.W. Bates, M.C.F. Proctor, C.D. Preston, N.G. Hodgetts and A.R. Perry, Occurrence of Epiphytic Bryophytes in a 'Tetrad' Transect across Southern Britain 1: Geographical Trends in Abundance and Evidence of Recent Change, *Journal of Bryology* 19, 4 (1997), 685–714.

24 Whitelaw and Burton, Diversity and Distribution of Epiphytic Bryophytes, 382; Stevenson and Rowntree, Bryophytes in East Anglian Orchards, 16.

25 Powell *et al.*, Lichen Ecology, 73–74.

26 S. Raven, Sandy Smith Nature Reserve – Wildlife and history of Plum Orchard. Unpublished report, The Greensand Trust, May 2012.

27 Powell *et al.*, Lichen Ecology, 69.

28 K. Alexander, *The Role of Trees outside Woodlands in Providing Habitat and Ecological Networks for Saproxylic Invertebrates: Part 1, Designing a Field Study to Test Initial Hypotheses*, Natural England Commissioned Report NECR225a (December 2016), 13.

29 K. Alexander, The Invertebrates of Britain's Wood Pastures, *British Wildlife* 11 (1999), 108–17.

30 K. Alexander, Colwall Orchards Invertebrate Survey: A Report for the Colwall Orchard Group (2009), https://ptes.org/wp-content/uploads/2016/07/Colwall-Orchards-Invertebrate-Survey-2009.pdf; K. Alexander, L. Bower and G. Green, A Remarkable Saproxylic Insect Fauna from a Traditional Orchard

in Worcestershire – but Are the Species Resident or Transient? *British Journal of Entomology & Natural History* 27 (2014), 221–29.

31 Lush *et al.*, *Biodiversity Studies*, 52, 200–2.

32 Lush *et al.*, *Biodiversity Studies*, 81.

33 Lush *et al.*, *Biodiversity Studies*, 23–25.

34 Alexander *et al.*, Remarkable Saproxylic Insect Fauna, 227.

35 Alexander *et al.*, Remarkable Saproxylic Insect Fauna, 227.

36 Barnes and Williamson, *Orchards of Eastern England*, 225–27.

37 Barnes and Williamson, *Orchards of Eastern England*, 227.

38 Alexander, *Role of Trees outside Woodlands*, 13.

39 K. Alexander, *Revision of the Index of Ecological Continuity as Used for Saproxylic Beetles*, English Nature Research Reports 574 (Peterborough, 2004).

40 H. Robertson, D. Marshall, E. Slingsby and G. Newman (eds), *Economic, Biodiversity, Resource Protection and Social Values of Orchards: a Study of Six Orchards by the Herefordshire Orchards Community Evaluation Project*, Natural England Commissioned Report NECR090 (Natural England, 2012), 86–87, http://publications.naturalengland.org.uk/publication/1289011.

41 Lush *et al.*, *Biodiversity Studies*, 48–49.

42 Barnes and Williamson, *Orchards of Eastern England*, 230–31.

43 Natural England, Traditional Orchards: Orchards and Wildlife, Technical Note TIN 020 (Natural England, 2010), http://publications.naturalengland.org.uk/publication/24006.

44 See, for example, D. Garcia, M. Minarro and R. Martinez-Sastre, Birds as Suppliers of Pest Control in Cider Apple Orchards: Avian Biodiversity Drivers and Insectivory Effect, *Agriculture, Ecosystems and Environment* 254 (2018), 233–43; C. Mols and M. Visser, Great Tits Can Reduce Caterpillar Damage in Apple Orchards, *Journal of Applied Ecology* 39 (2002), 888–99.

45 I. Newton, *Finches* (London, 1972), 64.

46 T. Browne, *Notes and Letters on the Natural History of Norfolk: with Notes by Thomas Southwell* (London, 1902), 25.

47 R. Baker, D. Howlett and K. Clarke, Mollusc and Diatom Surveys 2005, Norfolk. Unpublished report for the East of England Apple and Orchards Project, 2005.

48 O. Rackham, *The History of the Countryside* (London, 1986), 102.

49 FruitID, https://www.fruitid.com/#view/490, accessed 12 July 2020; M. Clarke, *Apples: a Field Guide* (Tewin, 2015), 54.

50 Clarke, *Apples: a Field* Guide, 10.

51 R. Austen, *A Treatise on Fruit Trees* (London, 1653), unpaginated introduction.

52 S. Wade Martins and T. Williamson (eds), *The Farming Journal of Randall Burroughes of Wymondham, 1794–99* (Norwich, 1995), 95–96.

53 Suffolk Record Office, Lowestoft branch, 109/E5/5; M. Pomfret, *Stones Orchard, Croxley Green* (n.d., Croxley Green), 8.

54 Bedfordshire Record Office, TW685.

CHAPTER 10

The importance of orchards: culture and history

Orchards have a cultural importance which is arguably as great as any significance they may have for biodiversity. In part this arises from the way that fruit and its production are deeply woven into the fabric of our cultural life, used as symbol and reference from earliest times – allusions which made more immediate sense in the past, when the world was full of orchards. In part it is because the sheer density of orchards that developed in some parts of England gave their landscapes a particular character, albeit one that now usually survives in a fragmentary, tenuous condition. But above all, it is because old orchards represent, or so it is suggested, a priceless genetic inheritance. The fruit varieties they contain, developed many generations ago, are a testimony to the horticultural skills of our ancestors. In fact, these latter two aspects – sense of place, and horticultural heritage – are closely connected. It is not only the antiquity of fruit varieties which many people find appealing, with their evocative names seeming to provide a connection with a distant, stable, rural past – Cornish Gillyflower, Cats Head, Pig's Snout, Slack-Ma-Girdle, Dr Harvey – it is also their association with particular localities, the names of varieties often referencing the place where they originated or the person who first developed or marketed them. Of a list of 728 cider varieties compiled in 2009, 152 have names which refer to their colour, 44 ones which describe an aspect of their taste, 18 ones which refer to seasonality, but no fewer than 368 have names that incorporate the name of a place or person.[1]

Genetics and varieties

The stated or unstated assumption in many accounts of old fruit and orchards is that, in the pre-industrial world, there were a large number of very local fruit varieties, each adapted to particular soils and climatic conditions, which were propagated over the centuries through the exchange of grafts between local people. Such ancient, 'traditional' varieties, moreover, can still be found growing in old orchards today, which thus represent a precious horticultural and genetic inheritance (Figure 54). These kinds of suggestion need, however, to be regarded with a measure of scepticism.

As we noted in Chapter 1, before the early eighteenth century, most people stocked their orchards with trees they had grafted themselves, using scion wood obtained from friends, neighbours or relatives, or they used young trees similarly acquired. Such exchanges were not necessarily local, however.

FIGURE 54. A phenomenal collection of old fruit varieties on display at an 'Apple Day' held at the Gressenhall Farm and Workhouse, Norfolk.

In 1716 Ralph Freman, of Hamels, in Hertfordshire, was sent '3 litle cherry trees' from Northamptonshire, almost certainly by his mother-in-law.[2] In 1659 grafts of pears and other fruit were being sent to Kirby in the latter county from properties in London.[3] By the end of the seventeenth century, moreover, fruit trees were also being supplied by commercial nurseries, with large ones in London, such as Brompton Park, selling to the social elite throughout the country, and a network of more modest businesses serving the local gentry and members of the middle classes – including, almost certainly, the more prosperous farmers. This further eroded the extent to which people planted varieties of local provenance in their orchards.

There are a number of difficulties involved in investigating the history of fruit varieties. The first is that it is the history of apples, rather than that of other fruit, that has been most intensively researched, and most of what we say in the following pages concerns apple varieties. The second is the complex and uncertain connection between a specific genetic type and a name given to an apple. One name might embrace several similar, but nevertheless genetically distinct, varieties. Conversely, one variety might be known by several different names in different parts of the country or, indeed, within the same locality. Charles Vancouver, writing about Devon in 1808, described how 'the range of names applicable to the same fruit in this and other districts and even in adjacent villages, preclude all chance of being understood at a distance'.[4] Even today, 76 Somerset apple varieties have at least one synonym.[5]

Lists of fruit trees, and in particular of apples, from seventeenth- and early eighteenth-century orchards – putting aside for a moment the cider-apple orchards of western England – tend to be dominated, not so much by a plethora of obscure local names, but by a relatively restricted number of shared national types. Names like Golden Pippin, Golden Reinette, Catshead, Golden Russeting, Nonpareil, Aromatic Russeting and Golden Pearmain occur with considerable regularity. It is by no means clear that these necessarily represent the kind of tightly defined, genetically specific varieties we are familiar with today. There are good reasons for believing that some of these names may have been used for rather broader types, with general characteristics of taste, use or storage. Even the less vague appellations, which also occur with monotonous regularity in early lists – Holland Pippin, London Pippin, Kentish Pippin – may have displayed a degree of variability, given the nature of contemporary communications and the fragmented and decentralised character of the supply network. The rector of North Runcton, in Norfolk, bemoaned in 1720 how 'The true Aromatick Golden Russeting is so scarce in this Countrey that I perceive they give the name to any ordinary fruit if it have butt a Russett coat.'[6]

In some early orchard lists, all the apple varieties mentioned are of these 'national' types, as here at North Runcton in 1720.[7] But those from great country houses often include some rare foreign varieties, imported and propagated by one of the big London companies, while examples from more lowly dwellings, in particular, often include otherwise unknown and in some cases clearly local or regional types. In 1734 Mary Birkhead listed the fruit trees growing in the gardens and orchards of two properties in Thwaite, in Norfolk – her daughter's new house and her own former home, a farmhouse now let to a tenant.[8] There were in all around 48 varieties of apple, of which around half were familiar 'national' types (Golden Pippin, Golden Pearmain, Nonpareil, 'Ariomatic Russeting', Dutch Pippin and the like) or were known products of national nurseries, such as the Spice Apple, raised a few decades earlier at Brompton Park. Four, however, were varieties which appear to have originated in East Anglia, and at this time were largely restricted to Norfolk, Suffolk and adjoining counties – Biefen (Beefing), Dr Harvey, Magiton (Majetin) and Colman. A small number were apparently even more local in character. The names Thwaite, Free Thorpe, Corton and Halvergate all reference Norfolk or Suffolk villages lying within 20 kilometres of the two properties. These presumably represent either genuine cultivars which had arisen in these places or, alternatively, names given to more common varieties whose real appellations had been forgotten. A local origin is possible for the large numbers of other varieties which appear to be unparalleled in other lists, nursery catalogues or later texts. Some have exotic names (Egypt Apple), some descriptive (Best Pearmain, Grey Pipen, White apple, Sower Apple, Bloody Apple), some fanciful (the Good Housewife, Maid's Pippin, Lady's Longing). Those bearing the names of individuals, such as 'Mr Walker's Apple', may refer to neighbours from whom a graft was obtained. But some of these obscure varieties were clearly not local at all, such as the Westbery Apple, the Lincolnshire Apple, the Arundel Apple, the 'Welch' Apple, the Gottenburg

Apple, the Oxford Apple, the 'Red Lyons, from France', the Keswick, the Isle of White or the Paris Apple.

Other lists from the seventeenth and early eighteenth centuries display a similar pattern, with a large number of well-known national types, some regional varieties, and a variable but often significant proportion of very obscure names, some of which appear to be very local cultivars. Amongst the latter we might note the Girton Pippin, growing in the parsonage orchard at Westmill, in north Hertfordshire, some 20 miles (*c.* 32 kilometres) to the south of Girton in Cambridgeshire, in 1710;[9] the Paston Pippin, referencing the great Norfolk family of that name or the village of Paston, on the north-east Norfolk coast, growing at the vicarage of Carleton Rode, in Norfolk, in 1758;[10] or the Wisbish Russeting, recorded at Ryston in the same county in 1672, presumably from Wisbech, just over the county boundary in Cambridgeshire.[11] But such specifically local names form a small minority, and many of the otherwise unknown varieties had clearly originated far away, like the Pickering Pearmain, recorded, alongside examples of Nonpareil, Golden Pippin, Golden Reinette and French Russet, in an orchard at Walton, in Warwickshire, in 1710.[12]

In the second half of the eighteenth century, with the steady increase in the number of provincial nurseries and the emergence of larger firms, such as Rivers of Sawbridgeworth or Mackies of Norwich, there were two important changes. First, orchard lists gradually lose otherwise unknown varieties, including those bearing the names of nearby villages. Second, a relatively small number of varieties once traditional to one part of the country, or which had been developed by provincial nurserymen in the first half of the eighteenth century, were now being planted everywhere. Typical are the lists made by William Wilshere of the fruit growing in his garden and orchard at Hitchin, in Hertfordshire, in 1809 and 1814.[13] These include some of the old national types – Nonpareils, a Lemon Pippin and a 'supposed Lemon Pippin', a Winter Pippin, a French Pippin, French Golden Pippins, Margil, Catshead, a Hollow Crown Pippin, Winter Pearmain, a Russet Nonpareil, Spice Pippin and a Spice Russet, all familiar from orchards half a century or more earlier. But there were also three Ribston Pippins ('a very good baking apple in November'), a variety which had been developed in Yorkshire in 1707, while the presence of two Norfolk 'Buffons' (Beefings) shows that this apple was now being marketed well beyond its East Anglian heartlands. Only two of the varieties listed are hard to identify, the 'Duncan Apple' and the 'Bedford Seedling', but the former does not sound local, and the latter may be a synonym for the old variety called 'Bedfordshire Foundling'. These lists, in other words, contain few surprises – nothing obscure or local – and simply reflect the range of apples available from the larger nursery companies. If the trees in question had not been bought directly from one of these, they may well have come as scion wood from a tree that had been so obtained.

The same features are exhibited by early nineteenth-century lists throughout the country. The trees planted at Packwood, in Warwickshire, in 1820 and 1822, for example, are dominated by varieties developed elsewhere in Britain over the previous century and which were now being planted everywhere, such as Dumelow's Seedling (Leicestershire, 1790s), Kerry Pippin (Ireland, 1802), Keswick Codlin (Lancashire, 1793), Hawthornden (Midlothian, 1780) and Ribston Pippin. These were accompanied by smaller numbers of the old 'national' varieties, such as Joaneting and Golden Pippin.[14] While the identity of one or two of the other apples is uncertain, this is again a list with few if any specifically 'local' characteristics. Around a third of the trees planted in the new orchard on a farm at Hasketon, in Suffolk, in 1814, were old 'national' types, such as Nonpareil (most numerous), Golden Reinette, Royal Russett, Golden Pippin, Winter Pearmain, French Pippin, Cats Head, Nonsuch and Golden Pearmain.[15] The others were mainly varieties from other regions, often first developed during the eighteenth century and now widely marketed: Ribston Pippin, Sykehouse Russet (Yorkshire, 1780), Wheeler's Russet (Scotland, *c.* 1780) and Scarlet Non Pareil (discovered in Surrey in 1770 and soon marketed by London nurseries). Only three – Hertfordshire Pearmain, Gray's Pippin and Red Bonum Magnum – appear otherwise unknown but do not sound local, and they may have been short-lived varieties developed by nursery firms or names bestowed by them on existing varieties. The apples listed are again essentially products of a national commercial industry, even if some of the individual specimens had been obtained from friends or neighbours.[16]

The national standardisation of varieties by the early nineteenth century is even more apparent in lists of fruit from commercial orchards. A list of apple trees growing in one at Melbourn, in Cambridgeshire, in 1826, to give but one example, is dominated by varieties developed, or recognised, elsewhere in England during the previous century or so – Ribston Pippin, Downton Pippin (Wiltshire, 1806), Blenheim Orange (Oxfordshire, 1740), Hawthornden (Midlothian, *c.* 1780).[17] The others are mainly examples of the old national types – 'Dutch Apple Trees' (presumably Holland Pippin), French Pippin and Nonsuch. The identity of the Wiltshire Pippin is unclear, but it was evidently not local.

The disappearance of obscure or local types, and the growing standardisation of fruit types, both well advanced by the early nineteenth century, were followed in the middle decades by another important change – the decline of standard national favourites, such as the Nonpareil and Golden Pippin. Whether, as suggested earlier, such names really refer to 'varieties' in the modern sense matters less than the fact that they now became rare. Indeed, as early as 1851, Hogg argued against the view that 'the Golden Pippin, and all the old varieties of English apple', were in a state of natural and terminal decay, suggesting instead that they had been 'allowed to disappear from our orchards' because they were 'not worth perpetuating, and their places supplied by others infinitely superior'.[18] Hogg and his colleagues at the Royal Horticultural Society were by this stage arguing that, whatever the value of local and old varieties in a domestic context, commercial growers needed to focus on a smaller number of varieties of proved worth, such as Ribston Pippin or Blenheim Orange. Standardisation of varieties and the decline of regional difference was now accelerated by improvements in transport, culminating in the development of the rail network. Not only the owners of great country houses, but also farmers and members of the middle classes might now obtain their fruit trees from a distance. In 1847 apple trees for the orchard at Oak Field Court, at Tonbridge, in Kent, were being purchased from Rivers Nursery at Sawbridgeworth, in Hertfordshire; the 1893 catalogue produced by Bunyards, the great Kentish nursery firm, included testimonials from satisfied customers living as far away as Hingham, Banham and Ketteringham, in Norfolk.[19]

With expanding market areas came increasing levels of competition, and rival companies introduced numerous new and improved varieties to tempt consumers. Many were short lived, but overall, the number of varieties available grew steadily, if slowly. At the start of the nineteenth century, firms like Pinkerton's of Wigan or Lauder of Bristol were already offering 120 or even 130 different varieties of apple.[20] Numbers were similar in the middle decades of the century: Lane's catalogue for 1862 includes no fewer than 100 varieties of apple;[21] Daniels were advertising 128 by 1878;[22] Rivers were supplying 113 in 1861. But the latter were offering 132 by 1870 and no fewer than 161 by 1914.[23] Pearsons of Nottingham were advertising the same number in 1906;[24] Bunyards of Kent were selling 192 in 1894, 179 in 1900.[25]

The gradual development of a wide range of standardised varieties, nationally available, and the demise of numerous obscure local cultivars was accompanied by an urge to classify and define both long-established types of fruit and the many new ones constantly being introduced by commercial nurseries. As early as 1815, the Horticultural Society of London began a research programme to resolve the 'synonymy in fruit varieties' (the manner in which one variety might have several different names), and in 1823 planted its own collection of fruit trees at Chiswick, which later became the National Fruit Collection at Brogdale, in Kent. The Pomological Society was founded in 1854 but was subsumed within the Horticultural Society, as its Fruit Committee, in 1858, and in 1883 the society held the National Apple Congress with the aim of improving and standardising classification.[26] These developments were accompanied by the appearance of a succession of 'Pomonas', volumes describing and illustrating different varieties of apple.[27] George Brookshaw's *Pomona Britannica* appeared in 1810, and Thomas Andrew Knight's *Pomona Herefordiensis* the following year, with William Hooker's *Pomona Londinensis* following in 1818 and John Lindley's *Pomologia Britannica* in 1841.[28] But the rate of publication increased markedly in the second half of the nineteenth century, with Robert Hogg's *British Pomology* appearing in 1851, the same author's *The Apple and Its Varieties* in 1859, and his *The Fruit Manual: Containing the Descriptions and Synonomes of the Fruits and Fruit Trees Commonly Met With in the Gardens and Orchards of Great Britain* in 1860, a volume which was revised and republished on a number of subsequent occasions.[29] John Scott's *Catalogue of Orchard Fruits* followed in 1872, with Robert Hogg and Henry Graves Bull's *The Herefordshire Pomona* appearing in annual instalments between 1878 and 1884 (Figure 55).[30] Classification and standardisation were the order of the day.

FIGURE 55. A page from *The Herefordshire Pomona*, written by Robert Hogg and Henry Graves Bull and illustrated by Alice Blanche Ellis and Edith Elizabeth Bull.

Plate LXXI

2. Bess Pool

Queen of Sauce

3. New Bess Pool

4. Minchall Crab

5. Brabant Belle-Fleur

6. Hambledon Deux Ans

7. Broad End

G. Severeyns, Chromolith. Brussels

Edith E. Bull del.
for The Woolhope Club.

The growth of large commercial nurseries with a national reach, the constant introduction of new varieties and the displacement of old ones, both local and national in character, ensured that by the end of the nineteenth century, the range of fruit found in orchards was radically different from a century earlier. The decline of old varieties was most marked in commercial orchards. Typical was an example at Shefford, in Bedfordshire which, when described just after the First World War, was almost entirely stocked with varieties introduced during the previous century: Allington Pippin (1870s), Lane's Prince Albert (1850), Bramley's Seedling (1867), Ecklinville (*c.* 1800), Cox's Pomona (*c.* 1825), Cox's Orange Pippin (*c.* 1825), Gladstone (1868), Diamond Jubilee (1893), Gravenstein (introduced into England in the 1820s), Lord Derby (1862), Worcester Pearmain (1872) and Stirling Castle (1820s). Only Dr Harvey, Ribston Pippin and Warner's King pre-dated the nineteenth century.[31] This abandonment of older varieties appears, based on surviving lists, to have occurred more slowly in the larger domestic orchards, but this may in part be because the listed trees included ones which were of some considerable age, and in part because of a continuing interest on the part of owners in planting a wide range of varieties. The orchard at The Pines, Mettingham, in Suffolk, in 1896, contained 56 varieties of apple, of which 41 were nationally available types first introduced in the later eighteenth and nineteenth centuries (albeit sometimes bearing unfamiliar versions of their name, and in some cases now lost – like Harvey's Wiltshire Defiance). Fourteen were older varieties, but ones which had long been nationally available, like Norfolk Beefing, Hanwell Souring or Golden Russet. Only two (Yellow Joist and Kathleen) are otherwise unrecorded, but were probably synonyms used by, or short-lived cultivars introduced by, local nurseries.[32] The orchard planted in 1890 at Salle Moor Hall, in Norfolk, contained 219 apple trees, of 29 varieties in all. Alongside recently developed varieties like Lord Grosvenor were old ones like Dr Harvey and Nonpareil, together with four which are unfamiliar and were probably short-lived products of local nurseries, to judge from their names: Bird's Seedling, Holkham Red, Raynham Pearmain and Thetford Monarch. All were acquired by the owner, Mr Benjamin Stimpson, from a firm in the nearby town of East Dereham.[33]

Most large domestic orchards planted in the later nineteenth century, however, were entirely composed of, or overwhelmingly dominated by, easily recognised, modern, nationally marketed commercial varieties of apple. Those listed in the grounds of Bretforton Manor, Honeybourne, Worcestershire, in 1875 were all like this: Keswick Codlin, Nelson's Glory, Lamb Abbey Pearmain, Lord Suffield, New Hawthornden, Blenheim Orange and Wyken Pippin. None of the old English varieties, like Golden Pearmain or Nonpareil, were represented, and there was nothing of obscure local provenance, hardly surprising given that at least some of the trees appear to have come from Pearson's Nursery in Nottinghamshire.[34] Even in remote Monmouthshire, the fruit growing in the orchards at The Hendre, the country house of the Rolls family, in 1899, mainly consisted of varieties first marketed within the previous five or six decades, such as American Mother (1844), Bismarck (1861), Belle du Pontoise (1879), Gascoyne's Scarlet (1871), Lord Derby (1862), Peasgoods Nonsuch (1858), Tyler's Kernel (1883), Newton Wonder (1870), and Worcester Pearmain (1872). Only a few were a little older (Lane's Prince Albert, Wellington (1780s), Bramley's Seedling, Cox's Orange Pippin, Baumann's Reinette (1811) and Ribston Pippin (1707)), and all were by now standard varieties, supplied and grown by nurseries throughout Britain.[35]

In smaller domestic orchards by the early decades of the twentieth century, a more limited and more standardised range was usually to be found. There was little to differentiate the fruit grown in the grounds of the rectory of St Giles, near Whitacre, in Warwickshire (Ribston Pippin, Bismarck, Ecklinville, Sturmer, Cox's Orange Pippin, Lane's Prince Albert, Bramley's Seedling and Allington Pippin) from that planted in the orchard of the suburban house called High Knoll, Ampthill, in Bedfordshire, three years later (Lane's Prince Albert, Peasgood's Nonesuch, Scarlet Gascoigne, Bramley's Seedling, Cox's Orange Pippin, Blenheim Orange, Newton Wonder, Worcester Pearmain, Fern's Pippin, and Keswick Codlin).[36] Both comprised what were now standard nursery types, nationally available. There is little or no overlap between the varieties that feature in such lists and those that were recorded in domestic orchards a century and a half earlier.

The development of West Country cider varieties is rather different from that of the culinary or dessert apples which dominated orchards elsewhere in England. As noted earlier, even in the early nineteenth century, many new trees were obtained by simply spreading the 'pomace' from cider making on the ground and allowing the pips to germinate. Those which, after six years or so, produced fruit suitable for cider making were transplanted to an orchard, while others of vigorous growth might be used as rootstock. Some of the more promising of the former might be propagated by grafting, but the overall result was at best a plethora of poorly defined varieties, at worst a mass of trees of individual genetic character. Celia Fiennes in 1685 thought that Somerset was '…very fruitful for orchards, plenty of apples and peares, but they are not Curious in the Planting the best sort of fruite'.[37] The situation at the end of the eighteenth century is clearly summarised by William Marshall:

> To describe, or even enumerate, *all* the present varieties of orchard fruit would be impossible. They are without number. In Herefordshire, more particularly, a very large proportion of the fruit that is grown is "kernel fruit": is produced from trees that have been raised from seed; and which have never been grafted. Consequently each tree is a separate variety; bearing the name, perhaps, of its planter, or of the field it grows in.[38]

This is not to suggest that long-lived and widespread varieties did not develop over time. Batty Langley, writing in 1729, thought that West Country apples were in general 'inferior', presumably because most were raised as 'kernel fruits', but described four specific types sent to him by a Devon correspondent, some at least of which had only recently emerged or been identified: the

Royal Wilding, the Mediate, the Whitflour and the Red Streak. Hugh Stafford in 1753 recommended the use of 'only fruits of an established reputation' in the making of cider and was able to list 30 different varieties from Devon and Herefordshire.[39] However, his descriptions of many betray a sense of uncertainty and fluidity which suggests that some were labels for broad groups of cultivars rather than single genetic 'varieties', and there was much doubt about particular classifications.

> The Elliot is of Herefordshire extraction, and, although it has a different name in some parts, is to all intents the same apple as the preceeding; for neither fruit nor tree can be distinguished from the WHITE-SOUR; the time of ripening of both, and the juices also are precisely the same. The *Elliot* was known in *Herefordshire* before the *Whitesour* had a name, as I am informed by very intelligent persons.[40]

Most of what we think of as traditional West Country cider varieties were, in fact, only developed in the course of the nineteenth and twentieth centuries, and only a small number, such as the Stubbard or the Royal Wilding, pre-date 1800.[41] The kinds of 'kernel fruit' apples produced by the old method were well enough suited to the production of rather rough, strong cider on a small scale.[42] The same was true of many of the more closely defined early varieties, such as the Mediate, which Stafford in 1753 thought good for 'Bramble Cyder', so named because 'of its roughness, which causes a sensation as if a bramble had been thrust down the throat and suddenly snatch'd back again. The lovers of rough cyder in this county generally give that of the *Midyate* the preference…'.[43] Stafford reported that there was already, by the 1750s, a growing taste for sweeter and smoother cider, but it was the rise of more commercial production for wider markets in the nineteenth century, and in particular the development of industrial cider making from the 1870s, that ensured the more widespread use of those established varieties with a high sugar content, such as Kingston Black; the development of many new types with this characteristic; and the abandonment of old methods, of growing trees from pips in pomace.

From the early twentieth century, these developments accelerated. Standardisation and reduction of varieties was spearheaded by the Long Ashton Research Station, which began trials of different varieties at the Burghill Mental Hospital Farm Orchard, in Herefordshire, in 1908. As H.V. Taylor, Horticulture Commissioner of the Ministry of Agriculture, explained in a lecture presented at Burghill in 1937, the cider industry had changed over the previous half century from a local cottage industry producing for local consumers, to one catering as much for the more refined tastes of an urban market.[44] Modern cider required the correct blend of sweet and bittersweet apples to ensure a good balance of sugar, acid and tannin, rather than the sharper varieties, more closely related to crabs, often dominant in old farm orchards, with high acidity but low tannin content.[45] Between 1933 and 1936, the Cidermakers Federation distributed cider-apple trees free of charge to growers at the rate of a tree for every ton of apples sent to the factories. The greater proportion consisted of sweet and bitter-sweet varieties, such as Sweet Alford, Woodbine, Langworthy, Ellis's Bitter, and

Tremlett's Bitter, mixed with Ponsford and Warburton as sharps.[46] Other factors fuelled this drive for improvement. By the 1950s Bulmers was working with the Long Ashton Research Station to identify a list of varieties that would be good, regular croppers.[47] The company were also active in developing varieties with good disease resistance, and also which cropped in mid- to late season.[48] Nevertheless, in spite of these efforts, as late as 1952, a Ministry of Agriculture report described how many of the older cider orchards in western England still 'contained as many varieties as there are trees'.[49]

The drive, in the course of the twentieth century, to reduce the range of fruit being cultivated also affected the culinary and dessert varieties grown in domestic and commercial orchards throughout England, bringing to an end the rapid proliferation fuelled by commercial competition in the later nineteenth century. In 1890 the garden designer and writer William Robinson described the average domestic orchard as:

> A museum of varieties, many of them worthless and not even known to the owner. This is wrong in the garden, and doubly so in the orchard … Too many varieties is partly the result of the seeking after new kinds in the nurseries. In orchard culture we should be chary of planting any new kind, and with the immense number of Apples grown in our country already, we may choose kinds of enduring Fame.[50]

The number of varieties advertised for sale by the larger commercial nursery companies seems to have gone into decline after 1900. At the beginning of the twentieth century, Daniels of Norwich regularly offered around 100 apple varieties for sale, but by 1910 this had dropped to 74 and by the 1920s to fewer than 60. Rivers of Sawbridgeworth, in Hertfordshire, advertised no fewer than 161 varieties of apple in 1906 but only 147 by 1926, and the number had fallen to 112 by 1931 and to 100 by 1935.[51] Pearsons of Nottingham's offering fell from 161 varieties in 1906 to 155 by 1908, 120 by 1911, and 82 by 1919, reaching a mere 64 by 1921, with only a slight recovery, to 78 varieties, in 1927.[52] Bunyards of Kent were an exception, with the number of varieties on offer falling from 179 in 1900 to 114 by 1914, before recovering to 136 by 1929.[53] But the overall trend is clear enough and continued after the war, with Daniels of Norwich, for example, advertising only 25 different varieties of apple by 1970.[54] The attrition, it should be noted, was largely of eighteenth- and nineteenth-century types, and, given that new varieties continued to be developed (most notably, perhaps, by Laxton's of Bedford), the ratio of new varieties to old being advertised for sale increased steadily. Of the apple varieties offered by Daniels in 1874, only 12 per cent were still available in 1917, 10 per cent in 1939 and just 1.5 per cent in 1974.

In commercial orchards, as we have already seen, the twentieth century saw a relentless effort to reduce the range of varieties being grown and, in particular, remove old types (above, p. 126). As early as 1920, when the Ministry of Agriculture and Fisheries initiated a scheme to provide fruit trees for county council smallholdings, the varieties offered were few and had almost all been introduced onto the market since 1860 – Bramley's Seedling (1867), Newton

Wonder (1870), Gladstone (1868), Early Victoria (a.k.a. Emneth Early) (1899), Beauty of Bath (1864), Grenadier (1862), Worcester Pearmain (1872), Allington Pippin (c. 1880), James Grieve (1893), and Rival (1920).[55] Only one – Lane's Prince Albert – was older, although not by much, having been first marketed in c. 1850. In the inter-war years, the dessert and culinary orchards of eastern and south-eastern England commonly grew only five or six varieties, in large blocks. An orchard in Upwell, in the Cambridgeshire Fens, put on the market in 1943, grew Bramley's, Newton Wonder and Grenadier; a 'capital fruit farm' in Walpole Highway, in Norfolk, advertised for sale the following year, grew Bramley's, Grenadier, Emneth Early, Newton Wonder, Lord Grosvenor and Allington Pippin.[56] By 1948, according to Stamp, only two dozen varieties of apple were widely cultivated on a commercial basis across the whole of Britain.[57] Cox's Orange Pippin had become, by the 1950s, by far the most commonly planted dessert variety and Bramley's Seedling the most popular culinary apple. In east Suffolk, just four varieties – Cox's Orange Pippin, Bramley's, Worcester Pearmain and Laxton's Superb – accounted for two thirds of the commercial acreage in 1951. The other third or so comprised a small range of types – Scarlet Pimpernel, George Cave, Beauty of Bath, Tydemans Early, James Grieve, Egremont Russett, Kidds Orange Red – all of which had been introduced since 1870, and mainly in the 1920s and 30s.[58]

It was in part this steady reduction in the range of fruit varieties available from commercial orchards, and from nursery suppliers, which, from the 1980s, stimulated an interest in old orchards and ancient fruit varieties and encouraged the idea that the former represented important repositories of the latter. But this suggestion is only true up to a point. As we discussed in the previous chapter, few orchards contain apple trees more than 125 years old, and the number of trees which are older than 150 years is extraordinarily small. Even the oldest surviving trees that we are likely to encounter in a farmhouse orchard were therefore planted in the late nineteenth century and, in most cases, after 1900. It is thus highly unlikely that we will encounter specimens of ancient, local provenance, and while some varieties of eighteenth- or even seventeenth-century origin can often be found – Ribston Pippin, Blenheim Orange – these will have come from a commercial nursery or been grafted using scion wood cut from a tree with nursery origins. In many old orchards, all the varieties present originated in the later nineteenth or twentieth centuries. Newton Wonder, Emneth Early, Beauty of Bath, Grenadier, Worcester Pearmain, Allington Pippin, James Grieve, Tydemans Early, Ellison's Orange, Gascoyne's Scarlet, Peasgood's Nonsuch or Tyler's Kernel may *sound* like survivors from some lost rural world, but in reality, they are products of a relatively recent, highly commercial and industrialised age. They are a testimony to the skills of Victorian and Edwardian nurserymen and, in most cases, a welcome contrast to the few bland varieties for sale in our supermarkets. It is for these reasons, rather than for any links with a deeper past, that our heritage of apple varieties should be conserved and celebrated.

Myth, art and literature

As should by now be apparent, until the middle decades of the twentieth century, orchards were everywhere – and everyone, except in the most urban and industrial areas, lived close to fruit trees. The kinds of fruit available shaped local and regional food traditions until remarkably recently: Norfolk 'Biffins' were still being sold by Norwich bakers into the 1950s, and rough farmhouse cider could be easily purchased, sold at the roadside, well within living memory.[59] The decline of domestic orchards, together with the wider decline of commercial fruit growing in Britain, is part of a more general divorce of people from any direct involvement in food production that has occurred over the past few decades, and that marks a radical severance from thousands of years of previous history. True, with orchards as with other forms of agriculture and horticulture, activists have fought hard, and with some success, to re-establish connections between people and the food they eat, but against the huge forces of international retail conglomerates and globalised trade networks, it is an uphill struggle.

In the case of orchards and fruit trees, there are other implications. Orchards were, in the past, familiar features which, in the case of domestic and farm orchards particularly, had histories often entwined with the fortunes of individual families, and they represented a more leisurely and pleasurable form of production than many forms of farming. There was hard work, but there were sensory pleasures of spring blossom and ripe fruit – and, across much of England, the mellow intoxication of cider. Not surprisingly, as we have already noted, orchards not only featured prominently in the design of early gardens, but also in story, religion and myth. The fruit picked by Eve from the Tree of Knowledge, its character unspecified in the Bible, was confidently interpreted by our ancestors as an apple, and in some descriptions, Eden is itself as much orchard as garden.[60] Fruit and orchards also loomed large in the classical texts that framed early modern culture, from descriptions of lost 'golden ages' of effortless production and abundance to the detailed accounts of fruit and grafting provided by Virgil in the *Georgics*.[61] In Liz Bellamy's words:

> Classical literature provides a range of stories and symbolic associations, as well as a series of generic forms, which contain assumptions about fruit cultivation and the relationships between fruit and people. Pastoral assumes a world of natural abundance, connoting a rural life of ease and idleness in contrast to the corruptions of urban living.... In georgic, rural life is described in terms of hard physical toil, but it is constructed as healthy and innocent precisely because of this.[62]

Early modern period writers, immersed in classical literature and themselves surrounded on all sides by orchards, developed such themes in diverse ways – not least in the later seventeenth century, when the trope of 'rural retirement' from the troubles of court and capital looms large in contemporary writing. Fruit was used to construct narratives of national identity: patriotism and nationalism, the desire to promote a drink made with English apples over one made with foreign grapes, underlies the relentless promotion of cider by writers like

Ralph Austen and John Beale as much as do economic considerations. Further developments occurred in the eighteenth century, as the distinction between exotic wall fruit and the indigenous apple and pear was employed as a symbol of class differences. 'The hardy fruits of the orchard are associated with the honest simplicity of rural labourers, whereas wall fruits connote the refinement of the elite', while the most exotic fruits, such as the orange and the pineapple – which required special facilities, such as hot houses, for their cultivation – came to represent, in many texts, an unhealthy dominance both of nature and of colonised populations abroad.[63] Fruit also expressed contemporary ideas of gender, biblical texts ensuring that fruit of all kinds was identified with female weakness and sexual appetites. All in all, as Bellamy so clearly demonstrates, fruit and orchards loom large in the symbolic worlds of the sixteenth, seventeenth and eighteenth centuries.

In the course of the nineteenth century, their cultural significance continued to develop, in part along old lines and in part along new, as has been demonstrated by Joanna Crosby.[64] There was a new emphasis, particularly in the last decades of the century, on the health-giving properties of fresh fruit, and especially apples.[65] This existed alongside a continuing emphasis on the biblical significance of the apple, as symbolic of the Fall, in this evangelical age, manifested in paintings like Anna Lea Merritt's *Eve Overcome by Remorse*, of 1885. Perhaps most importantly, associations of apples and orchards with 'Englishness' were now transformed by large-scale industrialisation and urbanisation. National identity was increasingly associated with the *rural*, 'with a cultivated landscape of small farms, provincial towns and clean cottages, all of which were further implicitly associated with strong community ties, stable families and productive leisure time', and was more generally bound up with nostalgia for a vanishing world.[66] The various 'Pomonas', which were published in the course of the nineteenth century and in particular after 1850, were in part a manifestation of this interest in and concern for an indigenous rural past. The *Herefordshire Pomona*, collated and written by Henry Graves Bull and Robert Hogg, included chapters on the history of, and folklore associated with, apples.[67] Above all, such concerns encouraged the depiction by fashionable artists of romanticised rural scenes which in some cases featured orchards, such as John Maler Collier's *In a Devonshire Orchard* (1896) or Frederick Morgan's *An Apple Gathering* (1880). Of particular note are the various depictions of orchards in south-eastern England by Helen Allingham (Figure 56). These certainly understate the intensity with which many English orchards were being managed by the last decades of the nineteenth century. But they continue to inform our images of what a real, 'traditional' orchard should be like.

Orchards, then, have long played an important part in English cultural life. Their wholesale loss has served to cut us off, not merely from everyday life as experienced by previous generations, but from an easy appreciation of the symbols and references that pervade the cultural products of both the distant and the recent past, visual and literary. This, as much as their importance in

FIGURE 56. *In the Apple Orchard*, from Helen Allingham's *Happy England*, of 1904. Images like this still shape our ideas of what an orchard should be.

sustaining biodiversity, is a powerful argument for the protection of old orchards and the planting of new ones.

The landscape significance

Since the 1980s, landscape historians, archaeologists and others have emphasised how the distinctive characteristics of local and regional landscapes provide a 'sense of place' and have an important role in giving a feeling of belonging and stability in a rapidly changing world. Features like field patterns, the location and abundance of woodland, patterns of settlement and architectural styles and building materials are as important as raw topography and geology in shaping the particular character of local and regional scenery. But all have proved vulnerable to the phenomenal speed of modern development. The adoption of more intensive agricultural practices in the 1950s, 60s and 70s, especially the bulldozing of hedges to create ever larger arable fields, served to erode the visual differences between regional landscapes, making the worst affected areas all resemble the arable prairies of Nebraska. Large-scale suburbanisation, with new houses designed in styles paying little regard to local vernacular traditions, has had – and continues to have – a similar homogenising affect. The destruction of orchards in areas where they had formed a prominent feature of the landscape arguably constitutes another critical aspect of this erosion of distinctiveness.

In many parts of England, a significant disjunction has developed between the countryside as we might imagine it, on the one hand, and its real character today, in the early twenty-first century, on the other. Devon and Somerset, where within living memory orchards were encountered at every turn, now have remarkably few examples. The extent of the change is brought home when, in areas where orchards were once ubiquitous but have been lost wholesale, we encounter a small area where they still survive in some numbers. The tract of land lying to the north-west of Hereford was until relatively recently rich in orchards, and many still remain. But it is when we encounter dense clusters – as in the northern parts of the parish of Burghill, where orchards of diverse types and sizes seem to appear around every bend – that the scale of the loss becomes starkly revealed.

During the 1990s and early 2000s, the whole issue of landscape 'character' began to be addressed by English Heritage. Working with the relevant local authorities and archaeological units, they undertook assessments of 'Historic Landscape Character', producing complex maps which attempted to capture some of the key features which combined to produce regional distinctiveness.[68] Some of these, such as that produced for the Chiltern Hills or Devon, included orchards as a significant element of the cultural landscape.[69] But many ignored them: even that for the quintessential 'cider county' of Somerset only mapped examples covering more than 20 hectares (*c.* 50 acres), that is, large commercial enterprises.[70]

The Historic Landscape Characterisation (HLC) programme was in part undertaken with the aim of informing the planning process, but the case of orchards highlights the kinds of problems, both practical and philosophical, that we encounter when we try to 'preserve' landscapes, or even when we attempt to perpetuate a proportion of their key elements. First, many districts where orchards are, or were until recently, prominent only developed a significant fruit-growing industry quite recently, in the 'orchard century', between 1850 and 1950. Few of the 'prune' orchards of south Buckinghamshire and Bedfordshire, for example – with which, to quote the relevant HLC report, the area around Eaton Bray has 'an historical agricultural association' – seem to have existed before 1860.[71] Many of our orchard *landscapes* are like this. They are not ancient or traditional but, like the streets of terraced houses in our major cities, are a product of the great industrial and economic expansion of the Victorian and Edwardian ages. They are a part of the historic landscape, but not a long-established and enduring part, and if such manifestations of practical, recent, commercial activity are worth preserving beyond the point where they are economically viable, what else might we feel obliged to protect and preserve? At this point, we are close to saying that because we have grown up with a thing, it should endure forever, close to saying that the landscape as this exists today should be frozen in time and undergo no further change, a position as philosophically untenable as it is practically impossible. In the West Country, where in many areas orchards have constituted a prominent element of the cultural landscape since the Middle Ages, the situation is clearly rather different. But even here, *wholesale* conservation of the orchard heritage, if enough of it yet remained, would be problematic. For these orchard landscapes, although old, were likewise shaped by practical considerations – by specific social and economic factors – whose time has passed. And on top of this, of course, we have the additional problem of the inherent instability, fragility, of orchards. They require active interventions to preserve them intact into the future, to prevent them developing into open pasture or secondary woodland. Old buildings, even ancient woods, will survive a measure of neglect much more readily. None of this is to counsel against the large-scale conservation of orchards. It is simply to note that such approaches are fraught with philosophical as much as practical problems, as indeed is the conservation of historic landscapes more generally.

Notes

1   D. Reedy, W.C. McClatchey, C. Smith, Y. Han Lau and K.W. Bridges, A Mouthful of Diversity: Knowledge of Cider Apple Cultivars in the United Kingdom and Northwest United States, *Economic Botany* 63, 1 (2009), 2–15.

2   A. Rowe (ed.), *Garden Making and the Freman Family: a Memoir of Hamels* (Hertford, 2001), xlv and 8.

3   Northamptonshire Record Office, FH/D/B/A/2453.

4   C. Vancouver, *A General View of the Agriculture of the County of Devon* (London, 1808), 239.

5   L. Copas, *A Somerset Pomona: the Cider Apples of Somerset* (Wimbourne, 2001), 75.

6   Norfolk Record Office, PD 332/20.

7   Norfolk Record Office, PD 332/20.

8   Norfolk Record Office, BRA 926/121/2 and BRA 926/122.

9   Hertfordshire Archives and Local Studies, DP/120/3/1.

10 Norfolk Record Office, PD 254/60.

11 Norfolk Record Office, MF/RO 218/7, 219/11 and 220/1.

12 Warwickshire Record Office, CR 1368 Volume4/86.

13 Hertfordshire Archives and Local Studies, 60158 and 61181.

14 Warwickshire Record Office, CR 298/6/3/28.

15 Suffolk Record Office, Ipswich branch, V5/11/4.2.

16 For these identifications, see J. Morgan and A. Richards, *The New Book of Apples*, revised edn (London, 2002); FruitID, https://www.fruitid.com/#main, accessed 1 December 2020.

17 Cambridgeshire Record Office, 296/B 661.

18 R. Hogg, *British Pomology* (London, 1851), 97.

19 Kent Archives, U442/E6/1–3; Bunyard Fruit Catalogue, Royal Horticultural Society Lindley Library.

20 J. Harvey, *Early Nurserymen* (Chichester, 1975), 116.

21 Lane's Fruit catalogue, Dacorum Heritage Centre, no catalogue number.

22 Daniel Brothers, *The Illustrated Guide for Amateur Gardeners* (Norwich, 1878), Gressenhall Rural Life Museum, Norfolk.

23 Rivers Fruit Catalogue, John Innes Library, Norwich.

24 Pearsons Fruit Catalogue, Royal Horticultural Society, Lindley Library.

25 Bunyard Fruit Catalogue, Royal Horticultural Society, Lindley Library.

26 J. Crosby, *The Social and Cultural Value of the Apple and the Orchard in Victorian England*. Unpublished PhD thesis, University of Essex, 2021, 99.

27 H. Frederic Janson, *Pomona's Harvest: an Illustrated Chronicle of Antiquarian Fruit Literature* (Portland, Oregon, 1996).

28 G. Brookshaw, *Pomona Britannica: the Most Esteemed Fruits at Present Cultivated in This Country* (London, 1810); T.A. Knight, *Pomona Herefordiensis* (London, 1811); W. Hooker, *Pomona Londinensis; Containing Coloured Engravings of the Most Esteemed Fruits Cultivated in the British Gardens; Pomologia Britannica* (London, 1841).

29 R. Hogg, *British Pomology: or the History, Description, Classification and Synonymes of the Fruits and Fruit Trees of Great Britain, Volume. 1: The Apple* (London, 1851); R. Hogg, *The Apple and Its Varieties: Being a History and Description of the Varieties of Apples Cultivated in the Gardens and Orchards of Great Britain* (London, 1859); R. Hogg, *The Fruit Manual: Containing the Descriptions and Synonomes of the Fruits and Fruit Trees Commonly Met With in the Gardens and Orchards of Great Britain, with Selected Lists of Those Most Worthy of Cultivation* (London, 1860).

30 J. Scott, *Scott's Catalogue of Orchard Fruits* (London, 1872); R. Hogg and H.G. Bull, *The Herefordshire Pomona* (Hereford, 1878–1884).

31 Bedfordshire Record Office, Z 740/108/10.

32 Suffolk Record Office, Lowestoft branch, 1117/285/29.

33 Norfolk Record Office, MC 65/1 and HEA 489.

34 Worcestershire Record Office, 705/273/27ii.

35 J. Basham, Fruit in Monmouthshire and South Wales, *Journal of the Royal Horticultural Society of London* 23, 3 (1899), 277.

36 Warwickshire Record Office, DRB 0072/13; Bedfordshire Record Office, HN7/1/AMP3.

37 E. W. Griffiths (ed.), *Through England on a Side Saddle in the Time of William and Mary: the Diary of Celia Fiennes* (London, 1888), 26.

38 W. Marshall, *The Rural Economy of Gloucestershire, Including Its Dairy; Together with the Dairy Management of North Wiltshire; and the Management of Orchards and Fruit Liquor in Herefordshire*, Volume 2 (London, 1796), 217.

39 H. Stafford, *A Treatise on Cider Making* (London, 1753), 17.

40 Stafford, *Treatise*, 18.

41 Copas, *Somerset Pomona*, 21.

42 Copas, *Somerset Pomona*, 19–29.

43 Stafford, *Treatise*, 21.

44 F. Mac, *Ciderlore: Cider in the Three Counties* (Eardisley, 2003), 47–48.

45 Anon., Cider Developments in the West, *Journal of the Ministry of Agriculture* 43 (1936–37), 213–15, at 214.

46 D. Manning, Commercial Horticulture in Devon, *Scientific Horticulture* 7 (1939), 143–49.

47 Mac, *Ciderlore*, 50–51.

48 Mac, *Ciderlore*, 57.

49 B.T.P. Barker, Cider: from Farm to Factory, *Journal of the Ministry of Agriculture* 59, 4 (1952), 192–96, at 194.

50 W. Robinson. *The English Flower Garden* (London, 1890), 380.

51 Daniels Brothers Catalogues, Gressenhall Rural Life Museum.

52 Pearsons Catalogues, Royal Horticultural Society, Lindley Library.

53 Bunyards Catalogues, Royal Horticultural Society, Lindley Library.

54 Daniels Brothers Catalogues, Gressenhall Rural Life Museum.

55 Bedfordshire Record Office, AO N1/1.

56 Cambridgeshire Record Office, KAR 115/38/2/48 and KAR 115/38/40.

57 L. Stamp, *The Land of Britain: Its Use and Misuse* (London, 1948), 110.

58 Suffolk Record Office, Ipswich branch, HD 285/2/5.

59 M. Askay and T. Williamson, *Orchard Recipes from Eastern England* (Lowestoft, 2020), 66.

60 L. Bellamy, *The Language of Fruit: Literature and Horticulture in the Long Eighteenth Century* (Philadelphia, 2019), 16.

61 Bellamy, *Language of Fruit*, 25–40.

62 Bellamy, *Language of Fruit*, 35.

63 Bellamy, *Language of Fruit*, 103.

64 J. Crosby, *The Social and Cultural Value of the Apple and the Orchard in Victorian England*. Unpublished PhD thesis, University of Essex, 2021.

65 Crosby, *Social and Cultural Value,* 84.

66 Crosby, *Social and Cultural Value,* 119.

67 Hogg and Bull, *Herefordshire Pomona*.

68 O. Aldred and G. Fairclough, *Historic Landscape Characterisation: Taking Stock of the Method* (London, 2003); J. Clark, J. Darlington and G. Fairclough, *Using Historic Landscape Characterisation* (London, 2004).

69 D. Green, The Changing Landscape of the Chilterns: Chilterns Historic Landscape Characterisation Project Final Report (2009), especially 28 and 167: https://www.chilternsaonb.org/uploads/files/AboutTheChilterns/HistoricEnvironment/The_Changing_Landscape_of_the_Chilterns.pdf; S. Turner, *Devon Historic Landscape Characterisation* (Exeter, 2005), 49 and 54.

70 O. Aldred, *Somerset and Exmoor National Park Historic Landscape Characterisation Project 1999–2000* (Taunton, 2001), 11.

71 Albion Archaeology, *The Chalk Arc Initiative: Historic Environment Characterisation* (2007): https://www.bedscape.org.uk/BRMC/chalkarc/low-res-pds/CA-HEC.pdf.

Afterword

In this short book we have provided no more than an introduction to the history of English orchards. Many aspects of this fascinating, multifaceted subject would benefit from further and more detailed research, and with further research some of what we have written may well turn out to be incorrect, or at least represent an oversimplification of a more complex reality. Nevertheless, the picture we have painted is perhaps broadly accurate. Orchards have existed throughout England for centuries – since medieval times they appear to have been a normal adjunct of most residences of any significant size, from farmhouses to great mansions. But they were generally larger and more numerous in the west of England, where a range of factors ensured that cider was the most important alcoholic beverage, than they were in the east. Most farmhouse orchards produced a surplus for local sale, but commercial orchards, forming the main or only business of their owner or occupier, also existed from an early date, especially in places close to major cities. By the seventeenth century, entire districts of specialised production had begun to develop in areas where conditions conducive to fruit growing existed within easy reach of the largest urban market – London. In Kent, Middlesex and parts of Hertfordshire, in particular, farmers began to expand this aspect of their business, and fruit growing became a major feature of the local landscape, and of social and economic life. So far as the evidence goes, the post-medieval period also saw a significant increase in the orchard area in the West Country, as the production of cider increased to supply urban markets and as the practice of growing fruit trees in hedges gradually declined.

But the greatest expansion in the number and extent of orchards occurred from the mid-nineteenth to the mid-twentieth century. It was initially driven by rapid population growth, large-scale urbanisation and the development of a national rail network. It was given further impetus in the late nineteenth century by agricultural depression and the consequent need for farmers to diversify production, and by the rise of commercial jam making and other food processing industries. However much we may like to think of orchards as something essentially rural in character, their history in England was closely bound up with urbanisation and industrialisation, with the development of the modern world. It was the 'orchard century' between *c.* 1850 and 1950, which saw the real emergence of many of our orchard *landscapes*, in places as diverse as the East Anglian Fenland and the Vale of Aylesbury.

Even in the ancient cider counties of the west of England, industrialisation – the rise of major producers, such as Bulmers of Hereford – had an important impact on the character and location of orchards. It did not, however, lead to any sustained expansion in their numbers or area. Indeed, by the middle decades of the twentieth century, many of the old, traditional cider orchards were in decline. The greatest growth in commercial orchards occurred in the east and south-east of England, where environmental conditions were better suited to the production of plums and cherries, and to that of apples for consumption rather than cider making. Although such fruit was also successfully cultivated in areas like Worcestershire and Gloucestershire, by the 1950s the western counties had lost much of their pre-eminence as an orchard region.

By this time, small farm orchards everywhere were in decline, and in the following decade, commercial growers of all kinds were confronted with a con-stellation of problems. Over the past six decades, the area of orchards in England has declined steadily, and vast areas have been cleared of fruit trees and built on or turned over to alternative agricultural uses. Yet at the same time, a large number of people have come to recognise the wider value of orchards – the older examples especially – in terms of biodiversity and the old varieties of fruit they contain. This has encouraged the planting of new 'heritage' and community orchards and an increasing drive to conserve old ones, including redundant commercial examples.

A simple distinction is sometimes posited between wildlife-friendly, 'tradi-tional' orchards, comprising tall-growing trees on vigorous rootstocks, planted in permanent pasture which is grazed by livestock or mown for hay, and the intensively managed commercial orchards which were planted in the second half of the twentieth century, with close-set, low-growing trees set in mown grass or bare earth. The slow attrition of the former, and the rise of the latter, forms a central thread in the narrative of decline that underlies much of the writing on orchards. While we would not want to entirely reject this familiar story, it needs to be nuanced in a number of ways. Even in the seventeenth and eighteenth centuries, not all orchards conformed to the tall-tree, 'traditional' model. Orchards of this kind allowed fruit trees to be grown on land which was also used to keep livestock and to provide a hay crop, and also in other ways: as we have seen, they were 'multi-use environments, appropriate to the rural economy of the small farmer. In other contexts, orchards could already take rather different forms. In Devon, Kent and almost certainly elsewhere, some comprised close-set rows of low-growing trees, similar in many respects to modern intensive orchards, except that the trees were mainly maintained as dwarfs through pruning, rather than rootstock choice. Like modern orchards, these early examples were not much used in other ways – they were primarily if not exclusively for the production of fruit. Very different – although equally removed from stock images of the 'traditional' orchard – were arable orchards, in which the trees stood within cultivated ground. Many orchards in Herefordshire and Gloucestershire especially were like this before the nineteenth century, underplanted with cereals or other crops. More widespread, and again from an early date, was the planting of soft fruit, vegetables or flowers beneath the trees, a practice which had become the dominant form of management across many parts of eastern and south-eastern England by the end of the nineteenth century. We must not, in other words, adopt a simple, linear narrative, in which 'traditional' orchards were replaced by modern, intensive commercial ones. There have been many different kinds of orchard over the centuries, variously used and variously conducive to the maintenance of biodiversity.

Perhaps of equal importance is the fact that even an intensive commercial orchard, if taken into less rigorous management or allowed to decline into a semi-derelict state, can have a high biodiversity value. Even low-growing trees on dwarfing rootstocks will soon veteranise, providing habitats for saproxylic insects and other organisms. Indeed, in more general terms, the relationship between an orchard's character in its productive heyday, and as a habitat today, is complicated. Most old orchards are probably more wildlife friendly now than they would have been in the past. This is most obviously the case with old commercial examples. But it is also true of 'traditional' farmhouse orchards, where – as we have suggested – veteran trees, with declining productivity, were regularly removed and replaced. But the most biodiverse orchards occupy a fine line between management and neglect; too great a reduction of management would lead either to degeneration to open pasture or to regeneration to secondary woodland. Orchards, as we have already noted, are thus rather odd habitats, their importance dependent on appropriate levels of intervention, which are generally lower than when they performed a primarily economic function. They are, nevertheless, a classic example of the 'wildlife gardening' that has, over recent years, come under sustained attack from advocates of re-wilding.

Until recently, there was general agreement that nature conservation in the UK was best achieved within the framework of the cultural, human-made landscape. Biodiversity was to be sustained through the preservation and management of long-established features of the countryside which had originally been created, or shaped, by practical and agricultural activities. These included both individual elements, such as hedges and field ponds, and more extensive, 'semi-natural habitats', such as heaths, ancient woods or hay meadows, most of which had been rendered redundant in practical terms by social, economic and technological change. This approach was based on a recognition of the fact that England's ecology had been critically shaped, and sustained, over many centuries, by human activities. To ecologists like Oliver Rackham, the rural landscape embodied both natural and human history, the two connected in complex ways.

The distinctive flora of hay meadows, for example, had developed as a direct consequence of the way they were managed over many centuries: they were depleted of nutrients by the annual cutting and removal of hay, and they remained ungrazed during the spring and early summer, allowing large, bulky species, such as globeflower (*Trollius europaeus*) or oxeye daisy (*Leucanthemum vulgare*), to flower and set seed. Heaths acquired their character in part from acidic soils, but also from intensive grazing and regular cutting, together with the repeated disturbance caused by digging heather for fuel; the extraction of sand and gravel; and, in some cases, sporadic ploughing and cultivation. When these activities cease, secondary woodland rapidly establishes itself. Old orchards, as essentially artificial and highly managed habitats, obviously form part of this wider picture.

Many people, however, now denigrate approaches to conservation based on the maintenance of historic land-use systems and believe instead in re-wilding.[1] This can mean a variety of things but, in essence, involves reducing or even removing altogether any form of human management. Ideally, we should be creating extensive tracts of unmanaged land in which 'natural' processes can reassert themselves and wildlife can flourish as it did before farming began. This approach is now being attempted at a number of places, most notably Knepp, in Sussex, where the aim is to recreate the kind of grazed and rather open woodland which, some researchers believe, characterised the primaeval landscape, although we should perhaps note that others believe that this was, in fact, probably rather more densely wooded. Either way, orchards, most artificial of environments and only sustained through continuous management, have no place in such an approach. A re-wilded orchard would very soon cease to be an orchard at all.

This is not the place to examine or critique such ideas. It is, however, worth emphasising that re-wilding does not represent a simple route back to some pre-Neolithic Eden. Re-wilded areas would host a mass of alien species which were absent from the pre-farming environment. These deliberate or accidental introductions include some of our most familiar flora and fauna – black and brown rat, rabbit, fallow deer, sycamore, poppy – as well as the more obvious and recent arrivals, such as grey squirrel, muntjac, Japanese knotweed and Himalayan balsam. Moreover, re-wilding, while it can certainly make an important contribution to nature conservation, can only ever be a part of the answer to the present crisis in biodiversity. With a population approaching 70 million, issues of food security alone will limit the extent of re-wilding projects and serve to concentrate them in areas both spatially and agriculturally marginal. While such wilderness areas would provide suitable places in which the more affluent might enjoy 'safaris', they would be of little use to the poor, the old or the infirm, who usually encounter nature rather closer to home, on country walks, or on the edges of urban areas. Once such re-wilded reserves became established on any scale, moreover, it would be harder to argue against the intensification of agriculture in the 'normal' countryside, for the work of sustaining biodiversity was being continued elsewhere.

In addition, the scope for re-wilding is, or should be, limited by the other roles that landscapes play. They have a cultural importance, through their association with visual art or literature. Would we really want re-wilding – the establishment of unkempt grazed woodland – to change the face of the bleak Howarth Moors, inspiration for Emily Brontë's *Wuthering Heights*, or of Dedham Vale, the subject of so many of John Constable's paintings? And landscapes can themselves be works of art. Would we want the greatest and best preserved of the works of Capability Brown or Humphry Repton to disappear under the trees? Moreover, ordinary rural landscapes – patterns of fields, roads, commons, woods – are historical monuments, like old houses or ancient churches. But keen advocates of extensive re-wilding are overtly hostile to such ideas. Over large tracts of land, complex mosaics of areas and features that are often many centuries in the making *should* be erased in order to foster the illusion and the experience of wilderness.[2]

Yet in spite of the current popularity of these new approaches to conservation, there is little hard scientific evidence that a re-wilded area is, in fact, more biologically diverse than a tract of countryside managed on something like 'traditional' lines. Indeed, the complex intermixture of human-made and intensively managed environments, such as coppiced woods, chalk downland, heaths and hedges, as well as orchards, arguably served to proliferate niches and opportunities, boosting biodiversity rather than reducing it.[3] Those who champion the future of orchards are clearly not uncritical supporters of re-wilding. While, like us, they may see its benefits in particular contexts, they will also believe in the importance of more traditional approaches to conservation. Orchards embody, perhaps better than any other feature of the landscape, the concept that what we think of as the 'natural' world has been critically shaped by human history and needs to be conserved within the physical and biological frameworks created by that history. In these crowded, long-settled islands, nature is not something that can usefully be regarded as separate and divorced from us, something to be curated, visited and observed on discrete reserves. Human management – and then a measure of neglect – has created in old orchards an important habitat for a variety of rare organisms. But perhaps more importantly, orchards are places where a wide range of less obscure wildlife can be sustained close to the human world, rather than isolated from it. Whether we are thinking of orchards located beside farmhouses; old 'institutional' examples; or new ones created in villages, suburbs or cities, orchards more than any other habitat have a close association with the places where people live. And on top of this, we should note again the cultural and historical importance of orchards, their symbolic significance, their role in perpetuating old varieties and tastes – to say nothing of the simple aesthetic appeal of blossom, tree shapes, birdsong. Until quite recently, the country was full of orchards, and their catastrophic decline constitutes a profound severance from our common past.

There are some problems, of course, with the current enthusiasm for old orchards, and for old fruit varieties. As we have seen, much that has been written on these topics is infused with nostalgia, and such things as the revival (or perhaps more accurately, re-invention) of the old custom of wassailing, in the context of a suburban community orchard, can seem odd.[4] But old orchards are – for all the reasons just given – unquestionably worth conserving on a significant scale and using in new ways where appropriate. And new orchards need to be planted, in large numbers, for the many benefits they provide. Such work is underway, by groups and individuals throughout the country. It needs to be intensified, and it needs to receive appropriate support and funding in planning, agricultural and conservation policies.

Notes

1   G. Monbiot, *Feral: Searching for Enchantment on the Frontiers of Rewilding* (London, 2014); S. Carver and I. Convery, Rewilding: Time to Get Down Off the Fence? *British Wildlife* 32, 4 (2021), 246–55.

2   T. Williamson, How Natural Is Natural? Historical Perspectives on Wildlife and the Environment in Britain, *Transactions of the Royal Historical Society* 29 (2019), 293–311.

3   P. Dolman, T. Williamson, R. Fuller and G. Barnes, What Does 'Traditional' Management Really Mean? *British Wildlife* 29, 2 (2017), 113–19; R. Fuller, T. Williamson, G. Barnes and P. Dolman, Human Activities and Biodiversity Opportunities in Pre-Industrial Cultural Landscapes: Relevance to Conservation, *Journal of Applied Ecology* 54 (2017), 459–69.

4   E. Wigley, Wassail! Reinventing 'Tradition' in Contemporary Wassailing Customs in Southern England, *Cultural Geographies* 26, 3 (2019), 379–93.

Bibliography

Books, articles, reports and theses

Albion Archaeology, The Chalk Arc Initiative: Historic Environment Characterisation (2007): https://www.bedscape.org.uk/BRMC/chalkarc/low-res-pds/CA-HEC.pdf.

Alcock, N. 1970. An East Devon Manor in the Later Middle Ages, Part 1: 1374–1420, the Manor Farm. *Devonshire Association Transactions* 102, 141–87.

Aldred, O. 2001. *Somerset and Exmoor National Park Historic Landscape Characterisation Project 1999–2000*. Taunton, Somerset County Council.

Aldred, O. and Fairclough, G. 2003. *Historic Landscape Characterisation: Taking Stock of the Method*. London, English Heritage.

Alexander, K. 1999. The Invertebrates of Britain's Wood Pastures. *British Wildlife* 11, 108–17.

Alexander, K. 2004. *Revision of the Index of Ecological Continuity as Used for Saproxylic Beetles*, English Nature Research Reports 574. Peterborough, English Nature.

Alexander, K. 2008. The Special Importance of Traditional Orchards for Invertebrate Conservation, with a Case Study of the BAP Priority Species the Noble Chafer *Gnorimus nobilis*. In I.D. Rotherham (ed.), *Orchards and Groves: Their History, Ecology, Culture and Archaeology*, 12–18. Sheffield, Wildtrack.

Alexander, K. 2009. Colwall Orchards Invertebrate Survey. A report for the Colwall Orchard Group: https://ptes.org/wp-content/uploads/2016/07/Colwall-Orchards-Invertebrate-Survey-2009.pdf.

Alexander, K. 2016. *The Role of Trees outside Woodlands in Providing Habitat and Ecological Networks for Saproxylic Invertebrates: Part 1, Designing a Field Study to Test Initial Hypotheses*, Natural England Commissioned Report NECR225a. Peterborough, Natural England.

Alexander, K., Bower, L. and Green, G. 2014. A Remarkable Saproxylic Insect Fauna from a Traditional Orchard in Worcestershire – but Are the Species Resident or Transient? *British Journal of Entomology & Natural History* 27, 221–29.

Anon., 1604. *The Fruiterer's Secret*. London.

Anon., 1640. *The Country-Man's Recreation, or the Art of Planting, Grafting, Gardening*. London.

Anon., 1652. *A Designe for Plentie by an Unrivalled Planting of Fruit Trees*. London.

Anon., 1937. Cider Developments in the West, *Journal of the Ministry of Agriculture* 43, 213–55.

Askay, M. and Williamson, T. 2020. *Orchard Recipes from Eastern England*. Bridge Publishing, Lowestoft.

Atkins, P.J. 2016. Vinegar and Sugar: the Early History of Factory-made Jams, Sauces and Pickles in Britain. In D.J. Oddy and A. Drouard (eds), *The Food Industries of Europe in the Nineteenth and Twentieth Centuries*, 41–54. Routledge, London.

Austen, R. 1653. *A Treatise on Fruit Trees*. London.

Bagenal, N.B. (ed.) 1939. *Fruit Growing: Modern Cultural Methods*. Ward, Lock and Co, London.

Bailey, J. 1813. *General View of the Agriculture of the County of Durham*. London.

Bailey, J. and Culley, G. 1797. *General View of the Agriculture of the County of Northumberland*. London.

Baker, R., Howlett, D. and Clarke, K. 2005. Mollusc and Diatom Surveys 2005, Norfolk. Unpublished report for the East of England Apple and Orchards Project.

Baker, T.F.T., Cockburn, J.S. and Pugh, R.B. (eds), 1971. *Victoria History of the County of Middlesex*, Volume 4. Victoria County History, London.

Barber, J.T. 1803. *A Tour through South Wales and Monmouthshire*. London.

Barker, B.T.P. 1952. Cider: from Farm to Factory, *Journal of the Ministry of Agriculture* 59, 192–96.

Barker, B.T.P. 1953. Long Ashton Research Station, 1903–1953, *Journal of Horticultural Science* 28, 149–51.

Barnes, G. and Williamson, T. 2011. *Ancient Trees in the Landscape: Norfolk's Arboreal Heritage*. Windgather, Oxford.

Barnes, G. and Williamson, T. 2021. *The Orchards of Eastern England: History, Ecology, Place*. University of Hertfordshire Press, Hatfield.

Bartos, J. 2021. Wilderness and Grove: Gardening with Trees in England 1688–1750. Unpublished PhD thesis, University of Bristol.

Basham, J. 1899. Fruit in Monmouthshire and South Wales, *Journal of the Royal Horticultural Society of London* 23, 3.

Batchellor, T. 1813. *General View of the Agriculture of the County of Bedford.* London.

Bates, J.W., Proctor, M.C.F., Preston, C.D., Hodgetts, N.G. and Perry, A.R. 1997. Occurrence of Epiphytic Bryophytes in a 'Tetrad' Transect across Southern Britain 1: Geographical Trends in Abundance and Evidence of Recent Change, *Journal of Bryology* 19, 685–714.

Beale, J. 1656. *Herefordshire Orchards, a Pattern for all England, Written in an Epistolary Address to Samuel Hartlib, Esq.* London.

Bear, W.E. 1899. Flower and Fruit Farming in England – Part 3, *Journal of the Royal Agricultural Society of England,* 3rd Series 10, 46.

Beech, G. and Mitchell, R. 2004. *Maps for Family and Local History:* the Records of the Tithe, Valuation Office, and National Farm Surveys of England and Wales, 1836–1943. The National Archives, London.

Bellamy, L. 2019. *The Language of Fruit: Literature and Horticulture in the Long Eighteenth Century.* University of Pennsylvania Press, Philadelphia.

Black, A. 1880. *Black's Guide to the Counties of Herefordshire and Monmouthshire,* seventh edn. Edinburgh.

Blackburne-Maze, P. 1986. *The Apple Book.* Hamlyn, London.

Blagrave, J. 1669. *The Epitome of the Whole Art of Husbandry.* London.

Blanc, R. 2020. *The Lost Orchard: a French Chef Rediscovers a Great British Food Heritage.* Headline Home, London.

Blomefield, F. 1805–10. *An Essay towards a Topographical History of the County of Norfolk,* second edn, 11 vols. London.

Bone, Q. 1976. Legislation to Revive Small Farming in England 1887–1914, *Agricultural History* 49, 653–61.

Brassley, P., Lambert, A. and Saunders, P. (eds) 1988. *Accounts of the Reverend John Crakanthorp of Fowlmere: 1682–1710.* Cambridge Record Society Volume 8, Cambridge.

Briault, E.W.H. 1942. *The Land of Britain, Parts 83 and 84: Sussex (East and West).* Geographical Publications, London.

Brookshaw, G. 1810. *Pomona Britannica: the Most Esteemed Fruits at Present Cultivated in This Country.* London.

Brown, D. and Williamson, T. 2016. *Lancelot Brown and the Capability Men: Landscape Revolution in Eighteenth-Century England.* Reaktion, London.

Brown, P. 2016. *The Apple Orchard: the Story of Our Most English Fruit.* Particular Books, London.

Browne, H. 1677. *Nurseries, Orchards, Profitable Gardens and Vineyards Encouraged.* London.

Bullein, W. 1595. *The Government of Health.* London.

Bulmer, E.F. 1937. *Early Days of Cider Making.* Privately published, Hereford.

Burdett, H.C. 1891. *Hospitals and Asylums of the World: Asylum Construction.* London.

Bush, R. 1951. *Tree Fruit Growing, Volume 1.* Penguin, London.

Butler, R. 1907. 'Social and Economic History'. In W. Page (ed.), *Victoria History of the County of Gloucestershire,* Volume 2, 127–72. Victoria County History, London.

Camden, W. 1637. *Britain, or a Chorographical Description of the Most Flourishing Kingdomes, England, Scotland and Ireland.* London.

Carver, S. and Convery, J. 2021. Rewilding: Time to Get Down Off the Fence? *British Wildlife* 32 (4), 246–55.

Chapman, G. 2002. *Chapman's Homer: the Iliad and the Odyssey,* ed. J. Parker. Wordsworth Editions, Ware.

Chauncy, H. 1826. *The Historical Antiquities of Hertfordshire,* second edn, Volume 1. London.

Clark, J., Darlington, J. and Fairclough, G. 2004. *Using Historic Landscape Characterisation.* English Heritage, London.

Clarke, J. 1794. *General View of the Agriculture of the County of Hereford.* London.

Clarke, M. 2015. *Apples: a Field Guide,* revised edn. Tewin Orchard, Tewin.

Clifford, S. 2008. Save Our Orchards: One Insight into the First Two Decades of a Campaign. In I.D. Rotherham (ed.), *Orchards and Groves: Their History, Ecology, Culture and Archaeology,* 32–45. Wildtrack, Sheffield.

Clutterbuck, J. 1864. *Agricultural Notes on Hertfordshire.* London.

Cobbett, W. 1830. *Rural Rides.* London.

Cocks, A.H. 1892. Vermin Paid For by Churchwardens in a Buckinghamshire Parish, *Zoologist, Series 3,* 16, 61–64.

Common Ground, *Orchards: a Guide to Local Conservation.* Common Ground, London.

Copas, L. 2001. *A Somerset Pomona: the Cider Apples of Somerset.* Dovecote Press, Wimbourne.

Corfield, P. 2004. From Second City to Regional Capital. In C. Rawcliffe and R. Wilson (eds) *Norwich Since 1550*, 139–65. Hambledon Continuum, London.

Cornille, A., Giraud, T., Smulders, M.J.M., Roldán-Ruiz, I., and Gladieux, P. 2014. The Domestication and Evolutionary Ecology of Apples, *Trends in Genetics* 30, 57–65.

Crosby, J. 2021. *The Social and Cultural Value of the Apple and the Orchard in Victorian England.* Unpublished PhD thesis, University of Essex.

Crossley, A. 1999. *Apple Years at Cockayne Hatley: the History of Coxes Orange Pippin Orchards ("COPO").* Privately printed, Cockayne Hatley.

Currie, C. 1990. Fish Ponds as Garden Features, *Garden History* 18, 22–33.

Cutler, W.H.R. 1908. Agriculture. In W. Page (ed.), *Victoria History of the County of Hereford*, Volume 1, 407–29. Victoria County History, London.

Davey, P. 1995. *Arts and Crafts Architecture.* Phaidon, London.

Davis, T. 1811. *General View of the Agriculture of Wiltshire.* London.

Defoe, D. 1722. *A Tour Through This Whole Island of Great Britain.* London.

Dilwyn, L.W. 1843. *Hortus Collinsonianus: an Account of the Plants Cultivated by the Late Peter Collinson.* Swansea.

Dobson, F. 2005. *Lichens: an Illustrated Guide to the British and Irish Species,* fifth edn. Richmond Publishing, London.

Dolman, P., Williamson, T., Fuller, R. and Barnes, G. 2017. What Does 'Traditional' Management Really Mean? *British Wildlife* 29 (2), 113–19.

Doubleday, H.A., Bund, J.W.W. and Page, W. (eds), 1901. *Victoria History of the County of Worcestershire*, Volume 1. Victoria County History, London.

Drake, L.J. 2008. *Wood & Ingram: a Huntingdon Nursery: 1742–1950.* Cambridgeshire Gardens Trust, Cambridge.

Ducumb, J.M. 1805. *General view of the Agriculture of the County of Hereford.* London.

Edelen, G. (ed.) 1968. *William Harrison's Description of England.* Cornell University Press, Ithaca, NY.

Ellis, W. 1733. *Chiltern and Vale Farming Explained, According to the Latest Improvements.* London.

Ellis, W. 1738. *The Timber-Tree Improved.* London.

Ellis, W. 1754. *The Compleat Cyderman: or, the Present Practice of Raising Plantations of the Best Cyder Apple and Perry Pear-Trees.* London.

Emmison, F.G. 1976. *Elizabethan Life: Home, Work and Land: from Essex Wills and Sessions and Manorial Records.* Essex County Council, Chelmsford.

Evans, E.J. 1993. *Tithes: Maps, Apportionments and the 1836 Act.* Philemore, Chichester.

Evans, J. 1954. *The Endless Web: John Dickinson & Co., Ltd., 1804–1954.* Jonathan Cape, London.

Fairchild, T. 1722. *The City Gardener.* London.

Farnell, M. 1972. The Neglected Aylesbury Prune, *Buckinghamshire and Bedfordshire Countryside*, March, 14–16.

Farrer, W. and Brownbill, J. (eds), 1907. *The Victoria History of the County of Lancaster,* Volume 3. Victoria County History, London.

Farthing, F.H. 1911. *Saturday in My Garden.* Richards, London.

Finberg, H.P.R. 1951. *Tavistock Abbey: a Study in the Social and Economic History of Devon.* Cambridge University Press, Cambridge.

Fisher, J.T. 1879. *The Peach and Nectarine: Their History, Varieties and Cultivation.* London.

Fuller, R.J., Williamson, T., Barnes, G. and Dolman, P. 2017. Human Activities and Biodiversity Opportunities in Pre-Industrial Cultural Landscapes: Relevance to Conservation, *Journal of Applied Ecology* 54, 459–69.

Fuller, T. 1662. *The History of the Worthies of England.* London.

Gee, M. 2018. *The Devon Orchards Book.* Halsgrove, Wellington.

Gerard, J. 1597. *The Herball, or General Histories of Plantes.* London.

Gerish, W.B. 1907. *Sir Henry Chauncy, Kt; Serjeant-at-Law and Recorder of Hertford.* Waterlow and Sons, London.

Gissing, T. 1857–58. Polstead Cherries, *The Phytologist* 2, 326.

Gooch, W. 1811. *General View of the Agriculture of the County of Cambridge.* London.

Green, D. 2009. The Changing Landscape of the Chilterns: Chilterns Historic Landscape Characterisation Project Final Report': https://www.chilternsaonb.org/uploads/files/AboutTheChilterns/HistoricEnvironment/The_Changing_Landscape_of_the_Chilterns.pdf.

Griffin, C.J. 2008. 'Cut Down by Some Cowardly Miscreants': Plant Maiming, or the Malicious Cutting of Flora, as an Act of Protest in Eighteenth- and Nineteenth-Century Rural England, *Rural History*, 19 (2), 29–54.

Griffin, C.J. 2014. 'Some Inhuman Wretch': Animal Maiming and the Ambivalent Relationship between Rural Workers and Animals, *Rural History* 25, 133–60.

Griffiths, E.W. (ed.) 1888. *Through England on a Side Saddle in the Time of William and Mary: the Diary of Celia Fiennes*. London.

Haggard, H. Rider 1906. *Rural England*, Volume II. Longman's, London.

Haggard, H. Rider 1910. *Regeneration: Being an Account of the Social Work of the Salvation Army in Great Britain*. Longman, Green and Co., London.

Hall, D. 1982. *Medieval Fields*. Shire, Princes Risborough.

Halsted, E. 1797. *The History and Topographical Survey of the County of Kent*, second edn, Volume 1. London.

Harrison, G.V. 1984. The South-West: Dorset, Somerset, Devon and Cornwall. In J. Thirsk (ed.), *The Agrarian History of England and Wales, V.I, 1640–1750: Regional Farming Systems*, 358–92. Cambridge University Press, Cambridge.

Hatcher, J. 1993. *The History of the British Coal Industry: Volume 1: Before 1700: Towards the Age of Coal*. Oxford University Press, Oxford.

Harvey, D. 1964. Fruit Growing in Kent in the Nineteenth Century, *Archaeologia Cantiana* 79, 94–108.

Harvey, J. 1972. *Early Gardening Catalogues*. Philemore, Chichester.

Harvey, J. 1974. The Stocks Held by Early Nurseries, *Agricultural History Review* 22, 18–35.

Harvey, J. 1975. *Early Nurserymen*. Philemore, Chichester.

Hassell, C. 1815. *General View of the Agriculture of the County of Monmouth*. London.

Hellier, H.E. 1935. *Practical Gardening for Amateurs*. Collingridge, London.

Henderson, A. 2008. Lichens in Orchards. In I.D. Rotherham (ed.), *Orchards and Groves: Their History, Ecology, Culture and Archaeology*, 76–85. Wildtrack, Sheffield.

Hindle, B.P. 1988. *Maps for Local History*. Batsford, London.

Historic England 2011. *Environmental Archaeology: a Guide to the Theory and Practice of Methods, from Sampling and Recovery to Post-excavation*. Peterborough, Historic England: https://historicengland.org.uk/images-books/publications/environmental-archaeology-2nd/environmental_archaeology.

Hitchmough, W. 1997. *CFA Voysey*. Phaidon, London.

Hoare, A.H. 1928. *The English Grass Orchard and the Principles of Fruit Growing*. Ernest Benn, London.

Hogg, R. 1851. *British Pomology: or the History, Description, Classification and Synonymes of the Fruits and Fruit Trees of Great Britain Volume 1: The Apple*. London.

Hogg, R. 1859. *The Apple and Its Varieties: Being a History and Description of the Varieties of Apples Cultivated in the Gardens and Orchards of Great Britain*. London.

Hogg, R. 1860. *The Fruit Manual: Containing the Descriptions and Synonomes of the Fruits and Fruit Trees Commonly Met With in the Gardens and Orchards of Great Britain, with Selected Lists of Those Most Worthy of Cultivation*. London.

Hogg, R. and Bull, H.H. 1878–1884. *The Herefordshire Pomona*. Hereford.

Homer, J. 2016. *Brewing in Kent*. Amberley Publishing, Stroud.

Hone, W. 1832. *The Year Book of Daily Recreation and Information*. London.

Hooker, W. 1841. *Pomona Londinensis; Containing Coloured Engravings of the Most Esteemed Fruits Cultivated in the British Gardens*. London.

House of Commons 1839. *Reports from Committees*, Volume 3. London.

Infante-Amate, J. 2012. The Ecology and History of the Mediterranean Olive Grove: the Spanish Great Expansion, 1750–2000, *Rural History* 23 (1), 161–84.

Jackson, J.E. 2003. *Biology of Apples and Pears*. Cambridge University Press, Cambridge.

James, M. 1932. *Complete Guide to Home Gardening*. Associated Newspapers, London.

Janick, J. 2005. The Origins of Fruits, Fruit Growing and Fruit Breeding, *Plant Breeding Review* 25, 255–320.

Janson, H.F. 1996. *Pomona's Harvest: an Illustrated Chronicle of Antiquarian Fruit Literature*. Timber Press, Portland, Oregon.

Jekyll, G. 1899. *Wood and Garden*. London.

Jekyll, G. 1919. *Colour Schemes for the Flower Garden*. Country Life, London.

Johnson, W. Branch 1977. *Industrial Archaeology of Hertfordshire*. David and Charles, Newton Abbot.

Kain, R.J.P. and Oliver, R.R. 1995. *The Tithe Maps of England and Wales: a Cartographic Analysis and County-by-County Catalogue*. Cambridge University Press, Cambridge.

Kent, E. 1825. *Sylvan Rambles, or a Companion to the Park and Shrubbery*. London.

Kent, N. 1796. *General View of the Agriculture of the County of Norfolk*. London.

Kiebacher, T., Keller, C., Scheidegger, C. and Bergamini, A. 2017. Epiphytes in Wooded Pastures: Isolation Matters for Lichen but not for Bryophyte Species Richness, *PLoS ONE* 12: https://doi.org/10.1371/journal.pone.0182065.

King, A. and Clifford, S. 1993. The Apple, the Orchard, the Cultural Landscape. In S. Clifford and A. King (eds), *Local Distinctiveness: Place, Particularity and Identity*, 37–46. Common Ground, London.

Kirby, T. 2000. 'Railways'. In T. Kirby and S. Oosthuizen (eds), *An Atlas of Cambridgeshire and Huntingdonshire History*, 68. Anglia Polytechnic University, Cambridge.

Kirk, S. 2005. *Philip Webb: Pioneer of the Arts and Crafts Movement*. Academy Press, London.

Knight, T.A. 1811. *Pomona Herefordiensis*. London.

Kropotkin, P. 1899. *Fields, Factories and Workshops*. Hutchinson, London.

Lambarde, W. 1576. *A Perambulation of Kent; Conyeining the Description, Hystorie, and Customes of the Shyre*. London.

Laundon, J.R. 1986. *Lichens*. Shire, Princes Risborough.

Lawson, W. 1618. *A New Orchard or Garden*. London.

Loudon, J. 1848. *Gardening for Ladies*. London.

Lovegrove, R. 2002. *Silent Fields: the Long Decline of a Nation's Wildlife*. Oxford University Press, Oxford.

Lush, M., Robertson, H.J., Alexander, K.N.A., Giavarini, V., Hewins, E., Mellings, J., Stevenson, C.R., Storey, M. and Whitehead, P.F. 2007. *Biodiversity Studies of Six Traditional Orchards in England*. Natural England Research Reports 25. Natural England, Peterborough.

Mabey, R. 1980. *The Common Ground: a Place for Nature in Britain's Future*. Hutchinson, London.

Mac, F. 2003. *Ciderlore: Cider in the Three Counties*. Logaston, Eardisley.

Manning, D. 1939. Commercial Horticulture in Devon, *Scientific Horticulture* 7, 143–49.

Markham, G. 1613. *The English Husbandman*. London.

Marshall, W. 1796. *The Rural Economy of Gloucestershire, Including Its Dairy; Together with the Dairy Management of North Wiltshire; and the Management of Orchards and Fruit Liquor in Herefordshire*, Volume 2. London.

Marshall, W. 1805. *The Rural Economy of the West of England*, Volume 1. London.

Masset, C. 2012. *Orchards*. Shire, Princes Risborough.

Middleton, C.H. 1922–23. The Orchards of Middlesex, *Journal of the Ministry of Agriculture* 29, 269–75.

Minchington, W. 1997. The British Cider Industry Since 1880. In H. Pohl (ed.), *Competition and Cooperation of Enterprises on National and International Markets*, 125–20. Steiner, Stuttgart.

Mingay, G. 1996. Agriculture. In A. Armstrong (ed.), *The Economy of Kent, 1640–1913*, 51–84. Boydell, Woodbridge.

Mitchell A. 1974. *Field Guide to the Trees of Britain and Northern Europe*. Collins, London.

Monbiot, G. 2014. *Feral: Searching for Enchantment on the Frontiers of Rewilding*. Penguin, London.

Moore, J.P. 2010. The Impact of Agricultural Depression and Landownership Change on the County of Hertfordshire, c. 1870–1914. Unpublished PhD thesis, University of Hertfordshire.

Morgan, J. and Richards, A. 2002. *The New Book of Apples*, revised edn. Ebury Press, London.

Mosby, J.E.G. 1938. *The Land of Britain, Part 70: Norfolk*. Geographical Publications, London.

Mowl, T. and Mayer, L. 2013. *The Historic Gardens of England: Cambridgeshire and the Isle of Ely*. Redcliffe Press, Bristol.

Muggleton, W. 2017. *The Apples and Orchards of Worcestershire*. Aspect, Malvern.

Norbury, C.P. 1952. Modern Developments in Fruit Growing, *Journal of the Royal Society of Arts* 100 (4881), 719–34.

Norden, J. 1608. *The Surveyor's Dialogue*. London.

Nourse, T. 1700. *Campania Felix; or, the Benefits and Improvement of Husbandry*. London.

Oldham, C. 1929. Payments for Vermin by Some Hertfordshire Churchwardens, *Transactions of the Hertfordshire Natural History Society* 18, 79–112.

Oldén, A. and Halme, P. 2016. Grazers Increase β-diversity of Vascular Plants and Bryophytes in Wood-Pastures, *Journal of Vegetation Science* 27, 1084–93.

Oliver, R.R. 1994. *Ordnance Survey Maps: a Concise Guide for Historians*. Charles Close Society, London.

Page, W. (ed.) 1914. *Victoria History of Hertfordshire*, Volume 4. Victoria County History, London.

Page, W. (ed.) 1914. *Victoria History of the County of York, North Riding*, Volume 1. Victoria County History, London.

Pam, J. 2004. Essex Agriculture: Landowners' and Farmers' Responses to Economic Change, 1850–1914. Unpublished PhD thesis, University of London.

Parkhill, G. and Cook, G. 2008. Hadleigh Salvation Army Farm: a Vision Reborn. Salvation Army, Hadleigh.

Parkinson, R. 1811. *General View of the Agriculture of the County of Huntingdon*. London.

Paye, P. 1986. *The Mid-Suffolk Light Railway*. Wild Swan Publications, Upper Bucklebury.

Paye, P. 2009. *The Wisbech and Upwell Tramway*. Oakwood Press, Tarrant Hinton.

Perren, R. 1995. *Agriculture in Depression 1870–1940*. Cambridge University Press, Cambridge.

Perrin, V. 2010. Cambridgeshire Orchard Survey: Phase 2 Survey, 2006–09. Traditional Orchards Habitat. Report for the Cambridgeshire and Peterborough Biodiversity Group, Peterborough.

Perry, P.J. 1974. *British Farming in the Great Depression: an Historical Geography*. David and Charles, Newton Abbot.

Petitt, G.H.N. 1941. *The Land of Britain, Part 74: Cambridgeshire and the Isle of Ely*. Geographical Publications, London.

Phibbs, J. 2016. *Place Making: the Art of Capability Brown*. Historic England, London.

Pinel, P. 1801. *Traité Medico-Philosophique sur l'Alienation Mentale*. Paris [translated into English in 1806, as *A Treatise on Lunacy*. London.]

Pitt, W. 1796. *General View of the Agriculture of the County of Stafford*. London.

Pitt, W. 1809. *General View of the Agriculture of the County of Northampton*. London.

Pitt, W. 1810. *General View of the Agriculture of the County of Worcester*. London.

Pomfret, M. n.d. *Stones Orchard, Croxley Green*. Privately published, Croxley Green.

Powell, M., Harris, A. and Hicks, M. 2012. Lichen Ecology in Traditional Hertfordshire Orchards and the Implications for Conservation, *Transactions of the Hertfordshire Natural History Society* 43 (2), 69–79.

Quinion, M. 2008. *Cider Making*. Shire, Princes Risborough.

Rackham, O. 1976. *Trees and Woodland in the British Landscape*. Dent, London.

Rackham, O. 1986. *The History of the Countryside*. Dent, London.

Raven, S. 2012. Sandy Heath Nature Reserve – Wildlife and History of the Plum Orchard. Unpublished report for the Greensand Trust, Haynes West End, Bedfordshire.

Reedy, D., McClatchey, W.C., Smith, C., Han Lau, Y. and Bridges, K.W. 2009. A Mouthful of Diversity: Knowledge of Cider Apple Cultivars in the United Kingdom and Northwest United States, *Economic Botany* 63 (1), 2–15.

Reynolds, S. 1962. *Victoria History of the County of Middlesex*, Volume 3. Oxford University Press and the Institute for Historical Research, London.

Ricketts, B. 2008. The Laxtons in Bedford (1879–1957), *Bedford Architectural Archaeological & Local History Society, Newsletter* 82, 14–28.

Roberts, M. 2018. *The Original Warden Pear*, revised edn. Eventispress, Bedford.

Roberts, W. 1937. Richard Milles' New Kitchen Garden, *Norfolk Archaeology* 62, 501–7.

Robertson, H., Marshall, D., Slingsby, E. and Newman, G. (eds), 2012. *Economic, Biodiversity, Resource Protection and Social Values of Orchards: a Study of Six Orchards by the Herefordshire Orchards Community Evaluation Project*, Natural England Commissioned Report NECR090. Natural England: http://publications.naturalengland.org.uk/publication/1289011.

Robinson, D.H. 1949. *Fream's Elements of Agriculture*. John Murray, London.

Robinson, J.M. 2012. *Felling the Ancient Oaks*. Aurum Press, London.

Robinson, W. 1890. *The English Flower Garden*. London.

Rotherham, I.D. 2008. An Introduction to Orchards and Groves. In I.D. Rotherham (ed.), *Orchards and Groves: Their History, Ecology, Culture and Archaeology*, 6–10. Wildtrack, Sheffield.

Rowe, A. (ed.) 2001. *Garden Making and the Freeman Family: a Memoir of Hamels 1713–1733*. Hertfordshire Record Society, Hertford.

Rudge, T. 1807. *General View of the Agriculture of the County of Gloucester*. London.

Rutherford, S. 2003. Landscapes of Lunatic Asylums. Unpublished PhD thesis, de Montfort University, Leicester.

Sabin, C.W. 1908. Agriculture. In W. Page (ed.), *Victoria History of the County of Kent*, Volume 1, 457–71. Archibald Constable, London.

Salisbury, W. 1816. *Hints Addressed to Proprietors of Orchards*. London.

Sanders, R. 2010. *The Apple Book*. Francis Lincoln, London.

Scarfe, N.V. 1936. *The Land of Britain, Part 82: Essex*. Geographical Publications, London.

Scott, J. 1872. *Scott's Catalogue of Orchard Fruits.* London.

Seabrook, W. 1933. *Modern Fruit Growing.* Ernest Benn, London.

Shapley, D. and Powell, C. 2014. *A Brief History of Fresh Produce's Role in the UK Supermarket Revolution.* London Produce, London: https://www.producebusiness.com/wp-content/uploads/Attachments/Retail-booklet-2014.pdf

Shoard, M. 1980. *The Theft of the Countryside.* Temple Smith, London.

Short, B. 1997. *Land and Society in Edwardian Britain.* Cambridge University Press,

Short, B., May, P., Vines, G. and Bur, A.-M. 2012. *Apples and Orchards in Sussex.* Action in Rural Sussex and Brighton Permaculture Trust, Lewes.

Silva, G.J., Souza, T.M., Barbieri, R.L. and de Oliveira, A.C. 2014. Origin, Domestication, and Dispersing of Pear (*Pyrus* spp.), *Advances in Agriculture* 20, 1–8.

Sinclair, J. 1818. *The Code of Agriculture.* London.

Sinden, N. 1989. Orchard and Place. In Common Ground, *Orchards: a Guide to Local Conservation.* Common Ground, London, 5–11.

Smith, A. Hassell 1994. The Gardens of Sir Nicholas and Francis Bacon: an Enigma Resolved and a Mind Explored. In P. Roberts (ed.), *Religion, Culture and Society in Early Modern England*, 125–60. Cambridge University Press, Cambridge.

Smith, C.W. 2005. *The Lichens of Britain and Ireland.* British Lichen Society, London.

Stafford, H. 1753. *A Treatise on Cider Making.* London.

Stamp, L. Dudley 1936. *The Land of Britain, Part 85: Kent.* Geographical Publications, London.

Stamp, L. Dudley 1948. *The Land of Britain: Its Use and Misuse.* Geographical Publications, London.

Stanyon, M. 2011. Papermaking. In D. Short (ed.), *An Historical Atlas of Hertfordshire*, 80–81. University of Hertfordshire Press, Hatfield.

Stevenson, C.R., Davies, C. and Rowntree, J.K. 2017. Biodiversity in Agricultural Landscapes: the Effect of Apple Cultivar on Epiphyte Diversity, *Ecology and Evolution* 7, 1250–58.

Stevenson, R. and Rowntree, J. 2009. Bryophytes in East Anglian Orchards, *Field Bryology* 99, 10–18.

Stoate, T.L. 1979. *A Survey of West Country Manors, 1525: the Lands of Cecily, Marchioness of Dorset, Lady Harington and Bonville in Cornwall, Devon, Dorset, Somerset, Wiltshire.* Stoate, Bristol.

Strickland, H.E. 1812. *General View of the Agriculture of the East Riding of Yorkshire.* London.

Switzer, S. 1724. *The Practical Fruit-Gardener.* London.

Tate, W.E. and Turner, M. 1978. *A Domesday of English Enclosure Acts and Awards.* University of Reading, Reading.

Taylor, C. 1974. *Fieldwork in Medieval Archaeology.* Batsford, London.

Taylor, C. 1983. *The Archaeology of Gardens.* Shire, Princes Risborough.

Temple, W. 1690. *Miscellanea: the Second Part.* London.

Thirsk, J. 1984. The South-West Midlands. In J. Thirsk (ed.), *The Agrarian History of England and Wales Volume 5.1,1640–1750: Regional Farming Systems*, 159–96. Cambridge University Press, Cambridge.

Turner, S. 2005. *Devon Historic Landscape Characterisation.* Devon County Council, Exeter.

Tusser, T. 1570. *A Hundreth Good Pointes of Husbandry.* London.

Upcher, H. 1946. Norfolk Farming, *Transactions of the Norfolk and Norwich Naturalists Society* 16, 37–105.

Vancouver, C. 1808. *A General View of the Agriculture of the County of Devon.* London.

Wade Martins, S. and Williamson, T. (eds), 1995. *The Farming Journal of Randall Burroughes of Wymondham, 1794–99.* Norfolk Record Society, Norwich.

Wade Martins, S. and Williamson, T. 2008. *The Countryside of East Anglia: Changing Landscapes, 1870–1950.* Boydell, Woodbridge.

Ward, A.J. 2003. *The Early History of Papermaking at Frogmore Mill and Two Waters Mill, Hertfordshire.* Dacorum Heritage Trust, Berkhamsted.

Waugh, E. 2009. *Rivers Nursery of Sawbridgeworth: the Art of Pomology.* Rockingham Press, Ware.

Waugh, E. 2012. Planting the Garden: the Nursery Trade in Hertfordshire. In D. Spring (ed.), *Hertfordshire Garden History Volume II: Gardens Pleasant, Groves Delicious*, 177–201. University of Hertfordshire Press, Hatfield.

White, J. 1997. What Is a Veteran Tree and Where are they All? *Quarterly Journal of Forestry* 91 (3), 222–26.

White, J. 1999. *Estimating the Age of Large and Veteran Trees in Britain*, Forestry Commission Information Note 250. Forestry Commission, Alice Holt.

White, W. 1845. *A History, Gazetteer and Directory of Norfolk.* Sheffield.

Whitelaw, M. and Burton, M.A.S. 2015. Diversity and Distribution of Epiphytic Bryophytes on Bramley's Seedling Trees in East of England Apple Orchards, *Global Ecology and Conservation* 4, 380–87.

Wigley, E. 2019. Wassail! Reinventing 'Tradition' in Contemporary Wassailing Customs in Southern England, *Cultural Geographies* 26, 3, 379–93.

Wilkerson, J.C. (ed.) 1974. *John Norden's Survey of Barley, Hertfordshire, 1593–1603*. Cambridge Records Society, Cambridge.

Wilkinson, L.P. 1987. *Bulmers of Hereford: a Century of Cider Making*. David and Charles, Newton Abbot.

Williamson, T. 1995. *Polite Landscapes: Gardens and Society in Eighteenth-Century England*. Suttons, Stroud.

Williamson, T. 2003. *Shaping Medieval Landscapes: Settlement, Society, Environment*. Windgather, Macclesfield.

Williamson, T. 2013. *An Environmental History of Wildlife in England, 1650–1950*. Bloomsbury, London.

Williamson, T. 2019. How Natural Is Natural? Historical Perspectives on Wildlife and the Environment in Britain, *Transactions of the Royal Historical Society* 29, 293–311.

Williamson, T., Barnes, G. and Pillatt, T. 2017. *Trees in England: Management and Disease since 1600*. University of Hertfordshire Press, Hatfield.

Wilson, E. 2007. *The Downright Epicure: Essays on Edward Bunyard 1878–1939*, reprint edn. Prospect Books, London.

Worgan, G.B. 1815. *General View of the Agriculture of the County of Cornwall*. London.

Worlidge, J. 1675. *Systema Agriculturae; The Mystery of Husbandry Discovered*. London.

Wormwell, P. 1999. *Essex Farming, 1900–2000*. Abberton Books, Colchester.

Worsley, G. 2002. *England's Lost Houses: from the Archives of Country Life*. Aurum Press, London.

Woudstra, J. 2016. Fruit Cultivation in the Royal Gardens of Hampton Court Palace 1630–1842, *Garden History* 44 (2), 255–71.

Woudstra, J. 2017. The History and Development of Groves in English Formal Gardens, 1600–1760. In J. Woudstra and C. Roth (eds), *A History of Groves*, 67–85. Routledge, London.

Wright, J. 1891. *Profitable Fruit Growing*. London.

Young, A. 1804. *General View of the Agriculture of the County of Hertfordshire*. London.

Young, A. 1807. *General View of the Agriculture of the County of Essex*, Volume 2. London.

Websites

Bedford High Street Project, 'Laxtons': http://virtual-library.culturalservices.net/webingres/bedfordshire/vlib/0.digitised_resources/high_street_history_laxton.htm.

Bishop's Stortford Council Website, 'History, Sir Walter Gilbey': http://www.stortfordhistory.co.uk/guide2/sir-walter-gilbey/.

Cauldwell Archives, the Caldwell Nurseries Project: https://www.caldwellarchives.org.uk/places/nursery-sites.html.

Deakins Jam and Fruit: http://www.deakin.broadwaymanor.co.uk/deakin/naunton-field-jam-factory.htm.

FruitID: https://www.fruitid.com/#view/670.

Hansard, Volume 586, April 1958: https://hansard.parliament.uk/Commons/1958-04-22/debates/ff751ea9-ba17-411c-9132-48d87b9702d4/Hospitals(Farms).

Herefordshire Council, Herefordshire Through Time: https://htt.herefordshire.gov.uk/herefordshires-past/the-post-medieval-period/agriculture-and-industry/herefordshire-industry/brewing-and-malting.

National Library of Scotland, Ordnance Survey, 1:25,000 maps of Great Britain (Regular series) – 1937–1961: https://maps.nls.uk/os/25k-gb-1937-61/info1.html.

Suffolk Traditional Orchards Group, 'Cobnuts in Suffolk': https://issuu.com/suffolkbis/docs/stogan__6_cobnuts_in_suffolk_v3_aug?ff=TRUE&e=25146667/41601866.

UK Agricultural Statistics: https://www.gov.uk/government/statistical-data-sets/structure-of-the-agricultural-industry-in-england-and-the-uk-at-june.

Vision of Britain, Land Use Maps: https://www.visionofbritain.org.uk/maps/series?xCenter=3160000&yCenter=3160000&scale=63360&viewScale=5805357.4656&mapLayer=land&subLayer=lus_stamp&title=Land%20Utilisation%20Survey%20of%20Britain&download=true.

Wilkins and Sons website, 'History': https://web.archive.org/web/20141112223240/http://www.tiptree.com/goto.php?ref=y&sess=+A5E5147191D51+F18435A52+9+B581D1058+E+357+9+25F1D1758&id=14.